Frommer's™

Maine Coast
day BY day™

1st Edition

by Paul Karr

WILEY

John Wiley & Sons Canada, Ltd.

Contents

Published by:

John Wiley & Sons Canada, Ltd.

6045 Freemont Blvd.
Mississauga, ON L5R 4J3

ISBN 978-0-470-67832-9
Editor: Gene Shannon
Production Editor: Pamela Vokey
Project Coordinator: Lynsey Stanford
Editorial Assistant: Katie Wolsley
Photo Editor: Photo Affairs, Inc.
Cartographer: Lohnes + Wright
Vice President, Publishing Services: Karen Bryan
Production by Wiley Indianapolis Composition Services

For information on our other products and services or to obtain technical support, please contact our Customer Care Department within the U.S. at 877/762-2974, outside the U.S. at 317/572-3993 or fax 317/572-4002.

Wiley also publishes its books in a variety of electronic formats. Some content that appears in print may not be available in electronic formats.

Manufactured in China

5   4   3   2   1

A Note from the Editorial Director

Organizing your time. That's what this guide is all about.

Other guides give you long lists of things to see and do and then expect you to fit the pieces together. The Day by Day guides are different. These guides tell you the best of everything, and then they show you how to see it *in the smartest, most time-efficient way*. Our authors have designed detailed itineraries organized by time, neighborhood, or special interest. And each tour comes with a bulleted map that takes you from stop to stop.

Hoping to go for a hike in Acadia National Park or visit one of Portland's renowned microbreweries? Planning to hunt for Maine's best steamed lobster or stroll along the coast's countless beaches? Whatever your interest or schedule, the Day by Days give you the smartest routes to follow. Not only do we take you to the top attractions, hotels, and restaurants, but we also help you access those special moments that locals get to experience—those "finds" that turn tourists into travelers.

The Day by Days are also your top choice if you're looking for one complete guide for all your travel needs. The best hotels and restaurants for every budget, the greatest shopping values, the wildest nightlife—it's all here.

Why should you trust our judgment? Because our authors personally visit each place they write about. They're an independent lot who say what they think and would never include places they wouldn't recommend to their best friends. They're also open to suggestions from readers. If you'd like to contact them, please send your comments our way at feedback@frommers.com, and we'll pass them on.

Enjoy your Day by Day guide—the most helpful travel companion you can buy. And have the trip of a lifetime.

Warm regards,

Kelly Regan

Kelly Regan, Editorial Director
Frommer's Travel Guides

About the Author

Paul Karr is a prize-winning journalist and travel editor who has authored more than 25 guidebooks around the world, including *Frommer's Vermont, New Hampshire & Maine, Vancouver & Victoria For Dummies, Insight Guide: Switzerland, Driving Northern Italy & The Italian Lakes, USA On the Road,* and *Scandinavia: The Rough Guide.* Now based in New York and Tokyo, he has twice served as writer-in-residence for the National Parks Service and once dined in the White House at the President's personal invitation. For real.

Acknowledgments

Gracious thanks to all who participated in the creation of this guide, including (but certainly not limited to) editor Gene Shannon and the ever-dutiful production teams at Wiley. Thanks, too, to the many PR agencies and local tourism officials who assisted me with increasingly arcane questions, and thanks to those hotel and restaurant owners, managers, and staff who took time to give me a tour, serve me a decent meal, pose for endless photos, and just generally allow me to roam around their properties at will. Special shout-out to Maine for being such an awesome place. And finally, as always, this goes out to my lovely girl. None lovelier.

An Additional Note

Please be advised that travel information is subject to change at any time— and this is especially true of prices. We therefore suggest that you write or call ahead for confirmation when making your travel plans. The authors, editors, and publisher cannot be held responsible for the experiences of readers while traveling. Your safety is important to us, however, so we encourage you to stay alert and be aware of your surroundings.

Star Ratings, Icons & Abbreviations

Every hotel, restaurant, and attraction listing in this guide has been ranked for quality, value, service, amenities, and special features using a **star-rating system.** Hotels, restaurants, attractions, shopping, and nightlife are rated on a scale of zero stars (recommended) to three stars (exceptional). In addition to the star-rating system, we also use a **kids icon** to point out the best bets for families. Within each tour, we recommend cafes, bars, or restaurants where you can take a break. Each of these stops appears in a shaded box marked with a coffee-cup-shaped bullet ☕ .

The following **abbreviations** are used for credit cards:

AE	American Express	DISC	Discover	V	Visa
DC	Diners Club	MC	MasterCard		

Frommers.com

Now that you have this guidebook to help you plan a great trip, visit our website at **www.frommers.com** for additional travel information on more than 4,000 destinations. We update features regularly to give you instant access to the most current trip-planning information available. At Frommers.com, you'll find scoops on the best airfares, lodging rates, and car rental bargains. You can even book your travel online through our reliable travel booking partners. Other popular features include:

- Online updates of our most popular guidebooks
- Vacation sweepstakes and contest giveaways
- Newsletters highlighting the hottest travel trends
- Podcasts, interactive maps, and up-to-the-minute events listings
- Opinionated blog entries by Arthur Frommer himself
- Online travel message boards with featured travel discussions

A Note on Prices

In the "Take a Break" and "Best Bets" sections of this book, we have used a system of dollar signs to show a range of costs for 1 night in a hotel (the price of a double-occupancy room) or the cost of an entree at a restaurant. Use the following table to decipher the dollar signs:

Cost	Hotels	Restaurants
$	under $100	under $10
$$	$100–$200	$10–$20
$$$	$200–$300	$20–$30
$$$$	$300–$400	$30–$40
$$$$$	over $400	over $40

An Invitation to the Reader

In researching this book, we discovered many wonderful places—hotels, restaurants, shops, and more. We're sure you'll find others. Please tell us about them, so we can share the information with your fellow travelers in upcoming editions. If you were disappointed with a recommendation, we'd love to know that, too. Please write to:

Frommer's Maine Coast Day By Day, 1st Edition
John Wiley & Sons Canada, Ltd. • 6045 Freemont Blvd. • Mississauga, ON
L5R 4J3

15 Favorite
Moments

15 Favorite **Moments**

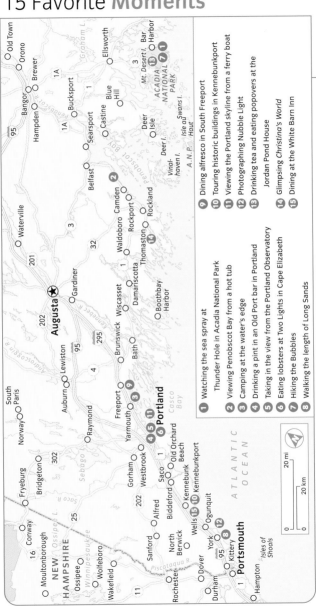

1. Watching the sea spray at Thunder Hole in Acadia National Park
2. Viewing Penobscot Bay from a hot tub
3. Camping at the water's edge
4. Drinking a pint in an Old Port bar in Portland
5. Taking in the view from the Portland Observatory
6. Eating lobsters at Two Lights in Cape Elizabeth
7. Hiking the Bubbles
8. Walking the length of Long Sands

9. Dining alfresco in South Freeport
10. Touring historic buildings in Kennebunkport
11. Viewing the Portland skyline from a ferry boat
12. Photographing Nubble Light
13. Drinking tea and eating popovers at the Jordan Pond House
14. Glimpsing *Christina's World*
15. Dining at the White Barn Inn

Previous page: A Maine farmhouse lies along the water's edge amid the autumn colors.

The Maine coast is a big place, though that's not immediately apparent from a map. But if you iron out all those kinks and peninsulas, there's a *lot* of room to roam—and that means plenty of special moments, though they tend to be lower-key and quieter here than in some other destinations. Here are some of my favorite Maine experiences.

1 Watching the sea spray at Thunder Hole in Acadia National Park. Mount Desert Island is full of active hiking, biking, kayaking, and camping adventures (see chapters 7 and 9 for a sampling), but sometimes you just want to sit back and watch nature do its thing. When the tides and waves are right, the huge spouts foaming up at Thunder Hole—a sea cave on a point of land at the southern tip of the island—are spectacular. *See p 142.*

2 Viewing Penobscot Bay from a hot tub. You can see beautiful Penobscot Bay from a windjammer, a skiff, a boardwalk, or the top of a mountain in Camden Hills State Park. But it's also nice, once in a while, to gaze upon it from the comfort of a heated pool or hot tub. At the Samoset resort, you can now do both, thanks to the recent installation of a pool and outdoor Jacuzzi on a hillside overlooking the bay. *See p 134.*

3 Camping at the water's edge. What's better than unzipping your tent to make breakfast and walking out to a view of a shiny, empty bay? Nothing, in my book. Throughout the Maine coast, you'll find campgrounds perched right beside the ocean, which is remarkable given how much of this coastline is privately owned. Look for waterside campsites on Mount Desert Island, in Freeport, and in York, for starters; but there are lots more, too. Just be sure not to pitch that tent *too* close to the water's edge. *See p 167.*

4 Drinking a pint in an Old Port bar in Portland. I've devoted one entire tour to the local bar and microbrewing options in Portland, and even that section covers just the basics; there are countless additional possibilities in the city and in the area. If you're a beer drinker, the go-to Portland evening experience is a pint of locally brewed beer inside one of the city's pubs, followed by a responsible walk or taxi ride back to your

The waves crash into Thunder Hole, a sea cave at the tip of Mount Desert Island.

Campgrounds right next to the ocean can be found throughout the Maine coast.

hotel. You might even meet some locals in the process. *See p 94.*

⑤ Taking in the view from the Portland Observatory. There are great views from walking paths on both ends of the Portland peninsula, but the ultimate view is glimpsed from the top of Portland's observatory at the crest of Munjoy Hill. It was built in the very early 19th century to signal ships at sea, but when that use became obsolete, the city suddenly gained a terrific tourist destination. The only catch is this: You need to hike up a whole bunch of steps to get that view. The out-of-shape or afraid-of-heights should probably pass. *See p 88.*

⑥ Eating lobsters at Two Lights in Cape Elizabeth. There's no food truer to Maine than

Digging into fresh lobster with a view of the water.

a steamed lobster with butter—preferably with a hunk of corn on the cob and a nice piece of blueberry cake on the side. And there's no more scenic place to eat this archetypal meal than right out on the windswept rocks behind Two Lights Lobster Shack in Cape Elizabeth. Bring your appetite, but hold onto your hat, too. *See p 115.*

⑦ Hiking the Bubbles. Sometimes, you don't have time to do the Appalachian Trail; sometimes, you just want a quick walk to get the blood flowing. The Bubbles are that sort of walk, if a bit too vertical to count as an "easy stroll." After a half-hour of hiking and clambering, you emerge on summit ledges with a view of pond, ocean, and islands. It's a great photo-op, and you can be done with the whole hike in an hour, though I'd recommend packing a light lunch from town and picnicking up top. *See p 165.*

⑧ Walking the length of Long Sands. There are countless beaches in southern Maine, but the first one you encounter after crossing the state line, York's Long Sands, might be the best. That's because it's long, flat, clean, and offers a huge slice of coastal scenery, plus consistently good waves. Bring Frisbees, dogs, a surfboard, kids, a pup tent—whatever you need—but take time for a long stroll

Finding Your Way around Like a Mainer

Folks on the Maine coast have their own way of referencing places, especially as you get farther north and farther from cities. "Downeast" means "far north and east along the coast"—way beyond Mount Desert Island, and the farther northeast, the better. "Upstate" means north, "up coast" northeast from wherever you're speaking. "Bean's" is either the closest L.L.Bean branch or (more likely) the flagship store in Freeport. "The City" is usually Portland (sometimes Boston), but "the County" *always* means Washington County—the one farthest (yes) "downeast" on this coast.

or power-walk at both the beginning and end of each day. You'll be glad you did. *See p 64.*

⑨ Dining alfresco in South Freeport. Among the small towns on the coast of Maine, Freeport is exemplary for its shopping options: a ton of outlets, plus the flagship L.L.Bean store (open 24/7/365). But few travelers realize there's a lovely little harbor just a few minutes' drive from the busy main street. South Freeport is a little village with a boatyard, some boat tours, and a great little lobster restaurant on the docks, Harraseeket Lunch & Lobster. It's well worth the quick detour for the peace, quiet, salt air, and lobster. *See p 130.*

⑩ Touring historic buildings in Kennebunkport. The town of Kennebunkport is far better known for its wealth and First Family summer residents than its history or architecture. But if it's handsome old buildings you crave, this town holds as good a concentration of them as any place in Maine. Three historic districts all lie within easy walking distance of each other and the center of town. Get a brochure from the local historical society explaining how to find the best churches and sea captains' homes. *See p 58.*

⑪ Viewing the Portland skyline from a ferry boat. I've said it before, and I'll say it again:

Kennebunkport is known for its concentration of historic buildings.

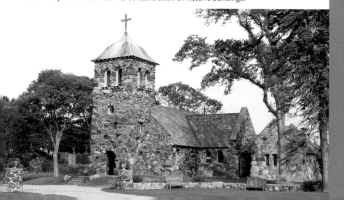

Photographers are drawn to the cheerful color palate of Nubble Light.

Portland the city is only half of the Portland experience. To really enjoy the place, you also need to get out on the beach—there are plenty of them just south of the city—on a good-weather day or out onto a boat. The Peaks Island ferry is one of the easiest ways, a salty 20-minute cruise from the waterfront over to a quieter, greener island. Bring a sweater. *See p 33.*

⑫ Photographing Nubble Light. Maine's full of scenic lighthouses, but the one near York Beach is especially scenic (and especially popular). The tableau of a bright white lighthouse beside a cute red barn and a big blue ocean never fails to bring the summer crowds. Pack your best camera and lenses (including a polarizing lens), and come early or late in the day when the light is best for shooting the scene. *See p 41.*

⑬ Drinking tea and eating popovers at the Jordan Pond House. The genteel days when Acadia was a Victorian-type resort, with horse-drawn carriages and steam trains bringing travelers from Boston, New York, and beyond are all gone. Scratch that: nearly gone. You still get a taste of that era at the

Jordan Pond House, a sort of tearoom plunked down in the middle of the park. The views are excellent, as are the popovers (the traditional snack), particularly when taken in a chair out on the lawn. *See p 148.*

⑭ Glimpsing *Christina's World.* The galleries of the Camden-Rockland area are the best in Maine, but for a real look at how artists painted what they saw here, consider a visit to the actual farmhouse where Andrew Wyeth painted his famous *Christina's World.* The Olson House, about a half-hour's drive from Rockland, is now owned by the excellent Farnsworth Museum in that city and can be visited by the public. *See p 39.*

⑮ Dining at the White Barn Inn. This Relais & Chateaux property is plenty luxurious, worth visiting for the plush bedding, decor, and service alone. But it's also wise to book at least one dinner in the dining room, considered by many to be the state's finest; it really was a barn once upon a time. Chef Jon Cartwright's New American cuisine draws heavily on local seafood, while incorporating bold new ideas. *See p 69.* ●

1 Strategies for Seeing the Maine Coast

The Maine Coast

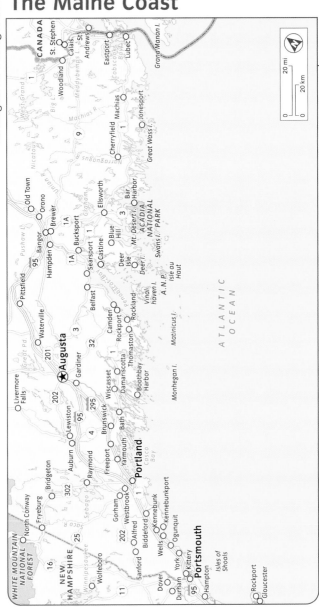

Previous page: Paying a little more for an ocean view is well worth the cost.

Going to the Maine coast for a week isn't like going to Daytona, Maui, or even Boston; it's far bigger, chillier, foggier, less expensive, and more thinly populated, to take just a few examples. Here are a few strategies and rules of thumb that can help you get the most enjoyment out of this unique place.

Rule #1: Get yourself some wheels.
Public transit in Maine exists, but it's frankly not all that great. (This is a big and mostly rural state, so you can't really blame them for that.) Unless you're planning to confine yourself to Portland—in which case you *could* use city buses, but even then, you'd still end up walking a lot—you're going to need bicycle, scooter, or automobile wheels almost anywhere that you want to go.

Rule #2: Think about visiting during the off-season.
Maine is a prime summer destination, of course, but it's pretty wonderful in late spring and fall, too. And you can sometimes save big on coastal hotel rooms by visiting the coast before July or after Labor Day. Weekdays, of course, also tend to be much cheaper than weekends—even in high summer season.

Rule #3: Don't try to do too much.
After all, the Maine coast is a place to *relax*. That means traveling and sightseeing *slowly*. Some of my very best memories here involve slow, solitary walks along beaches or up mountains when I had no itinerary and no watch on my wrist, and the next day's plans weren't pressing me to hurry back to my room or campsite. Staying in one town—and one room—for 3 days isn't a bad idea at all.

Rule #4: Adjust your expectations slightly downward.
Luxury inns and gourmet restaurants are here in increasing numbers, but there are also plenty of villages (Downeast and on out-of-the-way peninsulas) that still offer lodgings best described as throwbacks to the old days—days when a traveler would sleep in a sparely furnished room, sharing hallway bathrooms and communal breakfasts with fellow travelers. That's not an unpleasant experience at all, so long as you come in expecting it. Anyway, on this coast, Mother Nature is the star attraction.

Rule #5: Pay more for a view (or don't).
It's up to you, but know what you're getting before you get here. Even resort rooms on the Maine coast sometimes look out on

Renting a bike is a great way to see the sights along Maine's coast.

Water taxis are a convenient way to experience the sea in Maine.

gorgeous ocean vistas and sometime look out over big parking lots. Prices *usually* reflect these differences in scenery—but not always. When booking, always ask about your view and try to negotiate a better one if possible. You could scrimp, of course, but here's my take: Going to Maine and then skipping the views doesn't make much sense.

Rule #6: Get out on the water.
Maine is all about the sea, so at some point, you need to feel that salty, bracing sea spray on your face to really experience the place. Whether it's on a ferry boat, a deep-sea fishing excursion, a boogie board, or a friend's yacht, it doesn't especially matter; just get out there.

Rule #7: Engage locals.
You don't need to put on a fake accent and wear a Red Sox hat to fit in (in fact, *don't* do those things if you're not from New England). Mainers are surprisingly open and humorous, you'll find, even if they seem pretty quiet at first. It's a cultural thing. Get past that hard shell (here's where a little Red Sox knowledge really comes in handy), and people are usually pretty friendly deep down. And you can *always* talk about weather.

Rule #8: Get off the beaten track.
Throughout this book, I've tried to nudge you gently toward things that aren't obvious tourist stops—local coffee shops and diners, little-known historical spots, somewhat-secret beaches. You can see just the "greatest hits" if you want, but you'll probably have a better story to tell afterward if you deviate from them.

Rule #9: Bring a good camera.
I've traveled and photographed all over the world. Recently, I realized that many of my favorite shots came from right here on the Maine coast, often in anonymous places. The interplay of water, sunlight, fog, stone, snow, and sand never fails to create something I've never seen before—and won't see again, after the next ⅛th of a second.

Rule #10: Be like a Boy Scout.
You know, "Be Prepared"? I'm talking about the weather here. We all dream of perfect, sunny days on the beach, but in reality, Maine is a pretty humid place (it's next to a big pile of water called "the ocean," after all). You can expect to be rained out maybe a third of the time in summer, sometimes much more often than that in a bad year. Bring umbrellas, a sweater, a change of dry shoes, a *TV Guide*, and a thick novel, just in case. ●

The Best in **Three Days**

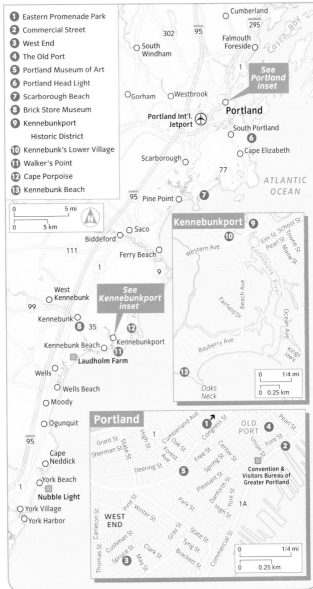

1. Eastern Promenade Park
2. Commercial Street
3. West End
4. The Old Port
5. Portland Museum of Art
6. Portland Head Light
7. Scarborough Beach
8. Brick Store Museum
9. Kennebunkport
   Historic District
10. Kennebunk's Lower Village
11. Walker's Point
12. Cape Porpoise
13. Kennebunk Beach

Previous page: The candy-striped West Quoddy lighthouse in Lubec.

You could spend a month on the Maine coast and still not see it all—heck, that's why people buy summer homes here, so they *can* see it all—but even a few days on the coast is enough to get a good taste. After Portland, we'll visit Freeport and the Kennebunks. Remember that you'll need a car for this tour, as well as the two that follow it. START: **Portland's Eastern Promenade.**

Day 1

❶ ★★★ Eastern Promenade Park. Morning is a great time to scale Munjoy Hill and make your way to this boulevard and the attached green park, which carries the same name. You'll want to take a walk along the shoreline path; sprawl out on the lawn with a book and the kids; and take pictures of the islands, boats, and changing light. Best of all, it's completely free—even the parking—a rarity in Portland. Hungry? A quarter-mile (.4km) uphill, there's **Hilltop Coffee** (90 Congress St.; ☎ 207/780-0025) and the attached **Rosemont Market** (88 Congress St.; ☎ 207/773-7888). ⏱ *1 hr. See p 77.*

Follow Fore St. downhill to

❷ ★ kids Commercial Street. As the heart of both Portland's working waterfront *and* its tourist trade, Commercial Street is the logical starting point for any tour of Maine—even if it's not exactly a quaint fishing village. Stroll, eat

croissants at **Standard Baking** (see p 99) behind the Hilton Hotel at Franklin Street, buy souvenirs, and watch the ferries coming and going at the Casco Bay Lines dock (Franklin and Commercial sts.; www.cascobaylines.com). Scoop up tourist information at the **Ocean Gateway Tourist Office** (14 Ocean Gateway Pier; ☎ 207/772-5800; www.visitportland.com), just north of the ferry dock, and ogle fragrant fish at **Browne Trading Co.** (see p 100)—fish being the reason this city became such a capital of commerce in the first place. The street's a bit of a carnival, but well worth a look. Also, take note of the abundant brick and stone commercial architecture. ⏱ *1½ hr. See p 77.*

Follow Commercial St. across the length of the Portland peninsula 2 miles (3.2km) to High St. Turn right and ascend. Turn left on Danforth St. and follow it to the

❸ ★★ West End. Portland's West End neighborhood offers more

The beautiful view of boats in the harbor from Eastern Promenade Park.

U.S. Custom House in Old Port.

great architecture in a small space than almost anywhere in New England. The whole neighborhood ought to be sectioned off as a Smithsonian-type museum of 19th-century opulence. Stroll west along Pine, Spring, or Brackett streets. Must-sees include the **John Calvin Stevens–designed homes** on Bowdoin Street (see p 93) and the **Victoria Mansion** on Danforth

Street (see p 79). Finish up at **Western Promenade Park,** which has splendid views of the western foothills. ⏱ *2 hr.*

<blockquote>Follow the Western Promenade downhill to Danforth St. Turn left and travel 1 mile (1.6km) to the end. Bear left slightly onto York St., then immediately right onto Fore St. and continue ½ mile (.8km) into the heart of</blockquote>

❹ ★ **The Old Port.** The compact grid of streets in Portland's waterfront district is known as the Old Port. The shopping is great (shops normally stay open until 6pm, sometimes later), and this is also the best place in northern New England to eat a gourmet dinner—**Fore Street** at 288 Fore St. (see p 113) and **Street & Co.** at 33 Wharf St. (see p 115) are two good picks—then grab a pint of locally brewed ale afterward at a place such as **Three Dollar Dewey's** (see p 96) or **Gritty McDuff's** (see p 107). Architecture buffs should take time to view the exterior of the **U.S. Custom House** (see p 87) at 312 Fore St. ⏱ *2–3 hr.*

<blockquote>Day 2
From the Old Port, walk or drive ½ mile (.8km) west along Fore St.</blockquote>

The Portland Museum of Art's collection features excellent paintings of the Maine coast.

Portland Head Light, one of the most striking lighthouses in Maine.

(which becomes Pleasant St.). Turn right on High St. and continue uphill to the top (park on High St., if possible). At the next right-hand corner is the

5 ★★★ Portland Museum of Art.
I can't even begin to list the great pieces of art in this downtown museum, thanks to a long line of part-time Mainers who funded the museum's establishment and expansion, and donated art to its collections. Suffice it to say that you'll move through the rooms with a growing awe—and a growing appreciation for the wonderful pictures that have been painted of the Maine coast. (The collection of European Impressionist work is equally impressive.) ⏱ *2 hr. See p 85.*

Turn left on Congress St. and continue 2 blocks to State St. Turn sharply left and go downhill on State St. (which becomes Rte. 77). Follow Rte. 77 for 1½ miles (2.4km) over the bridge and onto Broadway; once on Broadway, don't turn right to keep on Rte. 77, but take the *next* right onto Cottage Rd., instead. In 2 miles (3.2km), you reach

6 ★★★ Portland Head Light.
Given just a single day in Portland, I can't recommend strongly enough that you take a quick jaunt out to its beaches and lighthouses. I've covered some of them throughout this book—see Crescent Beach (p 104), Kettle Cove (p 104), and the Spring Point Shoreway's lighthouse (p 103), for example—but this one is perhaps the most accessible from downtown (a 10–15 min. drive) and the most picturesque. There's hiking, picnicking, and photo opportunities galore. ⏱ *1½ hr. See p 43.*

Exit the park, turn left onto Shore Rd., and travel 2 miles (3.2km) to Rte. 77. Turn left. Travel 7 miles (11km) to the junction of Rte. 207; bear left onto Black Point Rd. and continue 1 mile (1.6km) to

7 ★ Scarborough Beach.
There are plenty of great beaches south of Portland—so many that I've created an entire tour especially for those readers interested in seeing all of them (see p 62). But if you have to pick just one during this trip, Scarborough Beach is a pretty good choice—facilities, good swimming, lifeguards, watersports equipment for rent, and

even hot food for sale right at the beach. ⏱ *2 hr. See p 104.*

Overnight in Portland, Scarborough, or Cape Elizabeth.

Day 3
From the Portland area, drive south on I-295 (which becomes I-95, a toll road) 25 miles (40km) to Exit 25. Exit and follow Rte. 35 for 6 miles (9.7km) into Kennebunk. In the center of town, where Rte. 35 joins U.S. Rte. 1, is the

⑧ Brick Store Museum. This former brick store is clearinghouse central for Kennebunk historical archives, information, and walking tours; the on-site staff and a small army of local volunteers combine forces to collect and disseminate everything you ever needed or wanted to know about the town. And there are a lot of historical gems, many right in plain sight as you breeze down Route 35. ⏱ *45 min. See p 59.*

Continue several miles east on Rte. 35 to the intersection with Rte. 9 (Western Ave.). Turn left and cross the bridge. Park anywhere and stroll through the

An impressive 19th-century home in Kennebunkport's historic district.

⑨ ★ Kennebunkport Historic District. One of Maine's best historic districts, Kennebunkport's is split up into three distinct sections. The two best sections are the 3 blocks of Maine Street (from School St. to North St.), with numerous lovely 19th-century homes, and Church Street, which is just a block long but features the amazing meetinghouse-style **South Congregational Church** (see p. 61) at the end. You can reach either of these areas easily on foot from Dock Square. A third area is concentrated along Pearl and Green streets, a few blocks east of the square. Stop by the **Richard Nott House** (p 61), at 8 Maine St., to buy an inexpensive brochure describing local historic homes—or sign up for one of the excellent walking tours. ⏱ *1½ hr. See p 59.*

Walk across the short bridge to explore

⑩ Kennebunk's Lower Village. Lower Village is more working-class than Kennebunkport's downtown—at least, it feels that way, with its boatyard (hidden off the main street). Grab a drink and a bite at the microbrewery **Federal Jack's** (8 Western Ave.; ☎ 207/967-4322); sample the good fried-clam shack called **The Clam Shack** (2 Western Ave.; ☎ 207/967-3321); and poke through the various locally owned art, craft, and fashion shops such as **Green Tangerine** (8 Western Ave.; ☎ 207/967-8301) and **Zen & Co.** (13 Western Ave.; ☎ 207/967-8899). Finish at the general store **H.B. Provisions** (15 Western Ave.; ☎ 207/967-5762). Some of the best shopping in the Kennebunks is actually here, rather than in Dock Square. ⏱ *45 min. See p 60.*

Walk back across the bridge to Dock Square and retrieve your car. Turn right at Ocean Ave. and drive 2½ miles (4km) to

Kennenbunk's clean, sandy shoreline stretches for many miles.

⓫ Walker's Point. When you drive to Walker's Point, you not only get a peek at the lives of presidents, but you also get to sample free and breathtaking views of the sea that the families around here paid millions to enjoy every day. The Bush family has resided here since the late 19th century (the present-day compound was begun in 1903). World leaders have stopped by to dine with the presidents Bush (on lobster, I presume) and confer; today, you cannot enter the property, and it's still guarded by Secret Service agents at all times. But you can park on the road and snap long-lens photos of it. ⏱ *30 min. Ocean Ave. (across from Sandy Cove Rd.).*

Continue 1½ miles (2.4km) around the ocean point to Wildes District Rd. Turn right and continue 1 mile (1.6km) east to the village of

⓬ ★ Cape Porpoise. If you're going to see only one fishing village during a short trip to Maine, Cape Porpoise isn't a bad choice at all. There are *two* lobster pounds, **Nunan's Lobster Hut** on Route 9 and **Cape Porpoise Lobster Co.** (see p 41) right on the docks; active fishing operations; a small-town library and grocery store, **Bradbury Bros.** (167 Main St.; ☎ 207/967-3939); and even a few gourmet eateries that have popped up over the last decade to accommodate summer

people and second-home types. Don't forget to grab a snack or a dinner at a spot like **Pier 77** (77 Pier Rd.; ☎ 207/967-8500), near the docks, while you're here. This is prime cycling country, too, due to the absence of both traffic and any steep grades—get a bike from local outfitters **Cape Able Bikes** (☎ 207/967-4382), a few miles away at 83 Arundel Rd. (take North St. from downtown Kennebunkport). They're open daily year-round. ⏱ *1 hr.*

Turn around and follow Rte. 9 about 2½ miles (4km) back through Kennebunkport. Cross the bridge and immediately turn left on Beach St. Continue 1 mile (1.6km) east to

⓭ ★ Kennebunk Beach. The Kennebunk area's best beach is actually a string of beaches, running from Beach Street several miles south. The sand here is uniformly clean and white, coastal views are unimpeded, and you can even find tide pools to play in at a little rocky point of land. A sunset stroll here is a must. Important note: Unless you're staying at a local hotel or inn (they'll give you a pass), you will need a day parking permit from the town—purchase it at the police station or town offices back at the junction of U.S. Route 1 and Route 35—to park here. ⏱ *1½ hr. See p 60.*

The Best in One Week

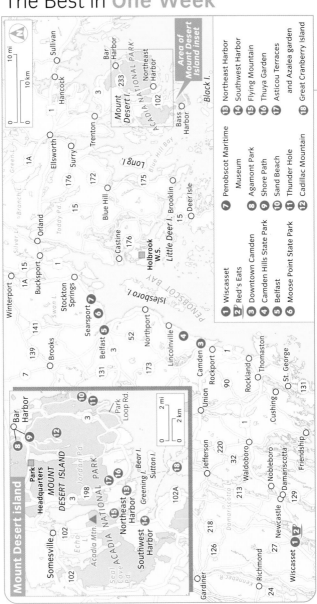

Mount Desert Island

Area of Mount Desert Island inset

1. Wiscasset
2. Red's Eats
3. Downtown Camden
4. Camden Hills State Park
5. Belfast
6. Moose Point State Park
7. Penobscot Maritime Museum
8. Agamont Park
9. Shore Path
10. Sand Beach
11. Thunder Hole
12. Cadillac Mountain
13. Northeast Harbor
14. Southwest Harbor
15. Flying Mountain
16. Thuya Garden
17. Asticou Terraces and Azalea garden
18. Great Cranberry Island

I f 3 days in Maine are good, a week is even better. Now, you'll get the chance to range far north of Portland, into the lovely Penobscot Bay region and onward to one of America's most wonderful natural treasures, Acadia National Park. You'll drive about 2 hours on each of the days of this tour, but during a Maine summer, that's no problem—it stays light until 9pm. (For the first 3 days of this tour, follow "The Best in 3 Days" itinerary, above.) START: **Kennebunk.**

Day 4

From Kennebunk, drive north on I-95 (a toll road) 25 miles (40km), taking Exit 44 to I-295. Continue north 20 miles (32km) to Exit 28. Exit and drive north along U.S. Rte. 1 for about 20 more miles (32km) to

1 ★ **Wiscasset.** The town of Wiscasset is "Maine's prettiest village," or so it claims. From U.S. Route 1, Wiscasset doesn't look like much—but once you delve deeper, you suddenly discover that it holds dozens of historic homes, commercial buildings, and even an old jail. Look for the 1824 **Lincoln County Courthouse** at 32 High St. (☎ 207/882-6311), the 1811 stone **jail** at 133 Federal St. (☎ 207/882-6817), and the 1808 Federal-style **Nickels-Sortwell House** on U.S. Route 1 at 121 Main St. (☎ 207/882-7619). Besides that, the town sits right on the bank of the pretty Sheepscot River. ⏱ *45 min. See p 123.*

2 **Red's Eats.** A lot of places claim to serve the best lobster roll in Maine. It's a subject for endless delicious debate, but my informal polling has consistently produced a ranking of Red's in the top three in the state. They're all about the meat here; for value and taste, it just might be the best. The fries and ice cream are really good, too. *U.S. Rte. 1 (at Water St.), Wiscasset.* ☎ *207/882-6128. $–$$.*

Continue east on U.S. Rte. 1 about 25 miles (40km). Turn left onto Rte. 90 and drive about 10 miles (16km) north until you rejoin U.S. Rte. 1. Turn left (east) and continue 2 miles (3.2km) into

3 ★★ **Downtown Camden.** The stretch of U.S. Route 1 running down Elm Street into the center of Camden and then back up out of

Downtown Camden has everything from nautical shops to bakeries.

town is one of the best in the Mid-coast for concentrating so many travel experiences into a small area. It's a mixture of old homes, B&B elegance, fishy chowder houses, tall ships, the sturdy **Camden Opera House** (29 Elm St.; ☎ 207/236-7963), and shops purveying anything from nautical souvenirs to T-shirts; it gets crowded but never feels artificial. The lovely **Camden Public Library** (☎ 207/236-3440), on the hill at 155 Main St., and its adjacent natural amphitheater (known as Camden Harbor Park), overlooking the harbor, only add to the fun. ⏱ *2 hr. See p 126.*

Window shopping in Belfast.

From downtown Camden, drive north 2 miles (3.2km) on U.S. Rte. 1 to the entrance to

4 ★ **Camden Hills State Park.** A good spot for sunset views of lovely Penobscot Bay, Camden's primo park lords over the water from some pretty impressive twin peaks. You can picnic down on the seaside section of the park (across U.S. Rte. 1 from the entrance), hike the flanks of the mountain along several trails (I recommend the easy to moderate, 3½-mile Megunticook Trail), or just drive up to good views. ⏱ *1 hr. See p 127.*

Day 5
Drive north on U.S. Rte. 1 about 20 miles (32km) to the clearly marked turnoff for

5 **Belfast.** The town of Belfast is a must-see detour when traveling north or south along U.S. Route 1; it's just a minute off the highway, yet has retained its likeable, small-town character thanks to careful traffic planning. Among the attractions here are a great natural foods store, **Belfast Co-Op** (☎ 207/338-2532) at 123 High St.; a few hip bars, such as **three tides** (☎ 207/338-1707) at 3 Pinchy Lane; gourmet restaurants like **Chase's Daily** (96 Main St.; ☎ 207/338-0555); and

a little main street running downhill to the working waterfront's edge. Explore its storefronts. ⏱ *1 hr.*

Return to U.S. Rte. 1 North. Cross the bridge and continue 3½ miles (5.6km); on the right side of the highway is the entrance to

6 **Moose Point State Park.** This big state park isn't on the radar of most coastal travelers bound willy-nilly for Acadia. Yet it contains lovely, invaluable waterfront property just steps off U.S. Route 1—the views of Belfast Bay from its several trails are almost matchless since most of the coastline in these parts is privately owned and carefully gated off from the public. Explore the tidal pools at water's edge, take a quick walk through the fragrant evergreens, and refuel for your trip north. ⏱ *30 min. 310 W. Main St. (U.S. Rte. 1), Searsport. ☎ 207/548-2882. Mid-May to mid-Oct admission $3 non-Maine resident adults, $1 seniors & children; off-season $1.50 adults, free for children.*

Continue 3 miles (4.8km) north on U.S. Rte. 1 into downtown Searsport, home of the

7 ★ **kids** **Penobscot Maritime Museum.** Though it's largely a working-class town today, Searsport was once one of the most important shipbuilding centers in the Midcoast. Sea captains built opulent mansions (many are B&Bs today), and coopers, brickyards, lumber mills, and factories followed. This museum-slash-campus recounts the history of the shipyards and fisheries; holdings include a sardine boat, a sea captain's home, scrimshaw work, and huge photographic archives. ⏱ *1 hr. 40 E. Main St. (U.S. Rte. 1), Searsport.* ☎ *207/548-2529 or 207/548-0334. www.penobscotmarinemuseum. org. Admission $8 adults, $3 kids 7–15; $18 families. May–Oct Mon–Sat 10am–5pm, Sun noon–5pm.*

Continue north on U.S. Rte. 1 about 30 miles (48km; joins with Rte. 3) to Ellsworth. Bear right onto Rte. 3 East and continue 15 miles (24km) onto Mount Desert Island and to Bar Harbor. At the corner of Mt. Desert and Main sts. is

⑧ ★ Agamont Park. Bar Harbor's best park looks out onto Frenchman Bay, with a glorious view of islands. The park is at the end of

the point, yet you can easily walk to all of Bar Harbor's bars, restaurants, and other attractions within 5 minutes. ⏱ *45 min. See p 137.*

From the park, on foot, follow the

⑨ ★ Shore Path. Bar Harbor's shore-way path is a little gem, passing huge opulent "cottages" as it tiptoes along a billion-dollar waterfront. It begins at the **Bar Harbor Inn** (p 149), itself a fine example of the form with knockout views from its dining room and many guest rooms. But on the Shore Path, you get nearly the same view—for the price of your pair of sneakers. ⏱ *30 min. See p 137.*

From Bar Harbor, head south on Main St. (Rte. 3) about 2½ miles (4km) to Park Loop Rd. You'll need to pay a park entry fee. Turn left and enter the loop road, following it 3½ miles (5.6km) to the parking lot for

⑩ ★ Sand Beach. One of Mount Desert Island's two or three best beaches, Sand Beach does actually have some sand—plus views of

Searsport's Penobscot Maritime Museum preserves the region's seafaring history.

several mountains and the open ocean. You might also enjoy the Sand Beach and Great Head walking trails that both depart from the east end of the beach itself. The easy to moderate Sand Beach trail threads a mile and a half (2.2km) gently inland through the woods away from the water, while the moderate, 1½ mile (2.2km) Great Head trail climbs the adjacent cliffs; you'll see plenty of plant, bird, and flower life on either one. ⏱ *45 min. See p 142.*

Continue south on the loop road 1 mile (1.6km) around the point to the parking area for

⓫ **Thunder Hole.** If you like big waves crashing against rocks and producing plenty of foam, vibration, and noise, you'll *love* Thunder Hole—at the right time of day, that is. The spectacle here can range from plumes up to 30 or more feet high (9.1m) to an absolute dud if there's no wave action in the bay. ⏱ *15 min. See p 142.*

Day 6
From Bar Harbor, travel west on Mt. Desert St. (which becomes Rte. 233) for 1½ miles (2.4km). Bear right on Paradise Hill Rd. and turn left at the intersection with Park Loop Rd. Follow Park Loop Rd. about 1 mile (1.6km) to the turnoff for Cadillac Summit Rd. Turn right and drive 3½ miles (5.6km) up to the top of

⓬ ★★ **Cadillac Mountain.** Drive to the top of this mountain, which is 1,528 feet (466m) from sea level to summit and made of pinkish and greenish granite. Trivia lovers note: Until 1918, this hill was known as Green Mountain, and a cog railway once ran to the top from a hotel. The engines are now used to haul travelers up Mount Washington in

New Hampshire, instead. ⏱ *1 hr. See p 143.*

Return down Cadillac Summit Rd. and along Park Loop Rd. to Rte. 233. Turn left and follow Rte. 233 about 5 miles (8km) inland (west) to Rte. 198. Turn left (south) and continue 5 miles (8km) to

⓭ **Northeast Harbor.** There's no doubt the main street of Northeast Harbor is one of the cutest on Mount Desert Island. It's worth a few hours to a half-day of exploring—easier if you're staying in town. But even if you're not, take time to sample the goods at the old-fashioned **Pine Tree Market** (121 Main St.; ☎ 207/276-3335); browse through shops and galleries; and dine in a local restaurant such as **Redbird Provisions** (11 Sea St.; ☎ 207/276-3006). ⏱ *3 hr. See p 145.*

Backtrack north 6½ miles (10km) on Rte. 198 to Rte. 102. Turn left and continue 6½ miles (10km) south to

⓮ **Southwest Harbor.** Southwest Harbor stands just a mile (1.6km) across the fjord from Northeast Harbor, but it takes almost half an hour to get from one to the other by car. Southwest has a different feel from Northeast. There are few "sights," per se, but plenty of agreeable small-town life. Highlights include the busy main street—check out **Little Notch Pizzeria** (☎ 207/244-3357) at 340 Main St., the excellent **Sawyer's Market** at 344 Main St. (☎ 207/244-3315), and fine-dining option **Fiddlers' Green** at 411 Main St. (☎ 207/244-9416)—then turn left onto Clark Point Rd., which passes a few inns (such as the **Lindenwood;** 118 Clark Point Rd.; ☎ 800/307-5335 or 207/244-5335) en route to the ferry dock, town pier, and **Beal's Lobster Pound** (182 Clark Point Rd.; ☎ 207/244-7178 or 207/244-3202). ⏱ *2 hr. See p 145.*

Day 7
From Southwest Harbor, drive north 1 mile (1.6km) on Rte. 102 to Fernald Point Rd. Turn right and continue 1 mile (1.6km) to the parking area and trail head for

⓯ **Flying Mountain.** This short, mile-long (1.6km) hike up to the top of a modest ridgeline supplies pretty good views of the fjord cleaving Mount Desert Island in two. Bird-watchers love it here, too—they often find unusual species passing through. No facilities to speak of; pack a snack. 🕐 *1 hr. See p 166.*

Backtrack to Rte. 102. Turn right and drive 5½ miles (8.9km) north to Rte. 3. Turn right and continue about 6 miles (9.7km) east and south (stay on Rte. 3) to the parking area for

⓰ ★ **Thuya Garden.** A wonderfully laid out flower garden full of bright perennials, Thuya is the testament of the landscape architect who once resided here. It's a wonderful spot for a picnic or snapping photos, best in mid-summer when blossoms are at their height. 🕐 *30 min. See p 144.*

Turn around and backtrack a half-mile along Rte. 3 to the parking area for the

⓱ ★ **Asticou Terraces and Azalea Garden.** Uphill from the busy loop road traversing this section of the island, these gardens are a fine surprise—and nearby (at the junction with Rte. 198) is a wonderful Asian water world where you step from stone to stone in a pond, admiring the seasonal blooms. It's very Zen. 🕐 *45 min. See p 144.*

Continue northwest on Rte. 3 for about ¾ mile (1.2km) to Rte. 198; turn left and continue 1 mile (1.6km) into Northeast Harbor. Turn left onto Harbor Rd. (before the downtown area) and continue to the docks. Board the mail boat for

⓲ **Great Cranberry Island.** This island gives you a real taste of Maine island culture, with its small **Preble-Marr Historical Museum** (Great Cranberry Rd. at McSorley Rd.; ☎ 207/244-7800), fishing boats, tiny general store, quiet dirt lanes, and outstanding views back onto the big mountains of Mount Desert Isle. 🕐 *2½ hr. 3–6 ferries per day year-round (winter Sun 1 per day). See p 37.*

Lush greenery at the tranquil Asticou Terraces and Azalea Garden.

The Best in Two Weeks

1 Seal Harbor
2 Jordan Pond
3 Day Mountain
4 Bar Harbor Village Green
5 Blue Hill
6 Stonington
7 Deer Isle Village
8 Castine
9 Rockport harbor
10 Center for Maine Contemporary Art
11 Farnsworth Museum
12 Bowdoin College
13 Downtown Freeport
14 L.L.Bean Flagship Store
15 Perkins Cove
16 Marginal Way
17 Ogunquit Museum of American Art
18 St. Peter's By-The-Sea
19 Long Sands
20 Nubble Light
21 Mason Park
22 Harbor Beach
23 Strawbery Banke
24 Prescott Park
25 Market Square

Consider this "a grand circle tour" of the coast, taking in not only its fantastic national park, but also a number of its cutest coastal villages. We'll travel from long strands of sand to lighthouses, museums, and quaint little harbors along the way. (For the first 7 days of your 2-week tour, follow the "Best in 1 Week" tour, above.) START: **Take a return ferry from Great Cranberry Island to Northeast Harbor. Drive 1 mile north to Rte. 3 and turn right. Continue 3½ miles west to Seal Harbor.**

Day 8

1 ★ Seal Harbor. Tiny but lovely, this harbor-side town features the free **Seal Harbor Beach** with restrooms, a green park known as the **Village Green**, a gas pump, plus more of those great views and gracious homes. It's a great spot to snap a photo and eat a picnic with food from the market in Southwest Harbor. ⏱ *1¼ hr. See p 143.*

From the parking lot, turn right and then immediately turn right again onto Stanley Rd. Drive north 1½ miles (2.4km) to the fork in the road. Bear left onto Park Loop Rd. and continue ½ mile (.8km) to

2 ★★ Jordan Pond. This small, attractive pond, framed by the hills and ridges of Acadia, is well worth a stop for the scenery and fresh air—it's one of the best photo opportunities on the island and requires only a 1-minute walk from a parking lot to reach. You can hike around the entire shore (it takes perhaps an

hour), but most travelers park in the huge parking lots and have a snack at the adjacent **Jordan Pond House** restaurant (Park Loop Rd.; ☎ 207/276-3244). ⏱ *1 hr. See p 143.*

Return along Jordan Pond Rd. to Seal Harbor. Turn left and follow Rte. 3 a mile (1.6km) to the parking lot on the right. Across the street is the trail head for

3 Day Mountain. This moderate, enjoyable mile-and-a-half (2.4km) hike affords you views of water, islands, geology, foliage—even horses and carriages, sometimes. The parking lot is clearly marked, and so is the trail. ⏱ *1½ hr. See p 166.*

Turn right onto Rte. 3 and continue 8 miles (13km) into Bar Harbor. On your left as you enter town on Main St. will be the

4 Bar Harbor Village Green. The town's central green space is a daily parade of tourists, ice-cream cones, kids, and guitar-strummers.

Enjoying a sunny afternoon at Seal Harbor's free beach.

Visitors to Blue Hill appreciate the calm, low-key nature of the town.

It's surrounded on all sides by shops and restaurants, and is an especially pleasant place to take in the scenery and plan your souvenir-shopping. ⏱ *45 min. See p 138.*

Day 9

From Bar Harbor, follow Rte. 3 20 miles (32km) north to downtown Ellsworth. Cross the town bridge and bear left onto Rte. 172. Continue 12 miles (19km) to

⑤ ★★ **Blue Hill.** Sitting on a pretty harbor at the junction of three roads, it's the preferred summer destination of many an out-of-stater precisely because it's so quiet and untouristed. The compact downtown features the general store (**Merrill & Hinckley**, on the green at 11 Union St.; ☎ 207/374-2821); a natural foods store (**Blue Hill Co-Op,** 4 Ellsworth Rd; ☎ (207/374-2165); the great little **Jonathan Fisher House** historical museum at 44 Mines Rd. (☎ 207/374-2459); a changing roster of galleries; and a smattering of fine eateries, such as **Arborvine** (33 Main St.; ☎ 207/374-2119). ⏱ *2 hr. Rte. 176 at Rte. 15.*

From Blue Hill's village center, follow Main St. (Rte. 176/15) south 5 miles (8km) to the end.

Turn left to keep on Rte. 15, continuing 12 miles (19km) to

⑥ **Stonington.** Stonington consists of one commercial street that wraps along a very scenic harbor's edge, plus a few side streets and fishing docks. It's still a somewhat rough-and-tumble fishing town, but gift, book, and craft shops have gradually taken over the main drag. Stop into **Bayside Antiques** (131 W. Main St.; ☎ 207/367-8714); **Dockside Books** (62 W. Main St.; ☎ 207/367-2652); or **Prints & Reprints** (31 Main St.; ☎ 207/367-5821), with its Wyeth (1917–2009) focus, for example. The **town opera house** (1 Opera House Lane, just off Main and School sts.; ☎ 207/367-2788) is home to a summer-stock theater company; check its schedule at www.operahousearts.org. ⏱ *45 min.*

Backtrack 5 miles (8km) north along Rte. 15 to

⑦ **Deer Isle Village.** The town of Deer Isle (as opposed to the island) is tiny and uncommercial; you barely notice it unless you know to stop, yet it's chock-full of artists' studios and galleries. Some of the better choices include the **Red Dot Gallery** (3 Main St.; ☎ 207/348-2733), a local collective; **Conary**

Cove Glass Works (3 Black Point Rd.; ☎ 207/348-9402); and **Deer Island Granite** (70 Center District Crossroad; ☎ 207/348-7714). Worth a look. 🕐 *30 min.*

Continue north on Rte. 15 12 miles (19km), staying straight (don't turn right) to the junction with Rte. 176. Go north 2½ miles (4km) on Rte. 176, then right onto Rte. 175. Continue 7 miles (11km) west to Rte. 199; stay straight on Rte. 199 (which becomes Rte. 166) for 8 more miles (13km) to reach

8 ★★ **Castine.** Often considered one of Maine's most attractive villages, Castine is best known to Mainers as the home of the **Maine Maritime Academy** (☎ 207/326-4311); in summer, the academy's training ship *State of Maine* can be toured for free whenever it's in port. Handsome mid-19th-century homes still fill the side streets, and towering elms overarch many of the avenues. The quirky **Wilson Museum** (☎ 207/326-9247), at 120 Perkins St., is worth a stop, as is the adjacent **John Perkins House** (same phone and address): It's Castine's oldest home. 🕐 *2 hr.*

Day 10
Follow Rte. 166 north 7 miles (11km) to Rte. 175. Stay straight to join Rte. 175 North and continue 8 miles (13km) to U.S. Rte. 1. Turn left and continue 40 miles (64km) south, through Camden; 2 miles (3.2km) beyond downtown, turn left onto Pleasant St. and go 1 mile (1.6km) to

9 ★ **Rockport harbor.** The coastal views, handsome commercial architecture, working fish pier, and gravity-like pull of this picturesque village to artists and photographers all make it as good a destination as any in Penobscot Bay. Park for free above the boat landing; the best spot for pictures is at Marine Park (free admission; open daily dawn–dusk); the best spot for picnic provisions is the **Rockport Corner Shop** (23 Central St.; ☎ 207/236-8361). And in the U.S. Route 1 section of town, less than a mile (1.6km) away, don't miss **Prism Gallery & Restaurant** (297 Commercial St.; ☎ 207/230-0061), featuring both blown glasswork and fine dining. 🕐 *1 hr. See p 125.*

10 **Center for Maine Contemporary Art.** The CMCA is one of the best little galleries in the Midcoast region, showcasing both boundary-breaking work (abstract painting, installations, and sculpture) and more time-honored work, such as handmade furniture and

The Center for Maine Contemporary Art exhibits the work of local artists.

crafts. It's especially known for showcasing the work of local and regional photographers. ⏰ *1½ hr.* *162 Russell Ave., Rockport.* ☎ *207/236-2875. See p 126.*

Continue ½ mile (.8km) south along Pascal Ave. to U.S. Rte. 1. Turn left and continue 6 miles (9.7km) south into downtown Rockland. Turn left on Elm St., then right on Main St. The next left goes down Museum St. and takes you to the

⓫ ★★ Farnsworth Museum.

This museum holds a superb collection of Maine-related art, including names like Kent (1882–1971) and Wyeth, but also some you might not have heard about. On a rainy day, a trip here is even better. ⏰ *2–3 hr. See p 125.*

Day 11
From Rockland, follow U.S. Rte. 1 south 50 miles (80km) to Brunswick. Exit onto Bath Rd. and turn right. In 2 miles (3.2km), turn left on Campus Dr. North and park in Visitor Parking for

⓬ ★ Bowdoin College. Maine's

best small college (it used to be harder to get into than Harvard) has a lovely central quad, sturdy chapel, and two museums of special note: the **Peary-MacMillan Museum** (inside Hubbard Hall; ☎ 207/725-3416), full of Arctic mementoes, and the **Bowdoin College Museum of Art** (5 College St.; ☎ 207/725-3275). ⏰ *1 hr. See p 121.*

Continue south 8 miles (13km) on U.S. Rte. 1 to

⓭ 🄺🄸🄳🅂 Downtown Freeport.

Some of Maine's best shopping is on and around Freeport's Main Street. There are dozens of brand-name outlet shops like—**The Gap** at 35 Main St. (☎ 207/865-4452), **Abercrombie & Fitch** at 55 Main St. (207/865-4641),

The L.L.Bean flagship store.

and so forth—plus local souvenir and craft shops like **Cool as a Moose** (100 Main St.; ☎ 207/865-4206) and historic homes such as **Jameson Tavern** (115 Main St.; ☎ 207/865-4196), where the papers that separated Maine from Massachusetts were signed. Parking is free in big lots just west of Main Street. ⏰ *3 hr.*

On the north side of Main St. is the

⓮ ★ 🄺🄸🄳🅂 L.L.Bean Flagship

Store. Bean is the patron saint of Freeport shopping, and has been so since Leon Leonwood Bean invented a waterproof boot and had the master stroke of marketing it to out-of-staters by mail. From there grew a business juggernaut, especially when L.L. decided to go 24-hours-open in 1951. ⏰ *1 hr. See p 108.*

Day 12
From Main St. in Freeport, get on I-295 and travel south 22 miles (35km); merge with I-95 (a toll road) and travel 24 miles (39km) to Exit 19. Pay the toll and turn left onto Rte. 9, following it 1½ miles (2.4km) to U.S. Rte. 1. Turn right and continue 5 miles (8km) to the 5-way intersection. Turn

left onto Shore Rd. and go 1 mile
(1.6km) to the end (bear left at
the split). This is

15 Perkins Cove. The densest
concentrations of galleries, views,
and restaurants in town. Among the
stars here are the wonderful eatery
MC Perkins Cove (111 Perkins Cove
Rd.; ☎ 207/646-6263), the coffee-
shop-with-a-view **Breaking New
Grounds** (3 Harbor Lane; ☎ 207/
641-0634), and the **Scully Gallery**
(116 Perkins Cove Rd.; ☎ 207/646-
2850), exhibiting the work of a local
watercolorist. ⏲ *1½ hr. See p 55.*

From road's end, backtrack about
900 ft. (274m), turn right onto Marginal Way Walk, and stroll onto

16 ★ Marginal Way. It's impossible to overstate my affection for this
little mile-long (1.6km) walking track,
which climbs along Ogunquit's cliffs
and passes in front of numerous
high-priced summer cottages on its
way from Perkins Cove down to the
great town beach. There are lots of
benches, hidden pocket beaches,
and scenic viewpoints along the
way. ⏲ *1 hr. See p 56.*

Turn left back onto Shore Rd. In
½ mile (.8km), on the left, you
reach the

**17 ★★ Ogunquit Museum of
American Art.** This is arguably
one of the dozen or so best museums (of any size) in New England. It
features important landscape works
reflecting the artistic colony that
sprung up here during the early
to mid-20th century, as well as a
rather impressive alcove of sculpture and plenty of modernist work,
too. ⏲ *1¼ hr. See p 55.*

Day 13
Continue south along Shore Rd.
1 mile (1.6km) past the Ogunquit
museum to

18 St. Peter's By-the-Sea. While
driving Shore Road south of Ogunquit, don't miss the big, handsome
stone St. Peter's By-the-Sea church,
a seasonal Episcopal church built
around 1898 which is only open
from early June through early September. It's a popular wedding spot
during its short season. ⏲ *15 min.
Shore Rd., Ogunquit.*

Continue 3½ miles (5.6km) south
to York's Main Street. Turn right
on Long Beach Ave. In about half
a mile (.8km), you reach the
northern end of

19 ★ kids Long Sands. One of
the state's longest, prettiest
beaches, Long Sands stretches in a
gentle two-part crescent for several
miles, open and exposed to the
Atlantic; waves are reliable, and the
bottom is mostly smooth enough
for swimming. ⏲ *2–3 hr. See p 64.*

From the southernmost end of
Long Sands, turn left (uphill) on
Nubble Rd. and travel about 1¼
miles (2km) to

20 ★ kids Nubble Light. There's
a reason why people come from all
over to photograph Nubble Light:
It's pretty and distinctive, and sits
on a headland with views that seem
to stretch all the way to Europe. You
won't be alone, but you'll be glad
you came. ⏲ *1 hr. See p 41.*

Day 14
From Long Sands, follow Rte. 1A
2 miles (3.2km) south to

21 ★ Mason Park. This park, right
across from the York Harbor Inn
(see p 52), would undoubtedly be
worth millions on the real estate
market. But it's free and public,
offers terrific views of Harbor Beach
(see below), and even connects to a
scenic, easy 2-mile walking trail
known as the Cliff Walk. ⏲ *45 min.
See p 52.*

Harbor Beach is clean and beautiful, with restrooms and changing facilities.

Walk 300 ft. (91m) from the park to reach

22 ★ **Harbor Beach.** This little sweep of sand is scenic and clean, and it comes with changing and restroom facilities—a big plus. You'll sometimes see shellfish, urchin, and seaweed divers wading into shore from the sea with their harvest. ⏱ *30 min. See p 64.*

Follow Rte. 1A west to U.S. Rte. 1. Turn right, then left at the next light. Merge onto I-95 South; travel 7 miles (11km) and take the first exit (Market St.). Turn left and continue 1 mile (1.6km) into Portsmouth. Park downtown and walk ¼ mile (.4km) downhill toward the tall steel bridge. Turn immediately left on Wright Ave. Walk east 1 block to State St. Turn right onto Marcy St. and stroll into

23 ★ **kids Strawbery Banke.** Everything from old museums and merchants' homes to blacksmith's shops and public houses are collected in this outdoor museum–slash–historical campus. Many of the buildings are open to the public, and re-enactors in costume help give a taste of life in colonial times. ⏱ *2 hr. See p 49.*

Walk 2 blocks farther along Marcy St. to

24 ★ **Prescott Park.** You can't go wrong with a visit to Prescott Park's many cultivated flower gardens, lawns, and riverside benches—it's an ideal urban park because it doesn't feel urban at all. Yet the city is just a couple of blocks away. ⏱ *1 hr. See p 49.*

Return along Marcy St. to State St. and turn left. Walk 3 short blocks and turn right on Pleasant St.; walk 1 block to the four-way intersection, which is

25 **Market Square.** Portsmouth's geographical and commercial heart beats strong in Market Square, where coffee shops like **Breaking New Grounds** (14 Market Sq.; ☎ 603/436-9555) fight for your attention with barbecue joints (**Muddy River Smokehouse**, 21 Congress St.; ☎ 603/430-9582), bakeries like **Popovers on the Square** (8 Congress St.; ☎ 603/431-1119) and the lovely **North Church** (2 Congress St.; see p. 48). There's also a city tourist office branch in a little hut during summer months. ⏱ *1½ hr. See p 48.* ●

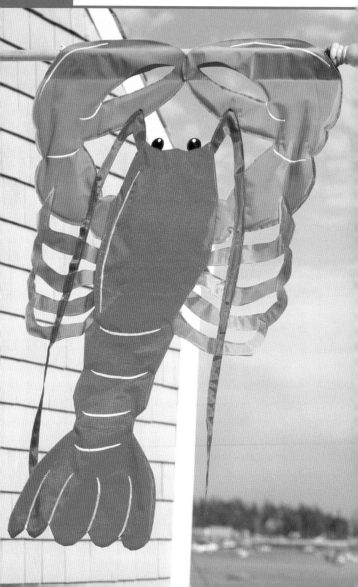

Island Hopping

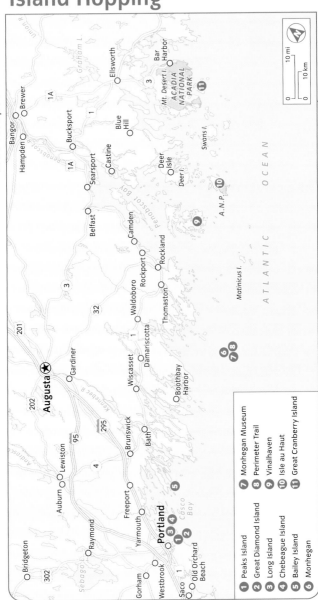

1 Peaks Island
2 Great Diamond Island
3 Long Island
4 Chebeague Island
5 Bailey Island
6 Monhegan
7 Monhegan Museum
8 Perimeter Trail
9 Vinalhaven
10 Isle au Haut
11 Great Cranberry Island

Previous page: There are many lobster pounds worth visiting along Maine's coast.

There are approximately 4,600 islands in Maine. Many of these are big, uninhabited rocks, mind you—but still, it's clearly impossible to see 'em all. So here are 17 to get you started. Nearly all of them are accessible by year-round ferry service. (With a private charter boat, your options expand exponentially.) But remember: Each of these islands is worth from a half-hour to most of a day.

START: **Portland's Casco Bay Lines ferry terminal at Commercial and Franklin sts.**

The Peaks Island ferry runs hourly.

DAY 1

❶ ★★ Peaks Island. Comfortable Peaks is by far the biggest of Casco Bay's islands, *population*-wise: As many as 6,000 people call it home each summer. It's also the closest—a 20-minute ride from the waterfront, and ferries leave on the hour. So it's ideal for a quick trip if you're pressed for time and can visit only one island during a short trip to Maine. It doesn't have the remote character nor artistic heritage of a Monhegan, but it does have a graceful loop road, ruined gun batteries in the center of the island, a microbrewery inside the **Inn on Peaks Island** (☎ 207/766-5100), and rocky beaches with open Atlantic views along the back shore. ⏱ *6 hr. Ferry tickets from (*☎ *207/774-7871; www.cascobaylines.com)*

$4.10–$7.70 adults; discounts for seniors & children. Ferries leave year-round, 1 per hr.

Overnight on Peaks Island.

DAY 2

In addition to a year-round, twice-a-day "mailboat run" that links the next three islands with Peaks (the 3-hr. run costs $7.25–$15 for adults; don't miss the second boat back, or you could be stranded overnight), there are always daily boats to and from each of these next 3 islands, up to 10 per day in peak summer.

❷ ★★ Great Diamond Island. Great Diamond is actually connected to Little Diamond at low tide. It's so thinly populated that many locals get around on golf carts, because there's no car traffic to worry about. The late-19th-century fort that was built here, Fort McKinley, was in ruins until a developer converted it into a controversial real estate development, Diamond Cove. Some of the history has been preserved in the small **Fort McKinley Museum** (☎ 207/766-5814), which has limited hours; you can tour the old battlements only by special appointment with the Diamond Cove development's museum staff. ⏱ *1 hr. McKinley Ct. (from the landing, walk up Diamond Ave. ½ mile/.8km & turn right).*

❸ ★★ Long Island. Next, the boat pulls into Long Island, which is

The Chebeague Island Inn was built in the 1920s.

a breed apart—literally. Its residents voted to secede from the city of Portland and all its support services in 1993, a famous case that drew nationwide media attention. This is a town of fishermen, rather than a summer-vacation haven. **South Beach** is managed by the state of Maine and is free to visit. 🕐 *1½ hr.*

❹ ★★ **Chebeague Island.** Also known as Great Chebeague, this island is last on the mail run and perhaps the biggest (physically) in the entire bay, although it remains thinly populated. More a summer vacation and second-home colony than a true year-round destination, Chebeague followed Long Island on the Maine secession train in 2007, separating from the coastal town of Cumberland. The island is

also notable for the 1920s-era **Chebeague Island Inn** (61 South Rd.; ☎ 207/846-5155), which is newly restored; if you're going to overnight in the islands, do it here. There's also a little general store. 🕐 *4 hr.*

Overnight on Chebeague Island.

DAY 3
Take the ferry back to Portland, then drive north on I-295 and U.S. Rte. 1 about 30 miles (48km) to Bath. Then, turn west on Rte. 24 and continue down the long peninsula to

❺ ★★ **Bailey Island.** Bailey Island can be reached by car from Bath or Brunswick via Route 24, and the drive over cribwork bridges out to the peninsula is positively gorgeous—as are the water views. Even though it's connected to land, it's a worthy side trip from U.S. Route 1. While here, take a boat ride, jump off, stroll around, and eat the lobster at **Cook's Lobster House** (68 Garrison Cove Rd.; ☎ 207/833-2818). From Portland harbor, you can book a cruise on Casco Bay Lines that stops on this island—it takes 6 hours in all. (You can also cruise *past* the island once per day on another routing that takes fewer than 2 hours and costs less, but it doesn't stop on the island

The secluded island of Monhegan remains untouched by modern life.

A few of the island's artifacts at the Monhegan Museum.

itself.) Fix a pre-ferry picnic with provisions from the **Browne Trading Co.** market on Portland's Commercial Street (p 100). *Casco Bay Lines* ☎ 207/774-7871. www.cascobay lines.com. Full cruise $24 adults, $21 seniors, $11 children; pass-by cruise $16 adults, $13 seniors, $7.25 children. Late June to early September; one island-landing cruise daily.

Return to U.S. Rte. 1 at Bath and turn north. Continue north about 45 miles (72km; about 1 hr.) to the town of Thomaston. Turn right onto Rte. 131 and go 15 miles (24km) to Port Clyde. Board the ferry for

⑥ ★★★ **Monhegan.** Monhegan might be Maine's *best* island. Visited by Europeans as early as 1497, it's wild, remote, and incredibly scenic. Artists discovered it in the 1870s, but it never developed; this is still a fisherman's island that hikers, painters, and photographers consider themselves lucky to stumble upon. Check into an inn such as the **Monhegan House** (1 Main St,; ☎ 207/594-7983. www. monheganhouse.com) or the **Trailing Yew** (Lobster Cove Rd.; ☎ 207/596-0440) and savor the solitude and sea air. You'll have to: There's only one ATM I know of here and a few pay phones—even electricity isn't a given. (If you can't stomach the complete quiet and the lack of phones, TVs, and

late-night takeout, overnight in the Tenants Harbor or Rockland areas and do a day trip in the morning.) ⏱ 4 hr. ☎ 207/372-8848. www. monheganboat.com. Round-trip $32 adults, $18 children 2–12. May–Oct daily 1–3 trips, Nov–Apr weekly 3 trips; June to mid-Oct last island-bound ferry 3pm. No cars; parking at dock $5 per day.

DAY 4

⑦ ★ **Monhegan Museum.** One of the few attractions on the island is this good museum next to the 1824 lighthouse on a high point above the village. The museum, open for a few hours in the middle of each day from late June through September, has a quirky collection of historical artifacts and provides context for this rugged island's history. Nearby is a small and select art museum that opened in 1998 and features changing exhibits showcasing the works of illustrious island artists, including Rockwell Kent. ⏱ 1 hr. 1 Lighthouse Hill. ☎ 207/596-7003. www.monheganmuseum.org. Free admission. July–Aug daily 11:30am–3:30pm, late June & Sept daily 1:30–3:30pm. Closed Oct–May.

After touring the museum, strap on walking shoes and explore the

⑧ ★★ **Perimeter Trail.** Much of Monhegan is ringed with high, open bluffs atop fissured cliffs; pack a picnic lunch and hike the trail that circles the island's shores, spending part of your time sitting, reading, and enjoying the surf rolling in against the cliffs. Take care—some of the trails are tricky or brush up against steep drop-offs. The island's interior trails are appealing in a different way: The deep, dark Cathedral Woods, for instance, are mossy and fragrant, and sunlight only dimly filters through the evergreens to the forest floor. To find this easy trail, descend Lighthouse Hill to Main Street and turn right, walk about ⅓ mile (.5km) north, and turn right onto the trail. It extends about a half-mile (.8km) to the island's eastern shore. 🕐 *1 hr.*

Take the return ferry to Port Clyde (4 hrs.). From Port Clyde, backtrack 15 miles (24km) to Thomaston and turn right on U.S. Rte. 1 North. In about 4 miles (6.4km), you come into Rockland. At the waterfront, follow signs to the state ferry to

❾ ★ Vinalhaven. One of Maine's most famous fishing islands, Vinalhaven is all about local character: The most popular restaurant here is called **The Harbor Gawker** (26 Main St.; ☎ 207/863-9365). It takes

more than an hour for the ferry trip, and there are no luxury lodgings once you do arrive (though there is now a coffee shop, **The ARC** [39 High St.; ☎ 207/863-4191] with Wi-Fi). This is a thriving town—with more than a thousand year-round residents—and locals have established a couple of galleries (**Five Elements** at 28 Main St. and **New Era** at 60 Main St.), plus a few simple rental cottages and the **Tidewater Motel** (☎ 207/863-4619) at 15 Main St. You can drive a car onto the ferry. Trivia note: Granite quarried here helped build the Brooklyn Bridge and the Washington Monument. 🕐 *1½ hr. Round-trip $18 adults, $8.50 children; $50 cars. 6 ferries per day year-round.*

DAY 5

Take the return ferry to Rockland. Continue 50 miles (80km) north on U.S. Rte. 1. A few miles past Bucksport, turn right (south) on Rte. 15 and continue 35 miles (56km) more across Deer Isle (p 26) to Stonington (p 26) and the ferry to

❿ ★★★ Isle au Haut. Famous for its hardy lobstermen and -women, rocky remote Isle au Haut

The rugged and remote Isle au Haut was discovered by Samuel de Champlain.

The views from Great Cranberry Island to the peaks of Acadia National Park can be magical.

is worth finding. The island was spotted and named by French explorer Samuel de Champlain, and it's half-owned by the Park Service and part of Acadia National Park (see Chapter 7). The ferry normally stops at **Town Landing**—convenient for groceries, with a small village, old homes, a handsome church, and a tiny schoolhouse, post office, and store. During summer, some boats stop instead at Duck Harbor, a few minutes' walk from five National Park lean-to's (uncovered shelters for camping, which must be reserved in advance and fill up quickly). Stroll the road circling the island or hike a rugged trail system stretching nearly 20 miles (30km) through towering, deep groves of spruce, fog, and boulders. The Western Head/Cliff Trail circuit, at the island's southwestern tip, is the best walk; follow unpaved Western Head Rd. to the trailhead. The 4-mile (3km) circuit takes 3 to 4 hrs. of moderate to difficult walking but rewards one with good ocean views. Be careful hiking over wet logs, stumps, and roots.
🕐 *3–4 hr. Isle au Haut Boat Services* ☎ *207/367-5193. www.isleauhaut. com. Tickets $32 adults, $16 kids*

under 12. 4–10 ferries per day year-round. Camping $25 per site; book through www.nps.gov.

DAY 6

Take the return ferry to Stonington. Follow Rte. 15 north to Rte. 176; after about 40 miles (64km; 1 hr.) more, you reach Ellsworth. Turn right onto Rte. 3 and follow it 20 miles (32km) south (joining up with Rte. 198) to Northeast Harbor. Board the ferry to

⓫ ★★ **Great Cranberry Island.** The biggest of the little Cranberries cluster has the **Preble-Marr Historical Museum** (☎ 207/244-7800) inside the village cafe at 163 Cranberry Rd., which has Wi-Fi, plus a general store at the docks. There's also an undemanding ½-mile (.8km) public trail (beginning at the town church) over bogs and boardwalks to empty Whistler Cove and its sandy beach. This is a flat and unspectacular island, but the views back across Sutton Island and on to the peaks of Acadia are magical. *Beal & Bunker ferry* ☎ *207/244-3575. Round-trip $24 adults, $12 children 3–12. 3–6 ferries per day year-round (except winter Sun 1 ferry per day).*

Maine Coast for Art Lovers

1 Congress Square
2 MeCA Institute of Contemporary Art
3 Westbrook College/UNE Art Gallery
4 Olson House
5 The galleries of Rockland and Rockport

I describe the "Big 4" museums of coastal Maine—the Portland
Museum of Art (p 85), Ogunquit Museum of American Art (p 55),
Bowdoin College Museum of Art (p 121), and the Farnsworth (p 125)—
elsewhere in these pages. All of them are must-visits for art aficiona-
dos. When you're finished visiting those four, take time to explore
some of these lesser-known museum and gallery gems, too. START:
Begin in Portland at Congress Sq. (corner of Congress and High sts.).

1 ★★ Congress Square. Portland is chock-full of galleries showcasing Maine artists working in
landscape, modern art, and mixed
media. Some of the best are concentrated in the area of Congress
Square, at the corner of Congress
and High streets, which is considered the de facto arts capital of the
city. Stop by the long-standing **June
Fitzpatrick Gallery** (☎ 207/772-
1961) at 112 High St. (with an annex
inside MeCA; see below) and **Portland Photo Works,** inside the State

Theatre at 142 High St. (☎ 207/228-
5829). You could easily see a half-
dozen more local galleries in the
Old Port, given a little more time.
⏱ *1 hr.*

**On Congress St., in the heart of
downtown, is the**

**2 ★ MeCA Institute of Con-
temporary Art.** The Maine
College of Art's house gallery showcases lots of student work each
semester, plus the largely modernist work of distinguished college

MeCA's Institute of Contemporary Art features the work of notable alumni and current students.

alumni—from installations to digital art, sculpture, and beyond. ⏱ *1 hr. 522 Congress St.* ☎ *207/879-5742. www.meca.edu. Free admission. Wed–Sun 11am–5pm, Thurs 11am–7pm, some Fri 11am–8pm.*

From Congress St., follow High St. downhill to Forest Ave. Follow it 1 mile (1.6km), turn left onto Woodford St., then turn right onto Stevens Ave. After about 1 mile (1.6km) is the

❸ ★★ Westbrook College/UNE Art Gallery.

This virtually unknown gallery (now part of the University of New England) once housed two nearly priceless van Goghs (1853–1890) on long-term loan from the Payson family. But they were sold in the 1980s; today, the museum is back to quiet excellence, curating and showing an outstanding collection of American art and, especially, photographs. ⏱ *1 hr. 716 Stevens Ave.* ☎ *207/221-4499. www.une.edu/artgallery. Free admission. Wed & Fri–Sun 1pm–4pm, Thurs 1pm–7pm.*

From Portland, it's a bit less than a 2-hr. drive north via I-295, U.S. Rte. 1, and then Rte. 97 to Cushing and the

❹ ★★ Olson House.

Andrew Wyeth's (1917–2009) *Christina's World* is possibly the most famous painting of Maine ever made—though fans of Edward Hopper (1882–1967), Rockwell Kent, and Winslow Homer (1836–1910) might argue—and you can walk through the same farmhouse he painted so many times from an upstairs studio. The Farnsworth Art Museum (p 125) was given the farmhouse in 1991; for a small fee, you can tour it, though the famous field is privately owned and off-limits. ⏱ *45 min. Hathorne Point Rd.* ☎ *207/354-0102. www.farnsworthmuseum.org/olson-house. Admission $5 adults. Mid-May to mid-Oct daily 11am–4pm; closed the rest of the year.*

From Cushing, return to U.S. Rte. 1 and turn right (north). In 20 or 30 minutes, you'll reach

❺ ★★★ The galleries of Rockland and Rockport.

Even arty Portland can't match Penobscot Bay for sheer gallery greatness per capita. Visit the **Center for Maine Contemporary Art** (162 Russell Ave.; ☎ 207/236-2875) in Rockport; the **Caldbeck Gallery** (12 Elm St.; ☎ 207/594-5935) and the **Dowling Walsh Gallery** (357 Main St.; ☎ 207/596-0084) are the top places in Rockland. There are lots more to choose from, too. ⏱ *3 hr.*

Lobsters & Lighthouses

1. Nubble Light
2. Fox's Lobster House
3. Goat Island Light
4. Cape Porpoise Lobster Co.
5. Cape Elizabeth Lights
6. Two Lights Lobster Shack
7. Portland Head Light
8. Seguin Island Light
9. Harraseeket Lunch & Lobster
10. Pemaquid Point Light
11. Shaw's Fish & Lobster Wharf

For this itinerary, I'm picking out some of the dozens of scenic lighthouses along the coast—especially those that are close to great lobster pounds. Most of Maine's lighthouses were built of stone in the early to mid-19th century, and nearly all were automated in the 1960s or '70s. The lobsters? They were used chiefly for bait and prison meals in Maine for decades (really), until the wealthy discovered their succulent taste. It's impossible for me to include all my favorites, but here's a taste. START: **Begin in York. Follow Rte. 1A to the Long Sands Beach, then turn off on Nubble Rd.**

❶ ★★★ Nubble Light. Yes, it's over-photographed. So what? This was the first lighthouse I ever laid eyes on in Maine, and it's still my favorite. You can see it well before you get there, and it sits on its own island with a cute red barn for good measure. You can get almost close enough to the fabled light to touch it, with the best viewing point at the lobster docks at Cape Porpoise. The lighthouse is lit for the Christmas season in late November each year. 🕐 *1 hr. See p 6.*

Beside the light is

❷ ★ Fox's Lobster House. Fox's is unabashedly commercial and charges more than many other lobster pounds in Maine do. But, again: So what? You're sitting outside, breathing salt air, on a headland that would be worth zillions in real estate terms, looking straight at Nubble Light. It's been here since 1966. 🕐 *45 min. 8 Sohier Park Rd., Cape Neddick.* ☎ *207/363-2643. Entrees & lobster dinners $15–$35. May–Oct daily 11:30am–9pm; closed Nov–Apr.*

Fox's Lobster House has a clear view of Nubble Light.

Circle about a mile (1.6km) back around the point to U.S. Rte. 1. Turn right (north) and drive about 12 miles (19km). Turn right onto Rte. 9 and continue about 7 miles (11km) through both Kennebunks (p 58) and on to Cape Porpoise (p 17). Just offshore is the

❸ ★ Goat Island Light. The small Goat Island Light is just off-shore from the little hamlet of Cape Porpoise. The light has a storied history, including use as a command post for U.S. Secret Service agents defending the family compound of President George H. W. Bush (1924–); a keeper who did a 34-year stint of duty on the rock; a caretaker who died in a boating accident; and Maine's last lighthouse-keeping family, the Culps, who departed only in 1990. A local land trust maintains the 25-foot (7.6m) tower and keeper's house. You can visit by private boat, but you can also see the light from the Cape Porpoise pier. 🕐 *15 min.*

Right on the pier is

❹ ★★ Cape Porpoise Lobster Co. There are two lobster pounds near the prime viewing point for the Goat Island Light. In a compact spot overlooking the sparkling water, this pound doesn't take reservations, but does take credit cards—hardly a given at Maine pounds this simple. 🕐 *1 hr. 15 Pier Rd., Cape Porpoise.*

Harraseeket Lunch & Lobster draws many repeat visitors.

☎ 800/967-4268 or 207/967-4268. Mid May to late Oct daily 9am–7pm; closed Nov to mid-May.

Backtrack to Rte. 9 and turn right. Merge with U.S. Rte. 1 and continue 7 miles (11km) to Rte. 207 (Black Point Rd.); turn right. After 3 miles (4.8km), turn left onto Rte. 77 and go 5½ miles (8.9km) to the

➎ ★ Cape Elizabeth Lights.

The southernmost lights in the greater Portland area, Two Lights State Park's twin lighthouses cannot be visited directly, but they have a rich lore that runs to daring rescues of shipwrecked sailors and the wonderful work of painter Edward Hopper, who featured the lights in several of his early-20th-century canvases. One light's decommissioned and a private home; the other is state-owned, still operational, and off-limits. But you can picnic in the state park and take pictures of their exteriors. ⏱ 45 min. 7 Tower Dr., Cape Elizabeth. ☎ 207/799-5871. Park summer $4.50 non–Maine resident adults,

$1.50 seniors, $1 kids age 5–11; off-season $1.50 adults, free for kids.

Almost adjacent to the state park is

➏ ★★ Two Lights Lobster Shack.

This would probably be one of my very favorites in Maine because of its awesome location

Portland's iconic Head Light.

alone, but the lobster dinners are really good, too. ⏱ *45 min. See p 115.*

Return to Rte. 77 and go north 2 miles (3.2km); turn right on Shore Rd. and continue 2 miles (3.2km) to

7 ★★★ Portland Head Light. You see this lighthouse everywhere on calendars; it's that pretty. The lighthouse was the first constructed in the United States, commissioned by President George Washington (1732–1799). The grassy parklands surrounding it are free and lovely; the handsome lightkeeper's home is a small museum, and the scenic position will keep you snapping photos all afternoon. ⏱ *1 hr. 1000 Shore Rd., Cape Elizabeth.* ☎ *207/ 799-2661. www.portlandheadlight. com. Museum $2 adults, $1 children 6–18; free admission to lighthouse exterior & park. Museum May to mid-Oct daily 10am–4pm; park year-round dawn–dusk.*

Follow Shore Rd. north to Broadway and turn left. Cross the bridge into Portland and I-295 North. Take I-295 North 12 miles (19km) to exit 17 (Yarmouth/Falmouth) and exit onto U.S. Rte. 1. Travel north 1 mile (1.6km) to South Freeport Rd. and turn right; continue 1⅓ miles (2.1km) to Church Rd. and turn right. At the docks, book a cruise to

8 ★ Seguin Island Light. A few miles off Popham Beach (p 123), this lighthouse sports Maine's strongest lens: It's 12 feet high (3.7m) and super powerful to cut through the heavy fogs. The place has been operating since 1857, the same year the keeper's home and stone light tower were also constructed. You can also charter a boat from Bath, Phippsburg, or Boothbay Harbor out to the light. The only regular cruise is the 6-hour, once-weekly run by **Atlantic Seal Cruises** out of South Freeport (☎ 207/865-6112; May– Sept Thurs only). It costs $55 per

Cruising the lights of Monhegan

Of all the various lighthouse-spotting cruises on the Maine coast, Monhegan Boat Line's (☎ 207/372-8848; www.monhegan boat.com) tour is perhaps the cream of the crop. (Offered July to mid-Sept Wed–Fri; tickets $25 adults, $10 children.) First, you pass the whimsical, almost modernist Tenants Harbor Light guarding the entryway to the harbor. (Artist Jamie Wyeth owns this island and lighthouse.) Then, the cruise passes four more lights, including handsome little Marshall Point Light, Whitehead Island Light (classically attractive), and Two Bush Light (skinny, brick, and white). The ride takes 2½ hours in all. Of the four-pack, the Marshall Point Light is especially notable: Andrew Wyeth once painted in a studio in the bell tower, and the lighthouse really got famous when Tom Hanks (1956–) turned around here and headed back west during his hit film Forrest Gump. Marshall Point also happens to be one of the most peaceful, scenic lighthouses on the entire Maine coast, and you can drive there on your own (it's near the Port Clyde docks).

The pristine Pemaquid Point Light.

adult, $40 for children under 10. You can also hire a freelance captain, such as Ed Rice of **River Run Tours** in Woolwich (☎ 207/504-2628), who runs a pontoon boat out to the lighthouse, or Ethan DeBerry (☎ 207/841-7977) in Phippsburg. To do so, you'll usually need a party of three to six and pay by the hour—rates vary highly each year. Once on the island, caretakers (present from late May through early Sept only) happily give free tours of the lighthouse. ⏱ *6 hr.* ☎ 207/865-6112. *Free admission; donations accepted.*

Also at the South Freeport docks is

9 ★★ Harraseeket Lunch & Lobster. Many repeat visitors to Maine swear by this lobster pound, right off the pier and as good a pick-and-pay pound as you'll find in these

parts. ⏱ *1 hr. 36 N. Main St., South Freeport.* ☎ 207/865-4888. *Entrees market priced (lobsters typically $10–$15). Mid-June to early Sept daily 11am–8:45pm; May to mid-June & early Sept to mid-Oct daily 11am–7:45pm. Closed mid-Oct to Apr.*

Backtrack to Freeport and turn right onto U.S. Rte. 1. Follow it north about 35 miles (56km); turn right onto Rte. 129 and drive 3 miles (4.8km), then bear left on Rte. 130. Continue 12 miles (19km) to the

10 ★★★ Pemaquid Point Light. One of Maine's handsomest lighthouses, this classic white stone tower is tucked down another long point finger of land and stands on striking, weather-beaten rocks and cliffs beside a little red keeper's house. The Fishermen's Museum inside explains about the local fishing trade. Coin buffs: This is the light depicted on the U.S. "Maine" quarter. ⏱ *1¼ hr. Pemaquid Point Rd., New Harbor.* ☎ 207/677-2494. *Free admission. Daily 9am–5pm.*

Backtrack 2½ miles (4km) north on Rte. 130, then bear right onto Rte. 32. In half a mile (.8km), turn right to find the classic

11 ★★★ Shaw's Fish & Lobster Wharf. Shaw's attracts a good share of tour buses, but it's worth finding anyway thanks to the superlative lobsters and lobster rolls, and tranquil views from the open deck. This is one of the few Maine lobster pounds with a raw bar—and with a full liquor license. ⏱ *1 hr. 129 Rte. 32, New Harbor.* ☎ 207/677-2200. *Entrees market priced (typically $10–$15 per lobster). Mid-May to mid-Oct daily 11am–9pm; closed mid-Oct to mid-May.* ●

Portsmouth & Kittery

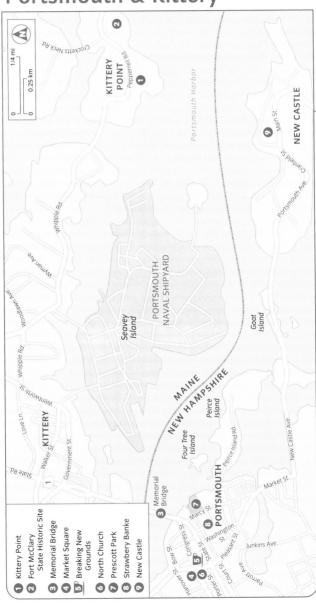

1 Kittery Point
2 Fort McClary State Historic Site
3 Memorial Bridge
4 Market Square
5 Breaking New Grounds
6 North Church
7 Prescott Park
8 Strawbery Banke
9 New Castle

Previous page: A young boy rides a boogie board at a beach in southern Maine.

Portsmouth, New Hampshire, and Kittery, separated by a river and state lines, are so close and yet so far apart. Both are of a similar colonial age and sprung from fishing origins; both contain plenty of saltbox homes. But while Portsmouth grew into an erudite, elegant little city, Kittery remains a quiet fishing village that also happens to be a bedroom community for Boston exurbites—one with a mile-long (1.6km) strip of outlet malls and restaurants.

START: **From I-95, take Exit 1, turning left onto Dennett Rd., which leads into Rte. 103. Stay on Rte. 103 East for about 3½ miles (5.6km).**

❶ Kittery Point. This tiny, historic district—a mile-long (1.6km) neck of land traversed by Route 103—is a scenic mélange of meadow, marsh, tides, military history, and colonial architecture. The man-made highlights include the extraordinary Georgian-style Lady Pepperell House at Follett Lane (where the road makes a sharp turn just before going into the water), built in 1760; and the waterside Old Burying Yard (behind the First Congregational Church, at the hairpin bend). Another home, the saltbox-style John Bray House at 100 Pepperrell Point Rd., is Maine's oldest (it's believed to be circa 1662). ⏱ *15 min. Rte. 103, Kittery.*

In the heart of Kittery Point, on Rte. 103 and Fort Rd., is the

❷ Fort McClary State Historic Site. This hidden historic park backs up against a lovely inlet and commemorates a spot that has been used for coastal defense since at least the late 1600s. The fort was built in 1808 but was little-used in wartime and eventually went to seed; in 1987, it was finally restored. The hexagonal blockhouse is now a small museum. ⏱ *30 min. Kittery Point Rd. (Rte. 103), Kittery.* ☎ *207/384-5160. Admission $3 adults, $1 seniors. Grounds and museum open year-round dawn–dusk; no staff Oct to mid-May.*

Follow Rte. 103 back to U.S. Rte. 1. Turn left and cross onto

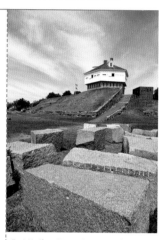

Fort McClary State Historic Site features a fort that dates from 1808.

Badgers Island. Continue ½ mile (.8km) to the

❸ Memorial Bridge. The iconic, 300-foot-long (91m), twin-towered drawbridge (built in 1923) connects two states. This was the first "vertical lift" bridge in New England, and the middle section still rises whenever a tall boat needs to pass through the inlet. The bridge is slated for replacement soon, although historic preservationists are fighting that decision; drive, walk, or bike over it while you can. ⏱ *15 min. U.S. Rte 1.*

Cross the bridge into Portsmouth. After 3 blocks, you'll drive through the heart of

Breaking New Grounds has free Wi-Fi and excellent coffee drinks.

❹ ★ Market Square. Market Square *is* the hub of Portsmouth's social life—an amalgam of coffee shops (including one with outdoor eating), bakeries, antique shops, historic buildings, and workaday traffic winding its way through the knot of the intersection. I'm told they used to practice military maneuvers out here back in the days of wine and muskets more than 200 years ago. Since you're visiting, you might like to know that the city's summer tourist office is housed in a little hut parked (naturally) right out front of the Breaking New Grounds cafe,

North Church was originally built in 1855.

roasting-coffee scent and all. ⏱ *30 min. Daniel St. (at Pleasant St.). Tourist kiosk open late spring to fall.*

❺ Breaking New Grounds. There must be a dozen coffee shops in Portsmouth, all of them pretty good, but this is the one to which I always seem to gravitate. The coffee drinks are excellent, the staff is hip, they have Wi-Fi, and you can usually find a quiet table inside or a noisy one outside. *14 Market Sq.* ☎ *603/436-9555. $.*

Right in Market Square, across Pleasant St. from Breaking New Grounds, is

❻ ★ North Church. There are many, many wonderful steeples in northern New England; well, this is one of my favorites. Portsmouth's massive, tall centerpiece church was built in 1855 to replace a smaller meetinghouse closer to the water. The stained glass, giant organ, and weathervanes here are distinctive. Step lively around the Harleys parked at its foot, though— knock one of those over and you could be in for a bad ending to your day. ⏱ *30 min. 2 Congress St. (at Market Sq.).* ☎ *603/436-9109.*

From the base of the church, walk 2 blocks down Pleasant St. to State St. Cross carefully at the crosswalk. Turn left and continue 3 blocks to Marcy St. Turn right and enter

7 ★ Prescott Park. Adjacent to Portsmouth's richest district of historic buildings, this is a flat-out great little park. From summertime musical performances to cultivated flower gardens to an ice cream shop, river views, and a playhouse, there's literally something for almost everyone. You can even just lay out on a blanket, read a book, and work on your tan if that's what you feel like doing. Ice cream, hot dog, and soda vendors set up shop on the Marcy Street side of the park in summer. ⏱ *1 hr. Marcy St. (at Court St., downhill from State St.).*

Continue 2 blocks down Marcy St. to find the visitor center for

8 kids ★★ Strawbery Banke. This is one of New England's most impressive concentrations of old buildings. Here, you get a true feel for the late-17th-century colonial period, not only because the actual buildings have been restored—but because they're actually open to the public for once, rather than privately owned. One ticket gains you entry to all. The district includes more than 40 buildings, about half of which admit the public to view period furnishings or historical exhibits. ⏱ *2 hr. Visitor's center at Hancock & Marcy sts.* ☎ *603/433-1100. www.strawberybanke.org. Summer admission $15 adults, $10 children 5–17, $40 family; winter rates lower. May–Oct daily 10am–5pm; Nov–Apr Sat–Sun 10am–2pm (must take 90-min. guided tour).*

Retrieve your car. Drive down State St. to Marcy St. and turn right (becomes Rte. 1B). After about 2 miles (3.2km), you arrive at

9 ★★ New Castle. Seven years before there was Portsmouth, there was New Castle (originally known as Great Island). When you arrive at a squat church and dollhouse-sized town hall, you've found "downtown" in the state's smallest town. This was once the site of a colonial jail, several forts, and a lighthouse. ⏱ *45 min. Rte. 1B, east of Portsmouth.*

Prescott Park's beautiful flower gardens are perfect for a relaxing stop.

The Yorks

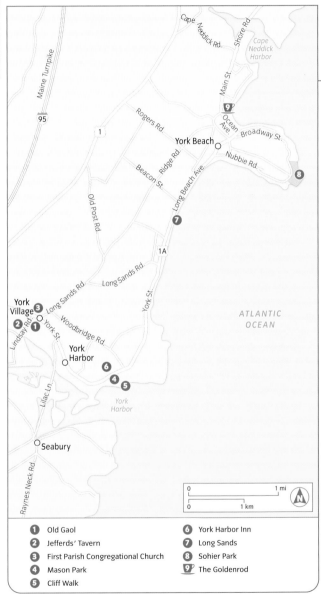

1. Old Gaol
2. Jefferds' Tavern
3. First Parish Congregational Church
4. Mason Park
5. Cliff Walk
6. York Harbor Inn
7. Long Sands
8. Sohier Park
9. The Goldenrod

Y ou won't find "The Yorks" on any map of Maine. York is one town, but it's composed of three or four neighborhoods, and each is quite distinct in character. The harbor is where the money is; the village is where you go for history, gas, and groceries; and there are two beaches, one long and overpoweringly scenic, the other as evocative of summer camp as they come. START: **From U.S. Rte. 1, follow Rte. 1A 1 mile into the center of York Village.**

York's Old Gaol used to be the state's only prison.

❶ ★★ **Old Gaol.** The big, reddish, vaguely barn-like structure (with a cannon in front of it) looming over York's main road is neither a barn nor a fort, but rather the state of Maine's former jail. Constructed here in 1719 with timbers scavenged from an earlier, simpler version of the local jail, it was both the state's only prison *and* a tiny home for the jail keeper and his family (talk about close quarters). Yes, some prisoners were whipped on a post outside. ⏱ *30 min. East side of York St. (at Lindsey No. 2 Rd., across from town hall).* ☎ *207/363-4974. Admission $5 adults, $4 seniors, $3 kids 6–15; $15 families. June to mid-Oct*

Mon–Sat 10am–5pm; closed the rest of year.

The York Historical Pass

One of southern Maine's outstanding historical bargains is the York Historical Pass, sold at Old York's headquarters inside the Remick Barn on Main Street in York. The pass costs $12 adults, $9 seniors, $5 kids 6 to 15, and $25 for families. It gets you into eight properties, including the Old Gaol and Jefferds' Tavern. *3 Lindsay Rd. (at Main St.).* ☎ *207/363-4974. www.oldyork.org.*

Cross Lindsey St. from the jail to find

❷ ★★ **Jefferds' Tavern.** This red tavern looks somewhat as it did when it was built in 1750, though it has since been both moved (from Wells), and considerably added onto (during the 1940s, when it was restored). The hive-shaped brick oven works and is sometimes used to bake simple breads. ⏱ *30 min. 6 Lindsey Rd.* ☎ *207/363-4974. Admission $5 adults, $4 seniors, $3 kids 6–15, $15 families; York Historical pass $12 adults, $9 seniors, $5 kids 6–15, $25 families. June to mid-Oct Mon–Sat 10am–5pm. Closed late Oct to May.*

Across the highway is York's white town hall. To the left of it is the

❸ **First Parish Congregational Church.** This meetinghouse-style church, built in 1747 (and quite similar to Portsmouth's North Church), features an attractively inlaid black clock face and graceful spire. This was actually the town's fourth meetinghouse to be built in a little over a century, each in a different location, and was originally oriented west (its back turned to the town hall)—until, in 1882, the whole thing was carefully rotated a quarter-turn to face the main road. Behind the town hall and church is a rather extensive parish cemetery dating from 1837; visitors are welcome to stroll through it during daylight hours, but pets and bicycles aren't welcome. ⏱ *15 min. 180 York St.* ☎ *207/363-3758.*

From York Village, bear right and follow Rte. 1A for 1 mile (1.6km). Pass the post office; at the top of the rise, on the right, is

❹ ★★ **Mason Park.** Technically called Hartland Mason Reservation Park, this lovely seaside plot was bequeathed to the York Harbor Inn by the local businessman who owned it. The small park features outstanding sea views, cultivated flower beds, a few benches, an

The pretty First Parish Congregational Church is more than 260 years old.

expanse of green lawn, some very informative historical plaques, and easy access to the pathway down to the Cliff Walk (see below). Note that the yacht club to the left is *not* part of the park; it's private property. ⏱ *45 min. U.S. Rte. 1, across from York Harbor Inn. Free parking.*

From the beach, enter the pathway and walk north along the

❺ ★ **Cliff Walk.** One of the best short walks in southern Maine starts here at the beach. Follow the sidewalk and dirt path as it ascends up a set of stairs (handrails help guide you), along the cliffs, and practically right through the front yards of multi-million-dollar mansions. Beach roses lend their scent to the ½-mile (.8km) pathway, while the views are breathtaking (but not too scary). Walk carefully and stay *on* the path—careless tourists have fallen from the 30-foot (9.1m) cliffs. ⏱ *45 min.*

Across Rte. 1A from the park's upper entrance is the

❻ **York Harbor Inn.** Once known as the Hillcroft, this rambling inn lords over the best views of York Harbor and the sea. It's also got some history of its own: The "Cabin Room" in the main building is made of original 1637 beams (once a sail loft) shipped over from the Isles of Shoals (just offshore), and lanterns came from a trolley line that once ran along what is now the highway here. The basement pub has original hitching posts where travelers tied up horses as they drank. The handsome blue Harbor Crest building uphill is from the early 18th century and contains wonderful tile work; another outbuilding, Yorkshire, dates from 1783. ⏱ *15 min. Rte. 1A, York Harbor.* ☎ *800/343-3869 or 207/363-5119. www.yorkharborinn. com.*

Long Sands beach offers great beachcombing and safe swimming.

Continue driving along Rte. 1A about 1½ miles (2.4km) north to

7 ★★ **Long Sands.** York's biggest and prettiest beach stretches 2 sandy miles (3.2km) alongside the Atlantic, is free to enter, and offers great surfing, beachcombing, and safe swimming. There's even a takeout seafood restaurant (Sun & Surf, at 266 Long Beach Ave., ☎ 207/363-2961) and changing facilities, as well as a bushel of cheap motels and cottages across from the water. *2 hr. Rte. 1A, York Beach.*

Drive 2 miles (3.2km) along Long Beach Ave. to the end of the beach (Nubble Rd.) and turn right. Travel 1¼ miles (2km) to

8 ★★★ **Sohier Park.** Finally, there's the small peninsula ending at an island capped by Sohier Park—which looks out onto scenic Nubble Light (p 41), probably one of the most photographed lighthouses in the world. The park is free; gawk from the safety of a

parking lot across the swift little inlet that separates it from the mainland. There are coin-operated viewers to get a better view, and a small gift shop and information kiosk in the park, as well. Expect a parking lot crammed with RVs and vans. *1½ hr. Nubble Rd. (off Long Sands Dr.), Cape Neddick. Free parking.*

9 **The Goldenrod.** There's only one place in Maine I know of where you can watch taffy being pulled on taffy machines, and that's at the Goldenrod. This iconic penny-candy store has anchored the Short Sands neighborhood of York since 1896, when electric trolleys first ran to this beach; the machines are positively hypnotic. There's also a diner on-site, but most folks come simply to ogle (or buy) the candy, which is made without preservatives. Eat up! *2 Railroad Ave. (at Ocean Ave.), York Beach.* ☎ *207/363-2621. Closed mid-Oct to mid-May. $$.*

Ogunquit & Wells

1. Ogunquit Museum of American Art
2. Perkins Cove
3. Ogunquit Beach
4. Marginal Way
5. Beach Plum Farm
6. Congdon's Donuts
7. Laudholm Farm
8. Carson Trail
9. Ogunquit Playhouse

35

Sea Rd.

1

Post Rd.

Coles Hill Rd.

Western Rd.

9

Elms ○ 7

95

9

Sanford Rd. ○ Wells

1

ATLANTIC OCEAN

6 Mile Rd.

Littlefield Rd.

0   1 mi
0   1 km

Moody ○

Ocean Ave.

Tatnic Rd.

5

95

Berwick Rd.   ○ Ogunquit

1

Shore Rd.

Area of Ogunquit inset

Ogunquit

Beach St.

3

Main St.

School St.

Shore Rd.

Marginal Way

ATLANTIC OCEAN

Obeds Ln.

1

4

Israels Head Rd.

Stearns Rd.

Bourne Ln.

Ogunquit Welcome Center

Perkins C.   Oarweed Cove

9

Pine Hill Rd. N

Shore Rd.

2

Perkins Cove

1

0   1/4 mi
0   0.25 km

Pine Hill Rd. S

Ogunquit is a lovely, genteel beach town that has attracted summer tourists and artists for years. Galleries abound, and there's a great art museum—but even if you're not an art lover, you'll adore the walking trail that climbs along the town's rocky cliffs and above its beach for outstanding views, not to mention the abundance of inns, cafes, and restaurants. Wells is uninspiring but contains several remarkable natural areas. START: **Take U.S. Rte. 1 north from York about 7 miles (11km) to Bourne Rd. and turn right. At Shore Rd., turn right again and continue for 1 mile (1.6km).**

The Ogunquit Museum of American Art has been called "the best small museum in America."

1 ★★★ Ogunquit Museum of American Art. It's been called "the best small museum in America," and it's certainly way up there on the list. The legacy of Ogunquit's artist-colony days is this terrific collection, housed in a tranquil, waterside complex. You'll see Maine-associated artists like Neil Welliver (1929–2005), Charles H. Woodbury (1864–1940), Marsden Hartley (1877–1943), Robert Henri (1865–1929), and more, plus modern sculpture, graphical art, and photography from artists across the country. Check out the sculpture nook overlooking the sea. ⏱ 1½ hr. 543 Shore Rd. ☎ 207/646-4909.

www.ogunquitmuseum.org. Admission $7 adults, $5 seniors, $4 students; kids under 12 free. July–Oct Mon–Sat 10am–5pm, Sun 1–5pm. Closed Nov–June.

From the museum, drive north on Shore Rd. ½ mile (.8km) to the intersection. Turn sharply right on Oarweed Rd. and continue ¼ mile (.4km) to

2 ★ Perkins Cove. Marginal Way might be more picturesque, but Perkins Cove is the "scene" in Ogunquit, and it's a must-visit—if you can find parking. An attractive collage of yachts, fishing boats, rowboats, narrow alleys, shops, restaurants, and even a small drawbridge combine to keep people shopping and snapping photos. Parking fees here are steep; if you're staying, park the car at your hotel and take the local trolley, which runs along Shore Road and costs less. From U.S. Route 1, it's a mile (1.6km) walk to the cove, though it feels longer due to crowds, traffic, and elevation changes. ⏱ 1 hr. Oarweed Rd. (off Shore Rd.). Metered & pay-lot parking.

From Perkins Cove, backtrack along Shore Rd. to the center of town. Park. On foot, follow any sign indicating access to

3 kids Ogunquit Beach. The longest and most popular beach in town, Ogunquit Beach is *the* reason many families reliably return to this town summer after summer. Situated on a sand bar by the harbor, the beach offers access to gentle waves and several miles of soft white sand, plus views of the town's mansions and cliffs. It's got facilities—bathrooms, snacks—that the other local beaches don't, making it the best choice for families. Lifeguards patrol in summer; birds and even seals are sometimes sighted here. ⏱ *2 hr. Parking $7–$15. From main intersection, follow Beach St. to end.*

④ ★★ **Marginal Way.** One of the best walking trails in coastal Maine is tucked into the little cliffs rising above Ogunquit Beach. It begins at the beach, then runs about 1¼ scenic miles (2km) up above sea level and out to a point of land, passing weird rock formations, little pocket coves, hotel balconies (see the **Beachmere Inn** [p 71]), and fancy summer cottages en route. About 30 benches are scattered along the path, all with great views. The trail ends near lovely Perkins Cove. ⏱ *1¼ hr.*

Marginal Way is one of the best walking trails in coastal Maine.

From the town's main intersection, follow U.S. Rte. 1 north ¾ mile (1.2km) to

⑤ **Beach Plum Farm.** You don't expect to find a farm/conservation area on busy U.S. Route 1, yet it's here; most travelers speed right by. It consists of peaceful grounds, a mile-long loop trail, gardens, river frontage, a farmhouse, and barns (one housing a small museum on local natural history, another the offices of local environmental organizations). Well worth a stop if you're tired of traffic and tourists. ⏱ *30 min. 610 Main St. (U.S. Rte. 1).* ☎ *207/646-3604. Daily dawn to dusk.*

⑥ **Congdon's Donuts.** While driving north along U.S. Route 1 from Ogunquit and through Wells, there are few reasons to pull over—but Congdon's is one of them. This has been a doughnut shop since the 1950s, and there's also a small sit-down diner. In a hurry? Use the drive-through window. *1090 Post Rd. (U.S. Rte. 1), Wells.* ☎ *207/646-4219). $.*

Continue north about 5¾ miles (9.3km) on U.S. Rte. 1 and bear right on Laudholm Farm Rd. to reach

⑦ **Laudholm Farm.** This former farm sits on 1,600 acres (647 hectares) and was once the home of powerful local railroad magnate George Lord; today, it's a national reserve dedicated to environmental research. You can hike on 7 miles (11km) of trails through marshes and woodlands, and out to sand dunes; stop in at the visitor center inside the grand Victorian farmhouse before you set out. (Tours are also available.) ⏱ *1 hr. 342 Laudholm Farm Rd.* ☎ *207/646-4521.*

The Rachel Carson National Wildlife Refuge has spectacular tidal creeks, salt pans, and bird life.

www.wellsreserve.org. Parking summer $2 per adult or $10 per car; free rest of year. Trails open daily 7am–dusk; visitor center open mid-May to mid-Oct Mon–Sat 10am–4pm, Sun noon–4pm.

Backtrack a half-mile along Laudholm Farm Rd. to Skinner Mill Rd. Turn right and follow it a half-mile to Rte. 9. Turn right and continue 600 ft. (183m) to the right-turn for the Rachel Carson Refuge and the

8 kids **Carson Trail.** Established in 1966, the Rachel Carson National Wildlife Refuge is named for the writer/scientist (1907–1964; a part-time Maine resident) who enlightened the world about the dangers of pesticides. This plot, adjacent to the refuge's headquarters office, is the most visitor-friendly because of the mile-long (1.6km) trail that loops through marshlands and wooded hollows, and alongside tidal creeks and salt pans, before returning to the parking area; it's notable for its bird life. ⏱ *30 min. 321 Port Rd.*

☎ *207/646-9226. http://rachel carson.fws.gov. Trails open daily dawn–dusk; offices open Mon–Fri 8am–4:30pm.*

Turn around and head south on Rte. 9 (Port Rd.) ¾ mile to U.S. Rte. 1. Turn left and continue 7 miles south until you reach, on the left, the

9 **Ogunquit Playhouse.** This 750-seat summer-stock theater sits right on U.S. Route 1, slightly south of the town's main intersection, but it has somehow retained its look and elegance through the years—notice the regal flagpoles, lawn, and landscaping. The theater has been entertaining locals since 1933, and famous thespians like Bette Davis, Tallulah Bankhead, and Sally Struthers have all acted here in shows like *A Chorus Line* and *Guys and Dolls*. ⏱ *3 hr. (for performance). 10 Main St. (U.S. Rte. 1).* ☎ *207/646-2402. www.ogunquit playhouse.org. Tickets generally $30–$45. Performances mid-May to mid-Oct.*

The Kennebunks

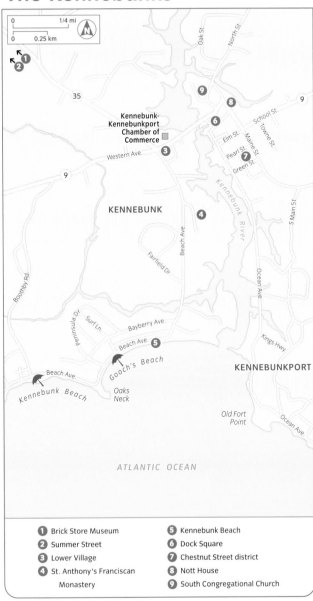

1 Brick Store Museum
2 Summer Street
3 Lower Village
4 St. Anthony's Franciscan Monastery
5 Kennebunk Beach
6 Dock Square
7 Chestnut Street district
8 Nott House
9 South Congregational Church

The Kennebunks: two towns, two main streets, and lots and lots of ocean and beach frontage. Both towns can easily be seen in a day or two. Workaday Kennebunk features a rich historic district, Maine's most luxurious inn, and great beaches, while Kennebunkport has better shopping and dining, its own impressive historic district, lots of B&Bs, one stunning church—and a couple of ex-President Bushes. START: **Rte. 35/U.S. Rte. 1 to Main St. in Kennebunk.**

❶ ★ Brick Store Museum. Kennebunk's best historical resource is very easy to miss even though it's in the dead center of town—you'll be too busy trying to read all the road signs. But don't think about skipping it if you're a history buff. The museum (actually a series of linked buildings) hosts exhibitions of art and artifacts throughout the summer and maintains comprehensive archives on the town's many historic mansions, churches, and cemeteries. Staff lead great local walking tours from spring through fall. ⏱ *45 min. 117 Main St. (junction of U.S. Rte. 1 & Rte. 35).* ☎ *207/985-4802. www. brickstoremuseum.org. Free admission (suggested donation $5); free parking on street. Tues–Fri 10am–4:30pm, Sat 10am–1pm. Closed Sun.*

From the center of town, drive southeast on Rte. 35, which soon becomes

❷ ★ Summer Street. In 1963, Kennebunk was the first town in Maine to establish an historic district, and Summer Street is the anchor of that district. Notable private homes here include Colonial-style homes at 13 and 15 Summer St.; the William Lord Mansion (which Lord didn't build, but lived in) on a rise at 20 Summer St.; the Doric Captain Nathaniel Lord Thompson House at 23 Summer St.; his brother Captain Charles Thompson's home, an 1846 Greek Revival structure next door at 25 Summer St.; and the so-called 'Wedding Cake House' at 104 Summer St. ⏱ *15 min.*

The Lower Village is a great place to buy artwork and tasty meals.

Kennebunk Beach is a popular place for beachcombing and dog-walking.

Continue along Rte. 35 2½ miles (4km) to the intersection with Western Ave. This is

❸ Lower Village. Kennebunk's lower village is the center of its tourist trade, if no longer its main engine of commerce. The shipyards are tucked out of sight, but you can still pick up information at the tourist office at 17 Western Ave. and buy artwork, clothes, takeout meals, Italian food, and baked goods. The bridge here over the Kennebunk River leads to Kennebunkport and Dock Square (see below). ⏱ *30 min. Western Ave. (Rte. 9) from Summer St. (Rte. 35) to Kennebunk River bridge.*

From the intersection of Rte. 35 and Western Ave., drive or walk ½ mile (.8km) on Beach Ave. to reach the

❹ ★ St. Anthony's Franciscan Monastery. This monastery is a peaceful spot for walks through quiet grounds and past elegant chapels, and sculptures. The estate and property were purchased by Lithuanian Franciscans in 1947, who then added the grotto, statuary, and worship spaces. There's a section of sculpture from the Vatican Pavilion at the 1964/1965 World's Fair, a chapel, an outdoor shrine, English gardens, statues, and a short (1 mile round-trip) walking trail with some of the best river views in town. Park in the visitor's lot and be respectful of the grounds. The **White Barn Inn**

(p 74) is across the road. ⏱ *1 hr. 28 Beach Ave. (less than ½ mile/.8km from Lower Village & the intersection of Rte. 9 & Rte. 35). ☎ 207/967-2011.*

Continue another ½ mile (.8km) along Beach Ave. to reach the beginning of

❺ ★★ kids Kennebunk Beach. Actually a string of several beaches broken up by a jetty or two—each section has its own name and devotees—Kennebunk Beach(es) is/are among Maine's finest. Sunrises, sunsets, swimming, beachcombing, and dog-walking are all superb here. There's even a section of rocky tide pools (keep an eye on the kids). ⏱ *1½ hr. Beach Ave. Local parking permit required ($15 per day, $25 per week; buy at town hall at 1 Summer St.).*

Return to the intersection of Western Ave. and Rte. 35. Turn right and cross the bridge into

❻ ★ Dock Square. Kennebunkport life revolves around this square, which in summer slows to a crawl of bumper-to-bumper sports cars pausing while shoppers cross at the lighthouse-shaped pedestrian walkway. Among the highlights are several excellent restaurants (such as **Hurricane,** p 68) and upscale specialty stores, galleries, and studios purveying everything from fine tableware and candles to furniture, pottery, antiques, ice cream, and even maps. ⏱ *1 hr. Ocean Ave. at Spring St. (Rte. 9).*

Turn down Ocean Ave. (at the milepost) and walk ⅓ mile (.5km) to

⑦ Chestnut Street district.
Bordered by a green, lawn-like park off Dock Square, this street marks the boundary of one of Kennebunk's historic districts. The district encompasses Chestnut, Elm, and Pearl streets—all of which contain many lovely 18th- and 19th-century historic homes, some converted into luxurious inns and bed-and-breakfasts. ⏱ *15 min. Reached via Ocean Ave. from Chestnut St. south 3 blocks to Green St.*

Continue 2 blocks up either Chestnut, Pearl, or Green sts. (all are attractive) to Maine St., lined with historic homes. Turn left. At the corner of Maine and Spring sts. is the

Chestnut Street is home to many 18th and 19th century historic homes.

⑧ ★★ Nott House.
The stout, Doric-columned Nott House (built in 1853) is a heavyweight, both literally and figuratively; it's not only a solid example of Greek Revival design, but it also holds the town's historical society. Period rugs, furniture, wallpapers, and other items keep one in that 19th-century state of mind. The society also offers excellent local walking tours of the neighborhood, which I highly recommend. ⏱ *1 hr. 8 Maine St. (at Spring St.). ☎ 207/967-2751. www.kporthistory.org. Admission $7 adults; free for kids 18 & under. Guided tours July & Aug Thurs & Fri 10am–4pm, 7–9pm; Sept to early Oct Thurs & Fri 10am–4pm; July to early Oct Sat 10am–1pm. Walking tours of neighborhood during Nott House season daily 11am; $7 adults.*

Turn back toward town on Spring St. and walk 1 block to Church St. Turn right and continue 1 block to the massive

⑨ ★★ South Congregational Church.
Kennebunkport's signal icon is the enormous clock face of this whitewashed, meetinghouse-style church (built in 1824), down a lane off Dock Square and close to the tidal river. The huge clock faces are the originals, and are made of wood (which is very unusual); they no longer keep the correct time, but this is still as lovely a church as you'll find in southern Maine. Inside, the simple spare theme continues but for some stained glass work and an outsized, impressively columnar pipe organ—though it's only from 2004. ⏱ *30 min. 2 North St. (at Temple St., just off Spring St.). ☎ 207/967-2793. Church open Mon–Fri 9am–2pm; Sun services 10:30am.*

Southern Maine's Best Beaches

Two Trails
Standish
25
302
1
11
Gorham
202
Westbrook
5
22
Portland Int'l. Jetport
Portland
North Waterboro
Buxton
South Portland
Cape Elizabeth
Scarborough
77
35
112
Waterboro
Pine Point
① Old Orchard Beach
Saco
Biddeford
Ferry Beach
Saco R.
② Biddeford Pool
Alfred
111
1
9
③ Goose Rocks Beach
South Sanford
West Kennebunk
99
Arundel
Kennebunk
35
Cape Porpoise
Kennebunk Beach
④ Kennebunkport
⑤ Laudholm Farm
4
Wells
ATLANTIC OCEAN
9
North Berwick
⑥ Wells Beach
Moody
Ogunquit
⑦
95
Cape Neddick
91
1
York Beach
⑧
⑨ Nubble Light
York Village
York Harbor
1A
⑩
Kittery
Portsmouth
NEW HAMPSHIRE

0   5 mi
0   5 km

Biddeford Pool Beach 2
Gooch's Beach 4
Goose Rocks Beach 3
Harbor Beach 10
Long Sands Beach 9
Mother's Beach 5
Ogunquit Beach 7
Old Orchard Beach 1
Short Sands Beach 8
Wells Beach 6

Probably three-quarters of Maine's best beaches are clustered in the far-southern reaches of the state. These beaches range from little, locally known pockets of sand and rocks to long, gorgeous strands that get just a little *too* popular on a sweltering July or August weekend. Here's a sampling. As a bonus, most offer views of boats, cliffs, or lighthouses, along with the sand and surf.

kids Biddeford Pool

Beach   On a little sandy peninsula even many Mainers have never set foot on, this is one of the southern coast's more scenic beaches—and it's good for families because there are some facilities here. There's an especially wide section of sand, plus dunes, fragrant beach roses, and assorted stuff washed in by the sea to comb through. You can pick from the longer, straighter stretch on Mile Stretch Road or the little pocket beach on Ocean Avenue at the very end of Mile Stretch. Regardless, though, you'll need to buy a nonresident permit from the city of Biddeford in order to park here without penalty. *Mile Stretch Rd. & Ocean Ave., Biddeford. Non-resident parking sticker $10 per day, $40 per week.*

★★ Gooch's Beach   One of my

favorite southern Maine beaches is this stretch, from Peninsula Drive until the road bends back toward town. Dogs adore this stretch, it's an outstanding place for a sunrise jog, and the photography is also sublime; you might even see surfers, local guys in wetsuits harvesting who-knows-what from the sea, and a visiting Hollywood actor or two trying to look incognito. Parking is free on the street, but again only by town permit in summer. *Beach Ave., from Lords Point Rd. north to Peninsula Dr., Kennebunk. Free street parking; town permit required in summer ($15 per day, $25 per week).*

Gooch's Beach is an excellent place to take photos.

kids Goose Rocks Beach   This

lovely 2-plus-mile-long (3.2km) crescent, on the northern edge of Kennebunkport, is a bit difficult to find, yet lovely. You approach via a path through the dune grasses. It's an uncrowded beach, with good views, little wave action, and safe shallow swimming. If you come between May and October, buy a parking sticker at the adjacent general store or the police station back in town (101 Main St., ☎ 207/967-2454) first. This beach doesn't have any facilities. *Kings Lane, Kennebunkport (off Rte. 9 via Dyke Rd./Goose Rocks Rd.). Non-resident parking sticker $12 per day, $50 per week.*

★ **Harbor Beach** Right at the foot of some of York Harbor's finest mansions and cottages, Harbor Beach is a tiny crescent of sand framed between two points of rocks. Pluses: a wonderfully quiet beach, free parking, restrooms, and outstanding views of boats out at sea and gentle waves. Minuses: A big hotel to one side detracts a bit from the scenic charm. And the cove is rocky and full of seaweed, which can crimp wading and swimming efforts. *Harbor Beach Rd. (just off Rte. 1A), York Harbor. Free parking.*

★★ **kids Long Sands Beach** The undisputed queen of York County's beaches, Long Sands has it all—sunrises, hotels, motels, panoramic views of ocean and lighthouse, 2 miles (3.2km) of hard-packed sand, a country store, even takeout seafood and ice cream. I can't think of a better place in Maine for a run on the beach (except when it's packed wall-to-wall with tanners); the northern half of the beach is a popular surfing zone, watched over by lifeguards during summer. Restrooms are located near the Oceanside Avenue turnoff. *Long Beach Ave. (Rte. 1A), York Beach. Metered parking.*

kids Mother's Beach The first of three little crescent beaches collectively known as "Kennebunk Beach," this is the one most aptly named: The durable playground here gets a workout from the little ones and their parents in the summer. There's a public bathroom, some rocks to scramble over, and a not-bad cove for swimming and sunning. Plenty of locals enjoy it—probably because you park by local permit only in summer. (You can also buy a non-resident permit at Kennebunk's police station at 101 Main St.; ☎ 207/967-2454). Out-of-season, you'll have it all to yourself. Also take time to walk from the beach to the golf club—there are some nice mansions here. *Beach Ave. (at Kennebunk Beach Rd.). Free parking in lot; town parking permit required in summer ($15 per day, $25 per week).*

★ **kids Ogunquit Beach** Ogunquit's main beach is more than 3 miles (4.8km) long, though its width varies with the tides. This beach appeals to everyone: the livelier scene at the south end near the

Mother's Beach and its playground are popular with locals.

A rare quiet moment on Old Orchard Beach, which draws thousands to its pier every summer.

town itself; the more remote and unpopulated stretches to the north, with their sand dunes; and the clusters of summer homes that lie beyond. The most popular access point is the foot of Beach Street. The beach ends at a sandy spit, where the Ogunquit River flows into the sea; you'll find a handful of informal restaurants. It's also the most crowded part of the beach. Restrooms and changing rooms are maintained at three points along the beach. *Accessed via Beach St., Ogunquit. Parking $7–$15.*

kids Old Orchard Beach

There's no other beach in Maine quite like OOB, not by a long shot: For sheer corny-ness, it still reigns supreme. Folks flock by the thousands to Old Orchard's pier each summer to gorge on the signature French fries and carnival-style attractions, or to play games of chance at the Palace Playland amusement. But don't overlook the 5-mile (8km) motel- and condo-covered beach extending north and south from the pier, either: It's great for a long, long walk. You'll hear lots of French-Canadian accents here—the place attracts them like a magnet, for some reason. *East Grand Ave. to West Grand Ave. (Rte. 9).*

kids Short Sands Beach   If

Longs Sands is York's queen beach, Short Sands is its impudent knave. This tiny strip of sand gets packed. It does offer great views of its little slice of ocean, framed at either end by various mansions, hotels, and summer homes. But the massive parking lot and corny-looking arcade right beside it feel more like New Jersey than New England. At least you're only steps from the Goldenrod candy shop (p 53). As does Long Sands, this beach is staffed by lifeguards in summer and has free restrooms adjacent. *Ocean Ave. (Rte. 1A), York Beach. Metered parking in lot.*

kids Wells Beach   Separated

from the main coastal land mass by a little tidal river, this sandspit is one of the longest beaches in Maine, and it's lined with what seem like hundreds (thousands?) of cookie-cutter summer cottages. (You'll see them long before you get here.) Ignore them, though: This beach is a decent choice for families because it's equipped with shops, food, bathrooms, lifeguards, a boardwalk, and even some shopping options. The dunes are attractive, too. *Atlantic Ave. (off U.S. Rte. 1, via Mile Rd.), Wells. Limited free parking in lot; $7–$15 in private lots.*

Southern Maine Dining

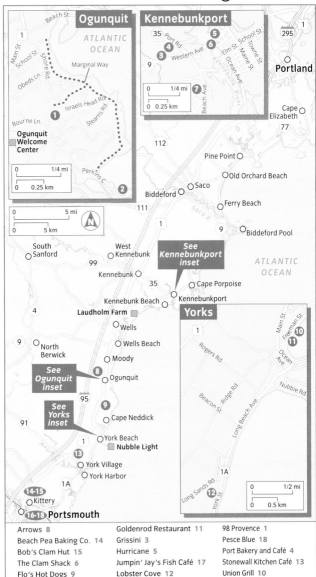

Arrows 8
Beach Pea Baking Co. 14
Bob's Clam Hut 15
The Clam Shack 6
Flo's Hot Dogs 9
Friendly Toast 16

Goldenrod Restaurant 11
Grissini 3
Hurricane 5
Jumpin' Jay's Fish Café 17
Lobster Cove 12
MC Perkins Cove 2

98 Provence 1
Pesce Blue 18
Port Bakery and Café 4
Stonewall Kitchen Café 13
Union Grill 10
White Barn Inn 7

Southern Maine Dining A to Z

★★ Arrows NEW AMERICAN
Mark Gaier and Clark Frasier do some of the most innovative cooking in the region, using local products, home-grown greens, and house-cured pro-sciutto. Expect roast chicken, local fish, steaks, lobster, and a great wine list. *41 Berwick Rd., Ogunquit. ☎ 207/361-1100. www.arrowsrestaurant.com. Entrees $41–$43. MC, V. June to late Oct dinner Wed–Sun; late Oct to Dec & mid-Apr to May dinner Thurs–Sun. Closed Jan to mid-Apr.*

Beach Pea Baking Co. BAKERY
In a house set back from busy U.S. Route 1, this little bakery serves gourmet sandwiches, soup and salad, and elaborate slices of cake, plus coffee, breads, and pastries. Eat inside or out on the front porch. *53 State Rd. (U.S. Rte. 1), Kittery. ☎ 207/439-3555. www.beachpea baking.com. Sandwiches $3–$7. AE, MC, V. Breakfast, lunch & dinner Mon–Sat.*

You can enjoy coffee, cake, and sand-wiches on the front porch of Beach Pea Baking.

kids Bob's Clam Hut SEAFOOD
This outlets-adjacent U.S. Route 1 staple does plump fried clams like nobody else in Maine. You can also get fish-and-chips and local ice cream at the window. *315 U.S. Rte. 1, Kittery. ☎ 207/439-4233. www.bobsclamhut.com. Sandwiches $4–$13, entrees $8–$29. AE, MC, V. Lunch & dinner daily.*

★ The Clam Shack SEAFOOD
On the bridge between the two Ken-nebunks, this is a place to eat fried clams, steamed lobsters, chowder, and meaty lobster rolls on round French bread. The owner has no pretense whatsoever; deal with it. *2 Western Ave. (on bridge), Ken-nebunk. ☎ 207/967-3321. www. theclamshack.net. Most entrees $10–$20. Cash only. May–Oct lunch & dinner daily. Closed Nov–Apr.*

Flo's Hot Dogs AMERICAN   The steamed hot dogs in a red-sided shack by the side of U.S. Route 1 are a throwback to an earlier era. There are only six seats, and you'll wait in line a *long* time even for takeout, but it's worth the wait. *1359 U.S. Rte. 1 (north of downtown), York. No phone. Hot dogs $2. Cash only. Lunch Thurs–Tues.*

Friendly Toast AMERICAN   This crazily decorated spot on Ports-mouth's main drag features all-day and -night breakfast (such as pump-kin and Almond Joy pancakes), plus heartier items like sandwiches and burritos. *121 Congress St., Ports-mouth. ☎ 603/430-2154. www.the friendlytoast.net. Breakfast, lunch & dinner entrees $4–$11. AE, MC, V. Breakfast, lunch & dinner daily.*

kids Goldenrod Restaurant
DINER   Here since 1896, this com-bination malt shop–candy

Grissini's trattoria serves excellent fire-grilled pizzas.

factory–diner anchors York's Short Sands neighborhood. Buy a box of taffy "kisses" or "birch bark" to take home. *2 Railroad Ave. (at Ocean Ave.), York Beach.* ☎ *207/363-2621. www.thegoldenrod.com. Breakfast entrees $2–$6, lunch & dinner entrees $5–$15. MC, V. Late May to early Sept breakfast, lunch & dinner daily; early Sept to mid-Oct breakfast & lunch Wed–Sun. Closed mid-Oct to late May.*

★ **Grissini** *ITALIAN* A trattoria gone upscale, spacious Grissini features a stone fireplace, very good pastas, and fire-grilled pizza, salmon, chicken, and steak. *27 Western Ave., Kennebunk.* ☎ *207/ 967-2211. www.restaurantgrissini. com. Entrees $14–$28, light menu $8–$14. AE, MC, V. Dinner daily. Jan–Mar closed Wed.*

★★ **Hurricane** *AMERICAN/ECLEC-TIC* Brooks and Luanne MacDon-ald's fusion restaurant is the best in Dock Square. Expect healthful sand-wiches and salads, boxes of sea-food, pan-roasted local fish, seared scallops, and lobster cioppino. *29 Dock Sq., Kennebunkport.* ☎ *207/ 967-1111. www.hurricanerestaurant. com. Entrees $15–$45, small plates $8–$22. AE, DC, DISC, MC, V. Lunch & dinner daily.*

★ **Jumpin' Jay's Fish Café** *SEA-FOOD* Jay's posts the catch of the day on blackboards; pick a fish, then pair it with one of the smooth sauces. Pasta dishes with seafood are also served. *150 Congress St., Portsmouth.* ☎ *603/766-3474. www. jumpinjays.com. Entrees $19–$25. AE, DISC, MC, V. Dinner daily.*

kids Lobster Cove *SEAFOOD* A fun spot for families to eat lobster dinners, broiled seafood, and fish platters right across the road from York Beach. Old-timey Maine des-sert choices include blueberry pie in season. *756 York St., York Beach (south end of Long Sands Beach).* ☎ *207/351-1100. Entrees $7–$21. AE, MC, V. Breakfast, lunch & dinner daily.*

★★ **MC Perkins Cove** *SEAFOOD/ NEW AMERICAN* Mark Gaier and Clark Frasier of Arrows (see above) run this bistro, featuring small plates, salads, mussels and oysters, and fish. Desserts are terrific. *111 Perkins Cove Rd., Ogunquit.* ☎ *207/ 646-6263. www.mcperkinscove.com. Lunch entrees $8–$19, dinner entrees $29–$31. DC, DISC, MC, V. Late May to mid-Oct lunch & dinner daily; mid-Oct to Jan & Feb to late May closed Tues. Closed Jan.*

★ **98 Provence** *FRENCH* A truly French menu that changes thrice yearly to reflect the seasons. Lobster is cooked in puff pastry; a fish stew is Provencal; and there's rabbit, escargots, cassoulet of duck, and rack of lamb. A bistro menu offers lighter meals. *262 Shore Rd., Ogunquit.* ☎ *207/646-9898. www.98provence.com. Entrees $23–$28; table d'hôte $29–$39. AE, MC, V. Summer dinner Wed–Mon; off-season dinner Thurs–Mon.*

★ **Pesce Blue** *SEAFOOD/ITALIAN* Seafood with a strong Italian accent: grilled flatbread topped with salmon; a salad of mussels, San Marzano tomatoes, and olives; pan-roasted haddock; salt-baked *branzino*. Desserts include *mascarpone* cheesecake, *panna cotta*, and olive-oil cake. *106 Congress St., Portsmouth.* ☎ *603/430-7766. www.pesceblue.com. Lunch entrees $9–$21, dinner entrees $14–$30. AE, DISC, MC, V. Lunch Wed–Sun, dinner daily.*

Port Bakery and Café *CAFE* This unpretentious bakery/cafe sits in the heart of Lower Village; it's owned by the same owners of Kennebunkport's Hurricane (see above). Inside, you'll find changing daily soups, salads, breads, and pastries—even homemade desserts. *181 Port Rd., Kennebunk.* ☎ *207/967-2263. Eentrees $3–$10. MC, V. Breakfast, lunch & dinner daily.*

Stonewall Kitchen Café *CAFE* This cafe serves Stonewall's own chowder, soups, and sandwiches, plus daily specials. Desserts, coffee, and takeout are also available. *2 Stonewall Lane (off U.S. Rte. 1), York.* ☎ *207/351-2719. www.stonewall kitchen.com. Entrees $7–$11. AE, DC, DISC, MC, V. Breakfast & lunch daily.*

★ **Union Grill** *AMERICAN/SEAFOOD* The Union Bluff Hotel's (p 74) dining room is a welcome upscale addition to York. Seafood predominates, but you can also eat duck wings, calamari, flatbread topped with Kobe short ribs, lobster "mignon," or boar with Béarnaise. Surprisingly good in a town of diners and fried foods. *8 Beach St., York Beach.* ☎ *800/833-0721 or 207/363-1333. www.unionbluff.com. Entrees $11–$30. MC, V. May–Oct breakfast, lunch & dinner daily; Nov–Apr dinner Sat & Sun. Pub open year-round for lunch & dinner.*

★★★ **White Barn Inn** *REGIONAL/ NEW AMERICAN* The White Barn Inn's (p 74) elegant dining room, a former barn, is Maine's best. Jonathan Cartwright serves lobster spring rolls, seared diver scallops, grilled chicken, steamed lobster over fettuccine, and other seasonally changing treats. *37 Beach Ave., Kennebunkport.* ☎ *207/967-2321. www.whitebarninn.com. Prix fixe dinner $91–$125 per person. AE, MC, V. Breakfast & dinner daily. Closed 2 weeks in Jan.*

Many consider the White Barn Inn Maine's best dining experience.

Southern Maine Lodging

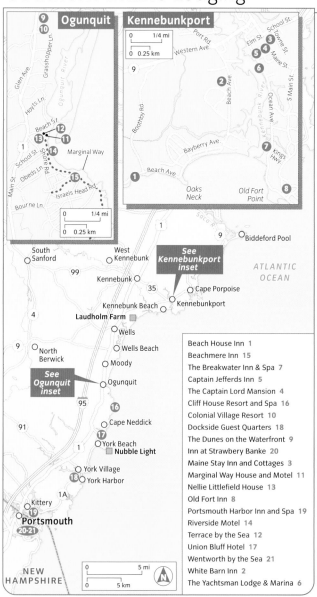

Ogunquit

Kennebunkport

Beach House Inn **1**
Beachmere Inn **15**
The Breakwater Inn & Spa **7**
Captain Jefferds Inn **5**
The Captain Lord Mansion **4**
Cliff House Resort and Spa **16**
Colonial Village Resort **10**
Dockside Guest Quarters **18**
The Dunes on the Waterfront **9**
Inn at Strawbery Banke **20**
Maine Stay Inn and Cottages **3**
Marginal Way House and Motel **11**
Nellie Littlefield House **13**
Old Fort Inn **8**
Portsmouth Harbor Inn and Spa **19**
Riverside Motel **14**
Terrace by the Sea **12**
Union Bluff Hotel **17**
Wentworth by the Sea **21**
White Barn Inn **2**
The Yachtsman Lodge & Marina **6**

Southern Maine Lodging A to Z

In addition to a cozy dining room, the Beach House Inn's rooms have panoramic views.

★★ **Beach House Inn** Owned by the White Barn Inn (see below) and right across from one of Kennebunk's best stretches of beach. Rooms are surprisingly comfortable, with panoramic views of the ocean; a front porch, bikes, and canoes are additional draws. *211 Beach Ave., Kennebunk.* ☎ *207/967-3850. www. beachhseinn.com. 35 units. Doubles* and cottage $125–$799 w/breakfast. 2-night minimum Sat & Sun. AE, MC, V. Closed Jan–May.

★★ **kids Beachmere Inn** A well-run cliff-top inn with a scenic lawn and access to Marginal Way (p 56). The original Victorian inn dates from the 1890s with turrets, porches, and angles. The other building is more modern. *62 Beachmere Place, Ogunquit.* ☎ *800/336-3983 or 207/646-2021. www.beachmereinn.com. 53 units. Doubles $95–$250 w/breakfast, suites & cottages $155–$460. 3-night minimum in summer. AE, DC, DISC, MC, V.*

★★ **The Breakwater Inn & Spa** A combination of inn rooms, spa rooms (close to the signature spa and fitness center), a cottage, and an apartment, the Breakwater has modernized with the times. Units are stylish; there's a good fancy seafood restaurant, Striper's, on the premises. *127 Ocean Ave., Kennebunkport.* ☎ *207/967-5333. www.thebreakwaterinn.com. Doubles & suites $100–$630 w/breakfast, cottage $429- $800. AE, MC, V.*

★ **Captain Jefferds Inn** An 1804 home in an historic section of

The cliff-top Beachmere Inn is close to the Marginal Way walking trail.

town, the Captain Jefferds was redone in 1997 to augment its antiques with luxury touches. Some units have whirlpool tubs. Breakfast is served before a fire or on the terrace. *5 Pearl St., Kennebunkport.* ☎ *800/839-6844 or 207/967-2311. www.captainjefferdsinn.com. 15 units. Late May to Oct doubles $160–$365 w/breakfast; rest of the year doubles $125–$330 w/breakfast. 2-night minimum weekends. AE, MC, V.*

★★ The Captain Lord Mansion

A pale yellow Federal-style home on a lawn, the Captain Lord's rooms are furnished in splendid antiques, stained glass, and gas fireplaces. One unit has a NordicRider stationary bike and foot massager. *6 Pleasant St. & Green St., Kennebunkport.* ☎ *800/522-3141 or 207/967-3141. www.captainlord.com. 20 units. Doubles $149–$379 w/breakfast, suites $249–$499. 2-night minimum weekends & holidays. No children 11 & under. DISC, MC, V.*

★★ Cliff House Resort and Spa

This complex of modern buildings replaced a former grand hotel. Views are stunning, and the Cliffscape wing features new beds and furniture. A spa, vanishing-edge outdoor pool, and restaurant look out on the sea. *Bald Head Cliff Rd. (off Shore Rd.), Ogunquit.* ☎ *207/361-1000. www. cliffhousemaine.com. 200 units. Doubles & suites $160–$385. AE, DISC, MC, V. Closed Dec to mid-Apr.*

kids Colonial Village Resort

This certainly is *not* a resort—but it's budget- and family-friendly with two pools, a Jacuzzi, tennis court, free doughnuts, coin-op laundries, and weekly rates for its cottages and apartments. Most rooms have kitchenettes and full-size refrigerators. *548 Main St. (U.S. Rte. 1), Ogunquit.* ☎ *800/422-3341. www. colonialvillageresort.com. Doubles & suites $54–$262 w/breakfast. AE, MC, V. Closed Dec–Mar.*

Dockside Guest Quarters

Off the beaten track, this family-owned compound features a private dock and shared, town-house–style cottages with private decks overlooking the harbor. *22 Harris Island Rd., York.* ☎ *888/860-7428 or 207/363-2868. www.docksidegq.com. 25 units. Doubles $117–$265 w/breakfast, suites $236–$312. 2-night minimum stay in summer. DISC, MC, V. Closed Jan–Apr; closed May, Nov & Dec Mon–Fri.*

★ The Dunes on the Waterfront

A fancy motor court? Indeed. These gabled cottages are decked in vintage maple furnishings, braided rugs, maple floors, louvered doors, full kitchens, and wood-burning fireplaces. *518 U.S. Rte. 1,*

Captain Jefford's Inn is located inside a historic 1804 home.

Ogunquit. ☎ 888/295-3863. www.
dunesonthewaterfront.com. 36 units.
Doubles $95–$345, cottages $160–
$435. MC, V. Closed Nov to late Apr.

Inn at Strawbery Banke
Tucked away a block off Strawbery
Banke (see p 49), this little inn feels
comfy, rather than luxurious. Rooms
are tiny and simply furnished, but
brightened by stenciling, pencil-
poster beds, wooden shutters, and
pine floors. 314 Court St., Portsmouth. ☎ 800/428-3933 or 603/436-
7242. www.innatstrawberybanke.
com. 7 units. Doubles $100–$150 w/
breakfast. AE, DISC, MC, V.

Maine Stay Inn and Cottages
Based around an historic home on
an historic street, this complex fills
the bill. Cottages are simple but kid-
friendly. The full breakfast is good,
and some rooms have Jacuzzis. 34
Maine St., Kennebunkport. ☎ 800/
950-2117 or 207/967-2117. www.
mainestayinn.com. 17 units. Doubles
& cottages $109–$319 w/breakfast.
2-night minimum stay on weekends.
AE, MC, V.

Marginal Way House and
Motel   A quiet, old-fashioned
compound centered around a four-
story guesthouse, this is a spare but
centrally located place with good
customer service. Some rooms have
little decks with views; all have
refrigerators and televisions. 22–24
Wharf Lane, Ogunquit. ☎ 207/646-
8801. www.marginalwayhouse.com.
30 units. June to late Sept doubles
$86–$208. MC, V. Closed Nov to
mid-Apr.

Nellie Littlefield House   Of
the many B&Bs in Ogunquit, this
might be the friendliest. Rooms are
carpeted and feature a mix of modern and antique reproduction
furnishings; several have refrigerators. One third-floor suite features a
Jacuzzi, another a turret. 27 Shore
Rd., Ogunquit. ☎ 207/646-1692.

The comfy Inn at Strawberry Bank is
bright and simply furnished.

8 units. Mid Apr-Dec doubles $102–
$267 w/breakfast. 3-night minimum
high-season & holidays. Children 13
& older only. DISC, MC, V. Closed Jan
to mid Apr.

★ Old Fort Inn   Not as well
known as other resorts and inns in
the Kennebunks, the Old Fort holds
its own in a picturesque neighborhood near the ocean. Units retain a
yesteryear charm, yet about half
have in-floor heated tiles in the
bathrooms and all have plush robes
and fridges. Breakfasts are good.
8 Old Fort Ave., Kennebunkport.
☎ 800/828-3678 or 207/967-5353.
www.oldfortinn.com. 16 units. Doubles & suites $125–$395 w/break-
fast. AE, DC, DISC, MC, V.

Portsmouth Harbor Inn and
Spa   Across the drawbridge from
Portsmouth, this inn features homey
rooms with harbor views and a comfortable spa in an adjacent building.
One of my favorite B&Bs in southern
Maine. 6 Water St., Kittery. ☎ 207/
439-4040. www.innatportsmouth.
com. 5 units. Doubles $120–$200
w/breakfast. Not recommended for
children 11 & under. MC, V.

Riverside Motel   The Riverside
offers wonderful marina and harbor
views, and free Wi-Fi, plus a convenient footbridge right over to Ogunquit's Perkins Cove (see p 55)—all at
a fraction of the cost of downtown
hotels. Rooms are spare and

The White Barn Inn features luxurious rooms and a spa.

whitewashed, but comfortable enough. *50 Riverside Lane, Ogunquit. ☎ 207/646-2741. www.riversidemotel.com. Doubles $99–$209. MC, V. Closed mid-Oct to mid-Apr.*

Terrace by the Sea The Terrace by the Sea is a fairly upscale choice, a nice surprise in a town (Ogunquit) where there's a lot of variability in the lodgings. Many rooms have great sea views, and there's also a heated outdoor pool; the innkeepers are friendly. Eight motel-style rooms have kitchenettes. *3 Wharf Lane, Ogunquit. ☎ 207/646-3232. www.terracebythesea.com. Doubles $52–$242. Children 5 & under welcome during off-season. MC, V. Closed mid-Dec to late Mar.*

★ **Union Bluff Hotel** It may look old, but this York Beach hotel was built in the 1980s. Recently, it's become something of a boutique hotel, thanks to the addition of the fancy Union Grill restaurant (p 69). Off-season, the property is deeply discounted. *8 Beach St., York Beach. ☎ 800/833-0721 or 207/363-1333. www.unionbluff.com. 61 units. Doubles & suites $59–$379. AE, DISC, MC, V.*

★★ **Wentworth by the Sea** Reopened in 2003, this grand resort features amazing views, excellent dining, two pools, a full-service spa, attractive rooms and suites, and a modern wing of townhouses by the water. *588 Wentworth Rd. (Rte. 1B), New Castle. ☎ 866/240-6313 or 603/422-7322. www.wentworth.com. 161 units. Doubles & suites $229–$459. AE, DISC, MC, V.*

★★★ **White Barn Inn** The White Barn pampers guests like no other in Maine, as it has done for years. The main inn features luxe rooms; a spa, parlor, and afternoon tea; and a prize-winning restaurant of the same name (p 69). The adjacent May's Cottage suites are spectacular, as is the outdoor pool. *37 Beach Ave., Kennebunk. ☎ 207/967-2321. www.whitebarninn.com. 29 units. Doubles $310–$620, cottages & suites $540–$925 w/breakfast & tea. 2-night minimum Sat & Sun. AE, MC, V.*

★ **The Yachtsman Lodge & Marina** The White Barn Inn owns this riverfront motel within walking distance of Dock Square. It features nice down comforters, CD players, and French doors that open onto patios—hardly your everyday motel. *59 Ocean Ave., Kennebunkport. ☎ 207/967-2511. www.yachtsmanlodge.com. 30 units. Doubles $189–$369 w/breakfast. AE, MC, V.* ●

Portland in **One Day**

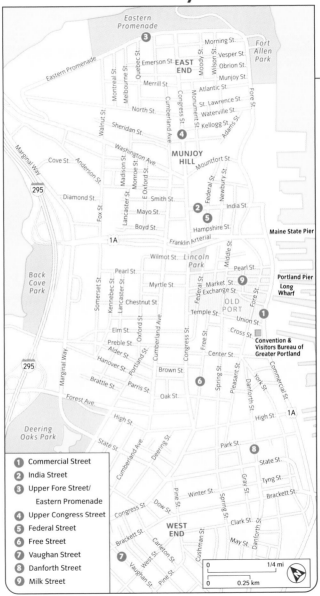

Eastern
Promenade

❸

Fort
Allen
Park

EAST
END

MUNJOY
HILL

❹

❷ **❺**

Maine State Pier

Lincoln
Park

Portland Pier

Long
Wharf

❾

OLD
PORT

❶

Convention &
Visitors Bureau of
Greater Portland

Back
Cove
Park

❻

Deering
Oaks Park

❽

WEST
END

❼

❶	Commercial Street
❷	India Street
❸	Upper Fore Street/ Eastern Promenade
❹	Upper Congress Street
❺	Federal Street
❻	Free Street
❼	Vaughan Street
❽	Danforth Street
❾	Milk Street

0   1/4 mi

0   0.25 km

Previous page: Cobblestoned Wharf Street is one of the most atmospheric parts of the Old Port.

Portland's a compact place, but that doesn't mean there's little to see here. Quite the opposite. Given even a single day in this lovely little city, you can stroll through a top-quality art museum, drink pints of ale in a working waterfront, climb towers, and feast on astounding views and architectural wonders. Here are 9 streets to get you started. START: **From Congress St., take Franklin St. to the base of the hill on Commercial St. in the Old Port.**

❶ kids Commercial Street. Portland's Old Port begins right here, *at* the port, and you can clearly smell the salt air down here. Commercial Street runs the length of the waterfront, passing by ferry and cruise slips, restaurants, bars, coffee shops, wandering mascots, and impromptu musical performances. The city's **main tourist office** (14 Ocean Gateway Pier; ☎ 207/772-5800)—stocked with free info—is on the cruise ship dock. Kids enjoy the mix of ice-cream shops, sailboats, and knickknack shops, while adults might wander down the various wharves with a camera. ⏱ *1hr.*

At the very northern end of Commercial St., turn away from the water onto

❷ India Street. It's only 5 blocks long, but India Street is one of the most interesting streets in the city. Why? Past, present, and future collide here. This was once the heart of Portland's Italian neighborhood,

though the street lost much of its identity when four-lane Franklin Street replaced most of their homes and apartments. Now, the excellent **Micucci Grocer** (45 India St.)—with a bakery in back—and **Amato's** (see p 100) are all that's left of it. On the same street: a good bakery (**Standard Baking Co.,** p 99), the **Rabelais** bookstore (p 108), and local coffee shop **Coffee By Design**, (67 India St.; ☎ 207/ 780-6767). Around the corner is the Belgian-fries shop **Duckfat** (p 113). ⏱ *15 min.*

From India St., climb Munjoy Hill along

❸ ★★ Upper Fore Street/Eastern Promenade. Rising gently from the Old Port, Fore Street (which becomes the Eastern Promenade about halfway up), takes you from marine/industrial enterprises and the **Maine Narrow Gauge Railroad Museum** (p 89) up past elegant mansions to the city's best park and its best views. Young and old alike enjoy the sunrises, sunsets,

India Street is home to Rabelais, one of Portland's better bookstores.

picnics, swing sets, and ball fields at the 70-acre (28-hectare) **Eastern Promenade Park** (p 89) topping the promenade. Its broad, grassy slopes extend down to the water and provide superb views of Casco Bay and its islands. ⏱ *45 min.*

From the midway point of the Eastern Promenade, turn left onto

④ ★ Upper Congress Street. The Munjoy Hill section of Congress Street has long suffered from a lack of respect, but it's catching up now thanks to a raft of new restaurants and an arts center. As you ascend and then descend the Hill via Congress Street, you can also drink coffee at **Hilltop Coffee** (p 101), climb the tower of the **Portland Observatory** (p 88) for bird's-eye views, and then catch a glimpse of big **Eastern Cemetery** (at the corner of Mountfort St.), which is Portland's oldest—it dates from 1668, believe it or not. The street descends to a level plain before passing a public park, Portland's massive **City Hall** (p 87), its **Public Library**, and finally the daily *Portland Press Herald*'s offices (at 390 Congress St.). ⏱ *45 min.*

At the library, turn left off Congress St. onto

⑤ Federal Street. This little street doesn't start out impressively, just a quick twist and a turn, but it takes you past a number of prominent elements in the downtown Portland mix: **Monument Square** (p 86), the resuscitated farmer's market under a roof known as the **Public Market House** (p 100), and **One City Center** (the city's tallest and most prominent office tower, with a small food court at ground level). A few blocks later, the street passes the columned stone building and additions housing the **Supreme Judicial Court** (entrance at 205 Newbury St.; ☎ 207/822-4146) and

Congress Street boasts a new arts center and a raft of new restaurants.

Superior Court (142 Federal St.; ☎ 207/822-4105), as well as the city jail. ⏱ *15 min.*

Circle back to Congress St. and turn left (west). Continue about 6 blocks to Congress Sq. Make a very sharp left (almost a U-turn) onto

⑥ ★ kids Free Street. Plenty to do here; for a short street, Free Street packs a punch. It starts out at Congress Square, itself a bustling little hub of activity, then quickly passes two of the city's heaviest-weight museums: the superb **Portland Museum of Art** (p 85) and then the **Children's Museum of Maine** (p 85). A block later, it passes the **Cumberland County Civic Center** (with semipro Portland Pirates hockey; 94 Free St., ☎ 207/828-4665) and **L.L.Bean's** Portland outlet store (p 108). The street ends in Monument Square at the excellent **Arabica** coffee shop (p 99). ⏱ *1½ hr.*

Make any left off Free St. (by car) or retrace your steps (on foot) to

Congress St. Turn left and proceed west on Congress ½ mile (.8km) to Bramhall St. Turn left, then immediately left again onto

7 Vaughan Street. You could throw a dart at the West End and hit an interesting street. I'm picking Vaughan Street as your jumping-off point just because it threads past so many interesting spots: the big **Maine Medical Center** (p 182), a series of increasingly large brick mansions, the **Western Promenade** (p 93) 2 blocks away, Bowdoin Street's dense concentration of John Calvin Stevens–designed (1855–1940) homes (p 93), and the **Western Cemetery** (p 93). ⏱ *15 min.*

At the foot of Vaughan St., turn left onto

8 ★ Danforth Street. This mile-long (1.6km) street is a major West End artery, and it gets busy. But it also takes you past some wonderful homes and neighborhoods. The mansions and school buildings of **Spring Street** (p 91) are a short block away, for instance, before passing the iconic **Victoria Mansion** (p 92) and a factory (at 20–36

Danforth St.) converted into artists' and photographers' galleries and studios. There are no high-rises along Danforth, so you can see vistas of the water, the Old Port, downtown's bank buildings, and **State Street's churches** (p 91) for much of its length. ⏱ *30 min.*

At the end of Danforth St., turn left onto York St. and then right onto Fore St. Continue to

9 ★ Milk Street. Circling back to the Old Port at the end of the day isn't a bad idea at all: The best restaurants are concentrated here, places like **Fore Street** (p 113), **Hugo's** (p 114), **Street & Co.** (p 115), and the **Grill Room** (p 113). But it's on little 3-block, cobblestoned Milk Street where you can really feel how Portland was a 19th-century powerhouse. Handsome brick commercial architecture leads you from busy **Exchange Street** (p 87) to the rotary plaza of the **Portland Regency Hotel** (p 118)—which was once a **Maine state armory** (p 107)—and on past a coffee shop, boutiques, and more quiet side streets of stone. ⏱ *15 min.*

Free Street's Children's Museum of Maine.

CHILDREN'S MUSEUM OF MAINE

Portland in **Two Days**

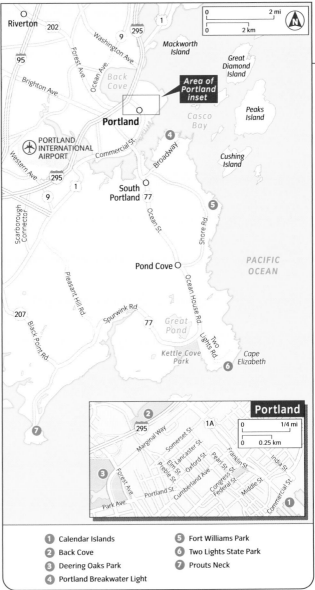

1 Calendar Islands
2 Back Cove
3 Deering Oaks Park
4 Portland Breakwater Light
5 Fort Williams Park
6 Two Lights State Park
7 Prouts Neck

An extra day in Portland is a serious bonus—and I'd urge you to use it to get outside the city. Paradoxically, half the charm of Portland lies in the beaches, marshes, forts, coves, and cliffs beyond its city limits. Get to these places on your second day, and you'll truly feel you've arrived in Maine. START: **Franklin and Commercial sts. in the Old Port.**

1 ★★ Calendar Islands. One of the don't-miss experiences of a Portland visit is a cruise around the bay on a Casco Bay Lines ferry that departs from the terminal at the foot of Franklin Street. You can take anywhere from a 20-minute run to Peaks Island (recommended) to a half-day mail-boat cruise through a bunch of the islands, collectively known as the Calendars because there's supposedly one for every day of the year. You'll get great views of the Portland skyline and peninsula, plus (if you make time) the chance to jump ship and explore an island for an hour—easy because ferries to many of the islands are frequent. ⏱ 1½ hr. Ferry terminal at Franklin & Commercial sts.

From the terminal, follow Franklin St. about 1 mile (1.6km) to merge with I-295 North. Take the next exit (Exit 8) to Baxter Blvd., which for the next several miles circles

2 kids ★ Back Cove. Portland's answer to Boston's Back Bay is overlooked by tourists but beloved by residents for its paved, 3½-mile (5.6km) walking/jogging/cycling circuit. And it's also nice to circumnavigate by car, a route that takes you over and under bridges, through graceful neighborhoods, and past rafts of seabirds. There are two parks on the cove, each with free parking: Payson Park (on the

northern side) and Back Cove Park (on the south side). Payson is more scenic; Back Cove Park has more parking. ⏱ 1 hr. Free parking in lots & on street.

From Back Cove Park (near Hannaford grocery), follow Preble St. to Bedford St. and turn left; continue onto Brighton Ave. At the 6-way intersection, make a very hard left onto Deering Ave. Continue ⅓ mile (.5km) to the left turn into

3 kids Deering Oaks Park. Portlanders don't often get down to this leafy, 50-acre (20-hectare) park just because its location is a bit inconvenient. But it's a good place for a picnic, tossing a ball, playing tennis, scooping up tourist info (one of the city's official kiosks is located here in summer), and enjoying the occasional festival. There's lots of stone work, the requisite oaks, a Spanish-American War memorial, and a big pond filled with geese, too. Trivia note: Skating scenes from the mid-'90s Denzel Washington film *The Preacher's Wife* were filmed on that (frozen) pond. ⏱ 30 min.

Exit the park on the east (State St.) side. Follow one-way State St. up- and downhill 1 mile (1.6km) to the Casco Bay Bridge (Rte. 77); stay on Rte. 77 across the

BACK COVE TRAIL

3½

MILES

5.6 km

Anthem ✚ FOUNDATION

The Back Cove trail is a favorite of local walkers and joggers.

82

bridge, turning left onto Broadway on the other side. Follow Broadway through all lights, about 1 mile (1.6km), to its very end; take the last possible left. Park at Bug Light Park and walk to the

④ Portland Breakwater Light.
Also known, in that colorful Maine way, as "Bug Light" (you'll know why when you see it), this iron-columned South Portland lighthouse is squat but important: It helps defend the cliffs, forts, and industrial concerns here from tankers, sailboats, and yachts cruising very close to shore. Or maybe it's the other way around. In any case, it's important enough that it was restored and reactivated in 2002. Visitors can (carefully) walk the stone breakwater out to the point and get a closer look at the lighthouse. ⏱ *15 min. Madison St.*

Backtrack out Breakwater Dr. to Broadway and turn right, then make the first left onto Preble St. Continue 1 mile (1.6km) and merge with Shore Rd. After another mile (1.6km), turn left into

⑤ kids ★★ Fort Williams Park.
Portland's most scenic lighthouse, hands-down, is the Cape Elizabeth stunner known as **Portland Head**

The Portland Breakwater Light was restored in 2002.

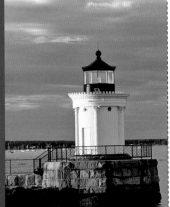

Cape Elizabeth's Portland Head Light.

Light, set in this town park and accompanied by an exceptionally attractive red-and-white keeper's house. It was commissioned by none other than George Washington (1732–1799) himself. Today, the park is a great place to snap photos and hang out with a lunch and a guitar or Frisbee. The ruins of the fort are adjacent. ⏱ *1½ hr. Shore Rd., Cape Elizabeth. Park free admission; keeper's house museum $2 adults, $1 children. Museum mid-May to mid-Oct daily 10am–4pm. Also sometimes open in spring and fall, weekends only. Park open year-round, dawn to dusk.*

Return to Shore Rd. and turn left. After about 2¼ miles (3.6km), turn left on Rte. 77 (Ocean St.). Continue almost 2 more miles (3.2km), bearing left at signs for Two Lights Rd. Follow the road 1 mile (1.6km) to

⑥ Two Lights State Park. Two Lights *sounds* scenic, but it's actually not as scenic as Fort Williams, and the pair of lighthouses erected near here are not open to the public. However, it's still a good spot to view the pounding waves of the coastline and said lighthouses. There are restrooms and plenty of picnic tables. The state cautions visitors to stand well back from the edge of the rocks because big "rogue" waves occasionally roll in. People have been swept away on this coast. ⏱ *30 min. 7 Tower Dr. (via Two Lights Rd.), Cape Elizabeth.* ☎ *207/799-5871. Admission mid-May to mid-Oct $4.50 non-resident adults, $1.50 seniors, $1 children; mid-Oct to mid-May $1.50 adults, free for children.*

Backtrack 1 mile (1.6km) to Rte. 77 and continue south about 5½ miles (8.9km) to its end. Turn left on Rte. 207 (Black Point Rd.) and continue about 2 miles (3.2km) onto

❼ ★ Prouts Neck. This stony little peninsula not only hosts an excellent inn; it also holds historic importance as the former studio home of painter Winslow Homer (1836–1910), who painted the dramatic sea waves here with an intensity rarely seen in the annals of American art. The studio is closed to the public, but you can see the cottages by car, as well as a bird sanctuary with a few very short public nature trails. Unfortunately, you can't park your car anywhere on the peninsula if you're not a resident. Solutions? Two: Sleep steps away at the fine **Black Point Inn** (p 117) or bicycle here from the plush **Inn by the Sea** (p 118), about 7 lovely miles (11km) away. ⏱ *45 mins. End of Black Point Rd., Scarborough.*

A painter's life: Winslow Homer

It's impossible to count the number of artists who have come to the Maine coast seeking just the right combination of sea, surf, coastal light, and fog — all the ingredients for making the definitive seascape. But perhaps no painter is more closely identified with Maine than Winslow Homer (1836–1910).

Homer came here from Boston by way of New York, Paris, and England, having first established a decent career as a magazine illustrator and a watercolorist. In his late 30s, however, he began living in remote coastal towns, and his style became immediately much bolder, more dramatic, and instantly identifiable.

Homer came to the family summer home in Prouts Neck with his paints at the age of 47 and set up a studio within sight of the crashing waves; he never moved again. And it was here that his final, and best, work began: the documenting of the difficult lives of Maine fishermen and their families. Famous paintings and etchings made here include: *Fog Warning; Driftwood; Incoming Tide, Scarboro Maine; Early Evening; High Cliff, Coast of Maine; The Life Line;* and *Eight Bells.*

Homer died in the Prouts Neck studio in 1910, and since 2006 the studio has been owned by the Portland Museum of Art (p 85). The studio is scheduled to open to the public in 2012, displaying the artist's personal effects and teaching visitors about his craft and lasting influence.

Downtown & the Old Port

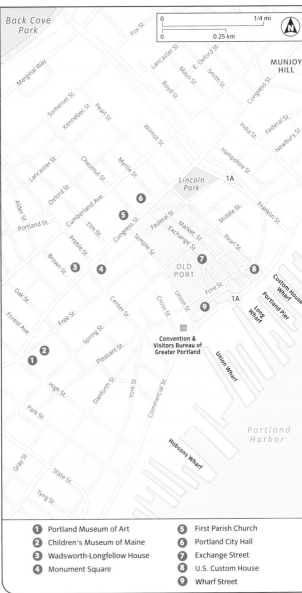

1 Portland Museum of Art	**5** First Parish Church
2 Children's Museum of Maine	**6** Portland City Hall
3 Wadsworth-Longfellow House	**7** Exchange Street
4 Monument Square	**8** U.S. Custom House
	9 Wharf Street

There's a surprising lack of historic sites in Portland's Old Port, mostly because the seaside district burned flat at least twice. Still, it's one of the most atmospheric parts of Portland, with plenty of great brick commercial architecture, cobblestones, shops, and blue-collar fishing enterprises on the docks. Downtown Portland is largely business-oriented and workaday, but there are a few excellent stops here, as well. START: **Junction of Free, High & Congress sts.**

❶ ★★★ Portland Museum of Art. This modern-looking, brick-faced museum holds one of New England's finest art collections. Holdings are particularly strong in American artists with Maine connections (Homer [1836–1910], Wyeth [1917–2009], Hopper [1882–1967]), but there are also rooms of Early American furniture and crafts; a section holding the likes of Renoir (1841–1919), Degas (1834–1917), and Picasso (1881–1973); and shows like the Hudson River School exhibit and a borrowed *Mona Lisa* that may have been a copy . . . or may be an original. Do *not* miss the adjacent McLellan House and its Sweat Galleries: They hold the best art. ⏱ *2 hr. 7 Congress Sq. (Congress & High sts.).* ☎ *207/775-6148. www. portlandmuseum.org. Admission $10 adults, $8 students & seniors, $4 children 6–17; free admission Fri 5–9pm. Tues–Sun 10am–5pm, Fri 10am–9pm; late May to mid-Oct also Mon 10am–5pm. Guided tours daily at 2pm.*

Exit the museum and walk next door to the

❷ ★ kids Children's Museum of Maine. The centerpiece exhibit in Portland's excellent kids' museum is a *camera obscura,* a room-sized "camera" on the top floor. Children gather around a white table in a dark room, where they see magically projected images that include cars driving on city streets, boats plying the harbor, and seagulls flapping by. This never fails to enthrall, providing a memorable lesson in the

workings of lenses. Other attractions might range from a simulated supermarket checkout counter to a firehouse pole or a "space shuttle" that kids can pilot from a mocked-up cockpit. ⏱ *1 hr. 142 Free St.* ☎ *207/ 828-1234. www.childrensmuseum ofme.org. Admission $8 per person (children under age 1 free). Apr–Nov Mon–Sat 10am–5pm, Sun noon–5pm. Closed Mon Nov–Apr.*

Cross over Congress St. (across the square from the art museum), turn right, and walk several blocks north to the

❸ ★ Wadsworth-Longfellow House. This 18th-century home is

First Parish Church has been operating since 1674.

Portland's City Hall is modeled after New York City's.

one of three connected townhomes that collectively house famed writer Henry Wadsworth Longfellow's (1807–1882) boyhood home *and* one of the state's best historical archives: a history campus, if you will. This home was built by Gen. Peleg Wadsworth, father of the poet, and is still furnished in early-19th-century style with some original furniture. Adjacent is the Maine History Gallery (open Mon–Sat 10am–5pm), a decent museum inside a former bank. ⏱ *45 min. 487–489 Congress St.* ☎ *207/774-1822. www.mainehistory.org. Admission $8 adults, $7 seniors & students, $3 children 6–18. May–Oct & Dec Mon–Sat 10:30am–4pm, Sun noon–4pm (tours on the hour). Closed Nov & Jan–Apr.*

Continue 1 block north along Congress St. to

④ **Monument Square.** Monument Square is the de facto outdoor lunch spot of Portland's downtown office workers. The most prominent feature here is obvious: the blocky monuments intended as memorials to Civil War dead—even if, today, they're mostly the resting places of pigeons and gulls. Farmer's markets, music concerts, and political protests and marches sometimes also occupy the square. ⏱ *15 min. Temple St. (at Congress St.).*

Continue north along Congress St. 1½ blocks to the attractive

⑤ ★ **First Parish Church.** Portland's oldest continuously operating house of worship (used since at least 1674, believe it or not) is here in the heart of the city, though the present-day structure was built in 1825 to replace the wooden building that had previously stood on the spot. Made of Maine granite, it's a narrow, graceful counterpoint to the modern high-rises encircling it; the rough stone blocks and clock tower are topped by a surprisingly graceful spire. ⏱ *15 min. 425 Congress St. (at Temple St.).*

Continue another 1½ blocks north on Congress St. to

6 Portland City Hall. Portland's massive city hall is an ode to the Second Renaissance Revival style; this could be a palace in the Loire valley—except for the bike messengers, SUVs, and pigeons out front. The hall was completed a year after the former city hall burned to the ground. John Calvin Stevens and his son John Howard helped design it, though the chief architects were from New York City (it's modeled after that city's City Hall). ⏱ *15 min. 389 Congress St. (at Exchange St.).* ☎ *207/879-0300. www.ci.portland.me.us. Free admission. Mon-Fri 9am-5pm.*

Cross Congress St. and walk several blocks downhill along

7 ★★ Exchange Street. Perhaps no street encapsulates modern-day Portland more than Exchange Street, even if it has become somewhat overrun with touristy shops, galleries, and restaurants. Running 4 short blocks downhill to bustling, beery Fore Street, this street physically and psychologically connects downtown to the Old Port. It's *the* go-to place for a souvenir, piece of jewelry, cup of gourmet coffee, or fancy meal. (You might see a few local skateboarders practicing moves, too; this isn't *only* a tourist district.) ⏱ *1¼ hr. Congress St. to Fore St.*

Turn left onto Fore St. In 3 blocks, on the right (diagonally across the intersection) is the massive

8 ★ U.S. Custom House. Dating from around 1870—right after a huge fire leveled nearly all of the Old Port—Portland's custom house is a towering example of Second Empire Renaissance architecture and takes up nearly 1 square block. Designed by Alfred B. Mullett, the U.S. government's Supervising Architect at the time, it's built of granite in a severe, columned courthouse style; even the twin cupolas and slate-hipped roof-work feel heavy. Fear of fire will do that to you. The marble work inside is quite remarkable, as is the ornamental work on the ceiling. It's still federally owned today. Ring the bell and ask the guards about a tour; if they don't have time to give one, book one by phone with the property manager. ⏱ *30 min. 312 Fore St. (at Pearl & Custom House sts.).* ☎ *207/780-3050. www.gsa. gov. Free admission. Tours by prior appointment or sometimes on admissions.*

Backtrack nearly to Exchange St. Turn left and walk a ½ block downhill on Moulton St. Turn right and find

9 ★ Wharf Street. It has become touristy, to be sure, but this little cobblestoned alley is also one of the Old Port's most atmospheric short jaunts (and it even smells like fish, sometimes). During a 2-block walk, you can dine on Italian or Thai food, drink beer and wine, and eat great seafood. Some of the bars and restaurants uphill on Fore Street have back entrances or terraces on this alley, adding to the fun. ⏱ *1 hr. Moulton St. to Union St.*

Exchange Street is one of the city's best shopping districts.

Munjoy Hill

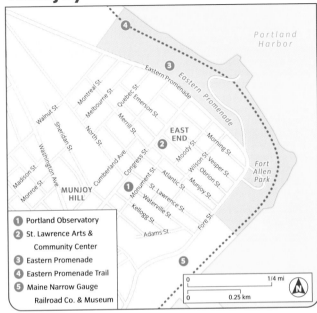

Portland Harbor

Eastern Promenade

Eastern Promenade

Walnut St.

Montreal St.

Melbourne St.

Quebec St.

Emerson St.

Merrill St.

Sheridan St.

North St.

EAST
END

Morning St.

Washington Ave.

Cumberland Ave.

Congress St.

Moody St.

Wilson St.

Vesper St.

Fort
Allen
Park

Madison St.

Monroe St.

MUNJOY
HILL

Monument
St. Lawrence St.

Atlantic St.

Obrion St.

Munjoy St.

Waterville St.

Kellogg St.

Fore St.

Adams St.

1 Portland Observatory
2 St. Lawrence Arts &
   Community Center
3 Eastern Promenade
4 Eastern Promenade Trail
5 Maine Narrow Gauge
   Railroad Co. & Museum

0   1/4 mi
0   0.25 km

N

For restaurants and bars, you head for the Old Port. But for the best actual *views* of lovely Casco Bay, ascend (by car, bike, or foot) Munjoy Hill at the eastern end of the hammerhead-shaped peninsula on which Portland sits. The view is breathtaking, almost San Francisco–like, and there's also history and dining on top of this hill—which was, long ago, a dairy pasture. START: **Congress St at North Street.**

1 ★ Portland Observatory.
One of the best bird's-eye views on Casco Bay is from the top of this shaggy, shingled observatory, which was originally a ship-signaling tower—a sort of hilltop, landlocked lighthouse—when it was built in 1807. The exhibits within give a taste of local history, but everyone comes for the views from that tiny deck up top. Climb it, and they're yours. ⏱ *45 min. 138 Congress St.*

☎ *207/774-5561. www.portland landmarks.org. Admission $7 adults, $4 kids 6–16. Guided tours daily late May to mid-Oct 10am–5pm, last tour at 4:30pm; late July to early Sept Thurs sunset tours 5–8pm. Observatory closed late Oct to mid-May & whenever no flags are flying.*

Walk 3 blocks northeast (toward the water) along Congress St. to the

The 200-year-old Portland Observatory was originally a ship-signaling tower.

much a walkway as an experience. You can jog or dog-walk the mile-long (1.6km) pathway, but Portlanders also love to toss Frisbees and plunk down picnics on the soft grass; meanwhile, wonderful views of boats and islands occupy a panoramic sweep. ⏱ *1 hr. At northeast terminus of Congress St. Free admission.*

Walk or drive to the bottom of the hill to reach the waterfront and the

④ ★ Eastern Promenade Trail. This pretty, little-known walking path runs 2 mostly flat miles (3.2km) all the way around the scenic Portland peninsula's hammerhead, from the Old Port's docks over to the circular estuarine inlet known as **Back Cove** (p 81). ⏱ *1 hr. Base of Eastern Promenade & Fort Allen Park.*

Return back up to the Promenade and turn left. Descend the hill along Fore St.; about ⅓ mile (.5km) down is the entrance to the

⑤ 🅺🅸🅳🆂 Maine Narrow Gauge Railroad Co. & Museum. Maine was once home to several narrow-gauge railways, operating on rails just 2 feet (.6m) apart. They have long since disappeared from practical use, but the small museum here preserves their memory. The admission fee is waived if you buy a ticket for the short ride on the narrow-gauge train that chugs along the foot of the Promenade. Bay views are outstanding, but the 3-mile (4.8km) ride is molasses-slow. ⏱ *1 hr. 58 Fore St.* ☎ *207-828-0814. www.mngrr.org. Museum $2 adults, $1 seniors & kids 3–12; train $10 adults, $9 seniors, $6 kids 3–12. Late May to early Oct daily 11am–4pm; early Oct to late May weekends 10am–4pm.*

② St. Lawrence Arts & Community Center. A granite and slate church built in 1897 in high Queen Anne style, the St. Lawrence Church is a National Historic Landmark but was badly decaying until a local benefactor took on the huge task of restoring it. The architecture is slowly coming back to life (the amazing stained-glass rose window glows once more), and the cathedral-like interior is a work in progress. The arts organization that owns the church holds live concerts in the Parish Hall Theater (see the website for its schedule). ⏱ *15 min. 76 Congress St.* ☎ *207/775-5568. www.stlawrencearts.org. Free admission; fee for performances. Daily 9am–5pm, plus performances.*

Continue downhill 4 blocks to the

③ ★★ Eastern Promenade. Portland's best bay view (short of going out on a boat) can be seen here from the sloping lawns of the Eastern Promenade, which is not so

The West End

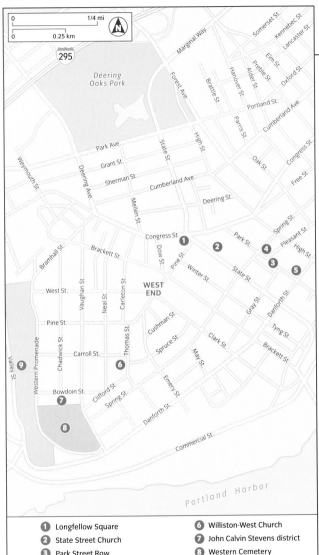

0   1/4 mi

0   0.25 km

295

Deering
Oaks Park

Marginal Way

Somerset St.
Kennebec St.
Lancaster St.

Elm St.
Preble St.
Oxford St.

Hanover St.
Alder St.

Portland St.

Forest Ave.

Brattle St.

Paris St.

Cumberland Ave.

Park Ave.

State St.

High St.

Oak St.

Congress St.

Weymouth St.

Grant St.

Deering Ave.

Sherman St.

Cumberland Ave.

Free St.

Mellen St.

Deering St.

Congress St. ➊

➋

Park St.

Spring St.

Pleasant St.

➍

Dow St.

Pine St.

Brackett St.

Winter St.

State St.

➌

High St.

Bramhall St.

➎

WEST
END

Vaughan St.

Neal St.

Carleton St.

West St.

Gray St.

Danforth St.

Pine St.

Thomas St.

Cushman St.

Clark St.

Tyng St.

Western Promenade

Chadwick St.

Carroll St.

Spruce St.

May St.

Brackett St.

Valley St.

➒

Emery St.

Clifford St.

➏

Bowdoin St.

Spring St.

➐

Danforth St.

➑

Commercial St.

Portland Harbor

➊ Longfellow Square
➋ State Street Church
➌ Park Street Row
➍ Holy Trinity Greek Orthodox Church
➎ Victoria Mansion

➏ Williston-West Church
➐ John Calvin Stevens district
➑ Western Cemetery
➒ Western Promenade

I f I had just a half-day to spend in downtown Portland, I wouldn't head for the Old Port—I'd head for the West End, home of the city's best architecture, a smattering of cafes, and a quiet grace. You won't find souvenir shops, lobsters, or ocean views here, but for the right traveler, it's perfection. START: **Junction of Congress & State sts.**

1 Longfellow Square. The West End's physical and psychological boundary is State Street, which runs right off the crest of Congress Street and down to the water. At the very crest of the hill is this square, half-blocked-off for pedestrians and marked by a bronze-and-granite statue of the writer Henry Wadsworth Longfellow—a son of Portland. Note the sculpted books beneath his chair. Artist Franklin Simmons (1838–1913) produced the work in 1888, funded by tens of thousands of coins donated by New England schoolchildren. Today, the square is ringed by restaurants and a small arts venue. ⏱ *15 min. State St. (at Congress St.).*

Walk downhill along State St. half a block to the grand

2 ★★ State Street Church. Gothic Revival in Portland? Oh, yes. One of the city's finest churches (on one of its most magnificent streets), this ruddy 1851 structure was designed by William Washburn (1820–1887) as a single, simple tower, but it was significantly redesigned by famed Portland architect John Calvin Stevens 40 years later after lightning struck the steeple. He created the stone facade, asymmetrical twin-tower design, and arched doors; the soaring, severe towers are especially magnificent. Now a Universalist church, it is also an arts venue of sorts, with occasional classical music performances, classes, and talks. ⏱ *30 min. 159 State St.* ☎ *207/774-6396. www.state streetchurch.org.*

Travel down State St. to Spring St., turn left, and continue 1 block. Turn right onto Park St. and the

This statue of Henry Wadsworth Longfellow was funded by thousands of coins donated by New England schoolchildren.

The State Street Church is an unexpected example of the Gothic Revival style.

❸ ★ Park Street Row. The outstanding row of Greek Revival brick townhouses marching down little Park Street dates from 1835, and these buildings even survived the terrible July 4th fire that ravaged huge chunks of Portland in 1866; today it's Maine's longest connected section of homes surviving from the early 1800s. (Another half-block of these homes, south of Gray St., was razed in the 1960s.) The homes across the street (on the east side of Park) aren't too shabby, either. ⏱ *15 min. 88–114 Park St. (btwn. Spring & Danforth sts.).*

At the corner of Park and Pleasant sts. is the

❹ Holy Trinity Greek Orthodox Church. This squared-off, brick church at the corner of two cute streets is unsung. But it's worth a look thanks to its age (second-oldest in the city), location, and history. Built in 1828 as a Methodist church, this is now the heart of Portland's Greek community: There's a big annual Greek festival every June. (Note the Byzantine cross, three arched doorways, and stained-glass work.) A

church bell cast in Paul Revere's Boston foundry resides here, though it no longer hangs in the tower. ⏱ *15 min. 133 Pleasant St. (at Park St.).* ☎ *207/774-0281. www.holytrinity portland.org.*

Continue 2 more blocks downhill along Park St. to Danforth St. On your left is the outstanding

❺ ★★ Victoria Mansion. Perhaps no building in Portland is more famous than this imposing High Victoria brownstone manse, built from 1858 to 1860 from plans by New Haven architect Henry Austin (1804–1891). It's the nation's premier showpiece of Victorian architecture. Details fill the interior, from wonderful and plentiful mural work to a grand staircase, gas-fueled chandeliers ("gasoliers"), Persian-style rugs hand-woven in Scotland, stained glass, nearly all the original furniture, and plaster work and cabinets by famed interior decorator Gustave Herter (1830–1898). Yes, it's pricey, but a must-see for anyone serious about architectural history. ⏱ *1¼ hr. 109 Danforth St.* ☎ *207/772-4841. www.victoria mansion.org. Admission $15 adults,*

Victoria Mansion is one of America's premier examples of Victorian architecture.

Mansions overlook the Western Promenade pathway.

$14 seniors, $5 kids 6–17; $35 families. May–Oct Mon–Sat 10am–4pm, Sun 1–5pm; Thanksgiving to Dec daily 11am–5pm. Closed most of Nov & Jan–Apr.

Go 6 blocks west along Danforth St. (away from downtown) to Emery St. Turn left and continue 2 blocks, then turn left on Spruce St. At the end is the

6 ★ Williston-West Church.
This lovely brick Victorian church, set in the residential heart of the West End, was built in the late 19th century with Queen Anne flourishes and a handsome spire. It was designed by architect Francis Fassett (1823–1908). (Fassett's prodigy, John Calvin Stevens, designed the parish house to the left 7 years later.) The organ inside is even older than the church, and there's some outstanding stained-glass work in Williston-West's Memorial Hall, much of it dedicated to former parishioners and deacons. ⏱ *30 min. 32 Thomas St. (at Spruce St.).* ☎ *207/774-4060. www.willistonwest.org.*

Facing the church, turn left on Thomas St., then immediately right on Bowdoin St. to find the

7 ★★ John Calvin Stevens district. Okay, this isn't actually the name of an historic district—but it *should* be. The prolific architect designed more than 300 buildings in Portland alone; the heaviest concentration is here in the West End along Bowdoin and Spring streets. Stevens' own house, in fact (in his signature style) was at 52 Bowdoin St. The fabulous brick Webb House up the block at 29 Bowdoin St. was also a Stevens, albeit in a Georgian style. ⏱ *45 min. Bowdoin St.*

From Bowdoin St., turn down Vaughn St. On your right is one side of the

8 Western Cemetery. The second-oldest public cemetery in Portland, these burial grounds are park-like and relaxed. Famous and not-so-famous folks were interred here from 1829 until around World War I. The partly recessed mausoleums are spooky and overgrown; some of the stone markers are damaged, but many of the names and dates remain remarkably legible. ⏱ *15 min. Vaughn St. & Western Promenade (from Danforth St. to Bowdoin St.).*

At the end of Bowdoin St. is the

9 ★ Western Promenade. This park, a ¾-mile-long (1.2km) strip of greenery with a pathway, is a good spot to eat a picnic on a bench or sun on the lawn as majestic Victorian mansions overlook your indolence. If you lift your eyes above the sprawl on a clear day, you can see the outlines of the White Mountains on the horizon—some 90 miles (145km) away. A simple 1910 monument honors Portland legislator Thomas Brackett Reed (1839–1902), while a staircase near the statue leads down the cliffs to Saint John Street. ⏱ *45 min. Free parking on street.*

Portland for **Beer Lovers**

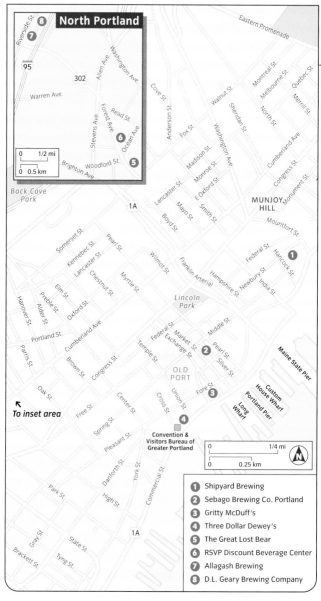

1 Shipyard Brewing
2 Sebago Brewing Co. Portland
3 Gritty McDuff's
4 Three Dollar Dewey's
5 The Great Lost Bear
6 RSVP Discount Beverage Center
7 Allagash Brewing
8 D.L. Geary Brewing Company

Portland can legitimately stake a claim to being the micro-brew capital of New England—in fact, of the East Coast. It's astonishing how many good breweries are packed into this one small city. A few more are a quick drive beyond city limits. **Note:** if you do this tour by car, borrow or hire a designated driver! START: **Newbury St, in the Old Port.**

1 ★ **Shipyard Brewing.** Shipyard has risen from a pile of contenders to become the Big Daddy of Portland brewing. What began as a single Kennebunk brewpub in 1992 quickly blossomed into a thriving, nationwide operation; the product line and sales volume grew steadily as Shipyard bought or partnered with rivals like Casco Bay Brewing (which it absorbed), Sebago, and Gritty's. You can't actually tour the brewery—instead, visit the attached store, watch a video of the brewing process, and taste the results. The fruit-punch soda is great, too. ⏱ *30 min. 86 Newbury St. (entrance on Hancock St.).* ☎ *800/789-0684 or 207/761-0807. www.shipyard.com. Store Mon–Sat 10am–5pm, Sun 11am–5pm; video tours Mon–Sat 11am–4pm, Sun noon–4pm.*

Shipyard Brewing grew from a single local brewpub to a nationwide operation.

Walk or drive 1 block downhill to Middle St. Turn right and continue 4 blocks to Market St. Across the street is

2 **Sebago Brewing Co. Portland.** Among Portland's best brew-pubs is this Old Port charmer, which goes all-out with its central location, indoor and outdoor tables, free Wi-Fi, friendly waitresses, and semi-gourmet menu of burgers, sandwiches, ribs, steaks, and fish. Oh yeah, the beer: The Boathouse Brown Ale, Frye's Leap IPA, and Lake Trout Stout are popular; or try the Full Throttle Double IPA for a more hopped-up experience. ⏱ *45 min. 164 Middle St.* ☎ *207/775-2337. Most entrees $9–$13. Daily 11am–1am.*

Walk 2 blocks downhill to Fore St., turn right, and continue 1 block to the corner of Exchange St. Across the street is

3 ★★ **Gritty McDuff's.** If I had time for just one beer in Portland before shipping out—this happens a lot—I'd end up at Gritty's, the second-ever brewpub to open in the city. Best beer in town? Maybe, maybe not. But the atmosphere is just right: a combination of geezers, ex-journalists, college kids, and tourists in an attractive space with big windows front and back (plus a patio on a cobblestoned alley). The Black Fly Stout is a fine example of the form, and the pub grub is fine. You can see the beer being born right below the brewpub: Those copper-and-bricked beer-works were designed in England. Yes, you can take a tour—ask the barman about it. ⏱ 1½ hr. See p 107.

Walk 1 block downhill to Commercial St. Turn right and walk 2 blocks to Union St. At the corner is

④ ★ Three Dollar Dewey's. The Old Port at its most Portland, Dewey's used to occupy a space on raucous Fore Street. The move downhill hasn't changed things much, though: This Portland institution still sports a row of perhaps three dozen taps dispensing wonderful microbrews, most of them from Maine, and still doles out free popcorn. (The bar probably stocks another 50 beers in bottles, as well.) They're not too big on imports, but that's okay; this is local beer at its best, and the bar food's not bad. You'll run into tons of locals here, from antiques dealers to councilmen to college kids. Ask a bartender about the name. ⏱ 1 hr. See p 107.

Now you need a car (or driver). Follow Commercial St. away from downtown 1 mile (1.6km). Turn left (onto the I-295 North on-ramp) and travel 1½ miles (2.4km) to Exit 6B (Forest Avenue/Rte. 302). Exit and drive west on Forest Ave. 1 mile (1.6km). Just past

the American Red Cross, turn left into the parking lot for

⑤ ★ The Great Lost Bear. The Bear feels more pubby than artisanal, but the beer card here tops Dewey's in quantity and, possibly, quality. With more than 60 tap lines and extensive storage space, they stock an extremely broad and well-chosen selection of brews from Montreal, Belgium, Brooklyn, Vermont, the other Portland (in Oregon), Germany, and other places. This is more of an international tasting than the Maine experience that Dewey's is. The layout is a bit dim and maze-like, but this place is often full. ⏱ 1 hr. 540 Forest Ave. ☎ 207/772-0300. www.greatlost bear.com. Daily 11:30am–11:30pm.

Continue another ¾ mile (1.2km) west on Forest Ave. (Rte. 302). On your right is

⑥ RSVP Discount Beverage Center. I'd be seriously remiss if I didn't mention the best place to find exotic beer in Portland. Hands-down, that's RSVP, which doubles as a soda, juice, and beer can and bottle redemption center and is plain-Jane in a nothing-special neighborhood. No matter. The beers here

Three Dollar Dewey's has three dozen microbrews on tap and free popcorn.

The Great Lost Bear stocks dozens of beers from around the world.

are amazing—they were stocking rows of Belgian browns and *krieks* long before most of the rest of the free world had caught on. Look for exotic European and West Coast beers. ⏱ *15 min. 887 Forest Ave.* ☎ *207/773-8808. Daily 9am–9pm.*

Continue 2½ more miles (4km) west out Forest Ave. At the 7-Eleven, turn right on Riverside St. In ¼ mile (.4km), turn right again onto Industrial Way to find

⑦ ★★ Allagash Brewing. Of the many locally brewed beers available in and around Portland, Rob Tod's Allagash Brewing holds a special place in my palate. I still remember the first glass of Rob's Belgian white I ever tasted—as crisp and clean as an orange rind. And, indeed, he uses citrus peels in the mix, as well as proprietary spices. Though that white is arguably his most famous, Tod brews other beers here, too: a Belgian double, a Belgian triple, and a bunch of specialty, limited-sale,

cellared, and barrel-aged beers. ⏱ *45 min. 50 Industrial Way.* ☎ *800/330-5385 or 207/878-5385. www.allagash.com. Store Mon–Fri 11am–4pm; tours Mon–Fri every 2 hr. 11am–3pm.*

Continue ½ mile (.8km) along Industrial Way to the end. Turn left and find the

⑧ ★ D.L. Geary Brewing Company. David Geary is usually credited with kick-starting Maine's microbrew bonanza in the 1980s when he opened this brewery after several years of research and "testing" (i.e. drinking) in the British Isles. And the city's first brewery is still one of its best-loved, pumping out their signature pale ale, plus about a dozen other (mostly hoppy) varieties. Tours are by appointment, but you can visit the gift shop any weekday. ⏱ *30 min. 38 Evergreen Dr.* ☎ *207/878-2337. www.geary brewing.com. Shop Mon–Fri 8am– 4pm; tours by appointment.*

Portland for **Foodies**

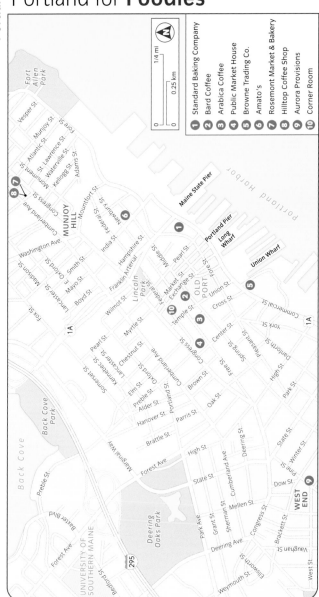

1 Standard Baking Company
2 Bard Coffee
3 Arabica Coffee
4 Public Market House
5 Browne Trading Co.
6 Amato's
7 Rosemont Market & Bakery
8 Hilltop Coffee Shop
9 Aurora Provisions
10 Corner Room

The secret, I think, is finally out. All the big travel and food magazines have caught on to what locals long knew: Portland's a foodie powerhouse. From fresh-caught fish and lobsters hauled out of Casco Bay daily to organic orchards and gardens, the area's food is a magnet for top chefs. Here's a tour of local tastes, both the raw and the cooked. START: **Old Port ferry docks.**

1 ★★ Standard Baking Company. Where better in Portland to grab a breakfast pastry than at Standard Baking, tucked right behind the **Hilton Garden Inn** (see p 117) in the Old Port? Nowhere, that's where. Allison Bray and Matt James wake 'n bake; all *you* need to do is show up early with an appetite. Even better, you can smell the bread and watch the bakers at work through big windows behind the counter. ⏱ 30 min. 75 Commercial St. (behind Hilton Garden Inn). ☎ 207/773-2112. Food items $1–$5. MC, V. Mon–Sat 7am–6pm, Sun 7am–5pm.

Head 3 blocks west down Commercial St. to Market St. Turn right and go 3 blocks uphill to Middle St. At the hub of the Old Port, turn left. On the left, you'll find

2 Bard Coffee. Some are already saying that Bard Coffee makes the best espressos in town—a mighty large boast, considering it only opened in 2009. So do they or don't they? I'm not sure, but it's certainly fun finding out. And no, the place isn't named for Shakespeare; one of the three owners is named Bard. ⏱ 30 min. 185 Middle St. ☎ 207/899-4788. www.bardcoffee.com. Coffee drinks $2–$5. Mon–Fri 7am–9pm, Sat 8am–9pm, Sun 9am–6pm.

Continue 2 more blocks west along Middle St. Turn right on Temple St., then make the next left onto Free St. In 1 block, at the corner of the intersection, is

3 ★ Arabica Coffee. Portland's coffee king? In my mind it's still Arabica, which has been here for awhile (although it recently moved a half-block down the street to this cool space, festooned with local art). If you can find better locally roasted coffee in town, go for it; but so far, this place wins, as far as I'm concerned. Head here for your

Standard Baking Company is a great place for a morning breakfast pastry.

mid-morning pickup. ⏱ 1 hr. 2 Free St. ☎ 207/899-1833. Food items $2–$6, coffee drinks $2–$5. MC, V. Mon–Fri 7am–6pm, Sat & Sun 8am–6pm.

Walk ½ block uphill to Monument Square, home of the new

4 Public Market House. The resurrection of a public market in Portland is nothing short of amazing and a very welcome development for Portlanders; entrepreneur Kris Horton, who had been located in a bigger, since-closed public market a few blocks away, got inspired and made it happen (with a lot of help). The stalls in this central Monument Square building include a beer and wine vendor (the Maine Beer Beverage Co.); a branch of the good Big Sky Bread Co. bakery (see p 113); Horton's greenmarket-slash-gourmet foods dealer, K. Horton Specialty Foods; and a simple Greek restaurant, Spartan Grill. A great place for lunch or just a snack. Prices vary by vendor. ⏱ 45 min. 28 Monument Sq. ☎ 207/228-2056. www.publicmarkethouse.com. Mon–Sat 8am–7pm, Sun 10am–5pm.

Follow the Square to the Temple St. garage, turn right, and continue 3 blocks downhill to Commercial St. Turn right and go 1 block to

5 ★★ Browne Trading Co. Family-run Browne's looks like just another of Portland's many fish markets on the various docks along the waterfront. But this one is special: it's actually world-famous for the quality of its seafood and flies fish out to big restaurants in places like New York, Las Vegas, and L.A. Pick up some smoked salmon, caviar, fresh-caught fish, or (seasonal) Maine diver scallops right at the source—and try something from the little cafe, too. ⏱ 45 min. 262 Commercial St. (store) & Merrill's

Wharf (fish market). ☎ 800/944-7848. www.brownetrading.com. Fish prices vary seasonally. Café items $5–$11. Store spring–fall Mon–Sat 10am–6:30pm, Sun noon–5pm; winter Mon–Sat 10am–6:30pm, call for Sun hr. (cafe closed Sun). Fish market open by appointment only.

Drive or walk ½ mile (.8km) east along Commercial St. At India St., turn left and continue 3 short blocks to

6 Amato's. This nondescript sandwich shop doesn't look like much, but it does actually hold one claim to fame—at least, I think so. The shops claims that it invented the "sub" sandwich, in a form known as an "Italian": a concoction of cold cuts, vinegar, peppers, tomatoes, and tons of onions. Amato's is a small New England chain now, but this is the original shop. ⏱ 15 min. 71 India St. (at Newbury St.). ☎ 207/773-1682. Sandwiches $3–$7. Daily 6:30am-11pm.

Continue uphill to Congress St. Turn right and climb. After about ½ mile (.8km), at the crest, is the

7 Rosemont Market & Bakery. Actually the third branch of two existing markets, this Rosemont is quite compact but fun to browse around in. Keep a sharp eye out for

Amato's claims to have invented the "sub" sandwich.

You'll find locally sourced cheese, bread, and meat at the Rosemont Market & Bakery.

local specialty and artisanal foods such as locally sourced cheese, bread, and meat; the changing-daily roster of specials might run to meatloaf, smoked ham and Colby, or beet sandwiches, plus soups like split-pea with ham or "smoky vegetable." A fun stop when you're on the Hill. They host wine tastings, too. ⏱ 15 min. 88 Congress St. ☎ 207/773-7888. www.rosemont market.com. Most food items $3–$7. Mon–Sat 9am–8pm, Sun 9am–6pm.

Beside the market is the

8 kids **Hilltop Coffee Shop.** There's been a lot of shaking up in Portland's coffee shops in recent years, but this one looks like a promising contender with staying power. A completely separate operation from the natural foods store to its left, this crest-top beanery brews up a mean latte, keeps plenty of cool local art on the walls, plays good music, hires good people, and serves pastries for snacking on. ⏱ 45 min. 90 Congress St. ☎ 207/780-0025. Coffee drinks $2–$5. Daily 6am–7pm.

Go down Congress St. for 1½ miles (2.4km) to State St. (Longfellow Square statue); make a hard left onto State St. and then an immediate right onto Pine St. Continue 3 blocks to

9 ★ **Aurora Provisions.** In another life, this was just a pedestrian convenience store. But then Aurora moved in and quickly transformed West Enders' shopping experience, stocking a mix of natural foods, gourmet products, and home-baked pastries, breads, and light meals. The sweets and cakes in the case are especially good. Even better, there's ample table space here to hang out over a cup of organic coffee with a friend. ⏱ 30 min. 64 Pine St. ☎ 207/871-9060. www.auroraprovisions.com. Mon–Sat 8am–6:30pm.

Backtrack along Pine St. to Brackett St. and turn right. After 1 block, turn left on Spring St. and follow it ¾ mile (1.2km) to Exchange St. Park and walk 1 block uphill to

10 ★ **Corner Room.** The acknowledged king of Portland mixologists is one John Myers. Myers concocts cocktails the way painters paint pictures: with subtlety and a thorough intimacy with his tools (i.e. spirits). Finish your tour here, in this combination Italian trattoria/drinker's paradise. ⏱ 1 hr. 110 Exchange St. (at Federal St.). ☎ 207/879-4747. www. thefrontroomrestaurant.com. Most cocktails $8–$10. Mon–Fri 11:30am–10pm, Sat 5–10pm, Sun 4–9pm.

Portland **Beaches & Marshes**

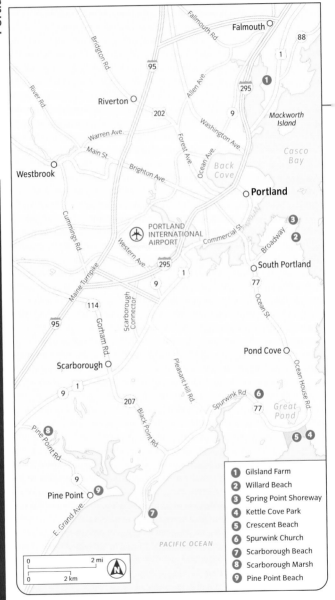

Falmouth Rd.

Falmouth

88

1

Bridgton Rd.

95

Allen Ave.

295

River Rd.

Riverton

202

Washington Ave.

9

Mackworth Island

Casco Bay

Warren Ave.

Main St.

Forest Ave.

Ocean Ave.

Back Cove

Westbrook

Brighton Ave.

Portland

Cummings Rd.

PORTLAND INTERNATIONAL AIRPORT

Commercial St.

Broadway

Western Ave.

295

1

South Portland

Maine Turnpike

9

77

Scarborough Connector

Ocean St.

114

95

Gorham Rd.

Pond Cove

Scarborough

Pleasant Hill Rd.

Ocean House Rd.

9

1

207

Black Point Rd.

Spurwink Rd.

77

Great Pond

Pine Point Rd.

Crescent Beach

9

Pine Point

E. Grand Ave.

PACIFIC OCEAN

1	Gilsland Farm
2	Willard Beach
3	Spring Point Shoreway
4	Kettle Cove Park
5	Crescent Beach
6	Spurwink Church
7	Scarborough Beach
8	Scarborough Marsh
9	Pine Point Beach

0   2 mi

0   2 km

One of the biggest surprises when visiting Portland is the discovery that there are numerous beaches—of various sizes, shapes, and compositions—within a quick 20-minute drive of the Old Port, plus several other intriguing natural areas ideal for bird-watching, canoeing, and strolling. This tour lays out the best of them in geographical order, but visiting one or two in one day is plenty; three or more, a stretch. START: **Take I-295 north to Exit 9, then exit onto U.S. Rte. 1 North (Falmouth). After about a mile (1.6km), turn left onto Gilsland Farm Rd.**

1 kids ★★ **Gilsland Farm.** The Maine Audubon Society could hardly have picked a better place for its headquarters: This rambling, 65-acre (26-hectare) property has a little of something for everyone, from grassy meadows to wetlands. Birders adore the place (tidal estuaries like this one tend to draw quite a variety of bird life), but it's also great for a long walk or picnic in the sea air—pathways are created by mowing out of the high grasses in summer. In winter, you can rent snowshoes at the adjacent nature center. ⏱ 1¼ hr. 20 Gilsland Farm Rd., Falmouth. ☎ 207/781-2330. www.maineaudubon.org. Property daily dawn–dusk; nature center Mon–Sat 9am–4pm, Sun noon–4pm. Free parking in lot.

Gilsland Farm is the headquarters for the Maine Audubon Society.

Return to U.S. Rte. 1 and merge with I-295. Continue south 2 miles (3.2km) to Exit 6A (Forest Ave.). Exit onto Forest Ave. and follow State St. uphill through Portland and over the bridge (becomes Rte. 77). At Ocean St. and Broadway, go straight through to Broadway. After 1½ miles (2.4km) turn right on Breakwater Dr. and park in Southern Maine Technical College visitors' parking lot.

2 kids **Willard Beach.** South Portland's Willard Beach is truly a "neighborhood beach," ringed by modest homes whose residents can stroll to the beach in a minute. You can also swim, check out the driftwood, and make sand castles here—families often come with picnics. ⏱ 45 min. Access via Willard St. or SMTC parking lot, South Portland.

Adjacent to Willard Beach is the

3 ★ **Spring Point Shoreway.** This 1½-mile (2.4km) one-way walking trail passes Willard Beach, but it also passes a few other points of interest: the granite breakwater running out to **Spring Point Light**; Southern Maine Technical College, renowned statewide for its culinary arts program; and the remnants of Fort Preble—a once-huge 1808 fort that protected the harbor through five wars. It's a good, energetic stroll. ⏱ 1 hr. Access via Fort Rd. or SMCC parking lot, South Portland. Free parking.

Backtrack to Broadway. After 1 mile (1.6km), at Ocean St. (Rte. 77), turn left and follow Rte. 77 for 5 miles (8km) to the Kettle Cove Dairy Bar ice cream shop. Bear left onto Ocean House Rd. and follow it to its end.

4 ★ Kettle Cove Park. Down a little side road in Cape Elizabeth, Kettle Cove is a town park and beach, though not the swimming kind. It's more a place to take a hike through the scrub and savor the views of fishing boats and pleasure craft moving through Maxwell Cove and the vicinity. There's a mile-long trail around the point and picnic tables. ⏱ *30 min. Kettle Cove Rd. (via Ocean House Rd.).* ☎ *207/799-5871. Limited free parking in lot.*

Backtrack to Rte. 77 and continue less than 1 mile (1.6km) south to entrance of

5 ★★ Crescent Beach. This beach (shaped just like, well, a crescent), is many Portlanders' favorite. It's a great place to walk a dog, clamber over rocks, or work on your tan, though not so great for swimming—lots of seaweed. There are restrooms, a tiny snack bar, barbecue grills, and picnic tables. The

adjacent **Inn by the Sea** (p 118) is a great place to take in the view over a drink or bite. ⏱ *2 hr. 66 Two Lights Rd. (Rte. 77), Cape Elizabeth. Non-resident parking $6.50 adults, $2 seniors. Grounds open year-round; parking lot closes early Oct to late May.*

Continue about 1 mile (1.6km) south on Rte. 77 to the junction of Spurwink Ave. and the lovely

6 ★ Spurwink Church. This 1802 meetinghouse-style church is the oldest building in town and a good peaceful stop after the beaches. The rather stark interior is marked by a 19th-century chandelier and working wooden pump organ, but it's the exceptionally handsome weathervane on the steeple that most are drawn to. The surrounding marshes, meadows, and stone walls are also lovely. ⏱ *15 min. Rte. 77 (at Spurwink Ave.), Cape Elizabeth.* ☎ *207/799-4197.*

Continue about 4 miles (6.4km) south to the end of Rte. 77 and turn left onto Rte. 207. Continue 1 mile (1.6km). On the left is

7 ★ Scarborough Beach. This beach—designated as a "state"

You can hike and watch the fishing boats in Maxwell Cove from Kettle Cove Park.

Canoeing at Scarborough Marsh.

park but actually operated by a private, for-profit company—might be the best swimming beach in the entire Greater Portland area; that's why, on summer weekends, it gets crowded indeed. Arrive early. There are lifeguards from mid-June through early September, but no dogs allowed during summer. You can also buy a surfing pass and hot dogs, and rent equipment at the beach shack. ⏱ *1½ hr. 414 Black Point Rd. (Rte. 207), Scarborough.* ☎ *207/883-2416. www.scarborough beachstatepark.com. Apr–Oct parking in lot $5 adults, $2 kids 5–11; Nov–Mar free parking on street. May to mid-Sept daily 9am–7pm, Apr & mid-Sept to Oct daily 9am–5pm.*

Backtrack to U.S. Rte. 1. Turn left and go 3 miles (4.8km) south to Rte. 9 (Pine Point Rd.). Turn left and continue ¾ mile (1.2km) to

8 kids ★ Scarborough Marsh. It's hard to do justice to the variety of activities at Scarborough Marsh, a huge wetland tucked between busy U.S. Route 1 and the beach. This is a true wildlife sanctuary, and the nature center operated by the Maine Audubon Society rents out

canoes for exploring the tidal river (harder than it looks when it's windy). Bird-watchers love the place, and you can hike 1½ miles (2.4km) of trails. ⏱ *1 hr. 136 Pine Point Rd. (Rte. 9), Scarborough.* ☎ *207/883-5100. www.maine audubon.org. Free parking in lot. Trails open daily year-round, dawn to dusk; nature center Mon-Sat 9am-5pm, Sun noon-5pm except closed on U.S. holidays.*

Continue on Rte. 9 (Pine Point Rd.) another 2½ miles (4km) until you can see the ocean. Turn left on Jones Creek Rd. then right on Ave. 5 to park at

9 kids Pine Point Beach. In a windy, slightly desolate spot with no changing rooms or bathrooms, long, sandy Pine Point is great for solitude-seekers or beachcombers. The beach is physically connected to **Old Orchard Beach** (p 65), about 3 miles (4.8km) away, but feels miles away in spirit. ⏱ *45 min. Pillsbury Dr. (at Ave. 5, off Rte. 9), Scarborough.* ☎ *207/730-4000. Late May to early Sept non-resident parking permit $10 per day; early Sept to late May free.*

Pine Point Beach is a favorite spot for beachcombers.

Shopping, A&E & Nightlife

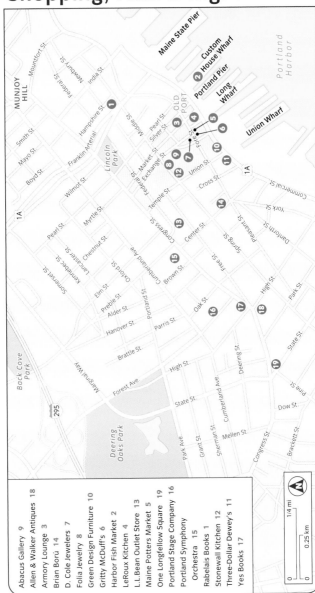

Abacus Gallery **9**
Allen & Walker Antiques **18**
Armory Lounge **3**
Brian Ború **14**
D. Cole Jewelers **7**
Folia Jewelry **8**
Green Design Furniture **10**
Gritty McDuff's **6**
Harbor Fish Market **2**
LeRoux Kitchen **4**
L.L.Bean Outlet Store **13**
Maine Potters Market **5**
One Longfellow Square **19**
Portland Stage Company **16**
Portland Symphony
   Orchestra **15**
Rabelais Books **1**
Stonewall Kitchen **12**
Three-Dollar Dewey's **11**
Yes Books **17**

Shopping, A&E & Nightlife
A to Z

Antiques
★ Allen & Walker Antiques
CONGRESS SQUARE The collection of Maine, New England, American, and Asian items for sale here is astounding: anything from oil paintings to historical prints, furniture, ceramics, china, and snuff boxes, plus the occasional odd item such as a massive box camera. *600 Congress St.* ☎ *207/772-8787. MC, V.*

Arts & Crafts
Abacus Gallery OLD PORT   A wide range of crafts—from furniture, jewelry, handbags, and watches to original prints and calendars—is displayed on two floors of this centrally located Old Port shop, which has been here since the early '70s. Great place to browse. *44 Exchange St.* ☎ *207/772-4880. www.abacusgallery.com. AE, MC, V.*

Maine Potters Market OLD PORT   Maine's largest pottery collective maintains a shop that's open daily in the Old Port, selling a variety of styles crafted by local potters. There are also other items, such as holiday ornaments. *376 Fore St.* ☎ *207/774-1633. www.maine pottersmarket.com. AE, MC, V.*

Bars & Cocktail Lounges
Armory Lounge OLD PORT   One of Portland's very best quiet spots for a drink is this bar hidden away in the basement of the **Portland Regency** (p 118). There's also a light pub menu served, and Mondays bring martini specials. *20 Milk St.* ☎ *207/774-4200. www.the regency.com.*

The Brian Ború pub features Irish music every Sunday.

Brian Ború OLD PORT   This slightly rowdy Irish pub on Center Street, in a bit of a wasteland between interesting areas, isn't far from the Old Port. The rooftop patio comes alive on nights with good weather—expect college kids and locals downing pints of Guinness—and there's Irish music every Sunday. *57 Center St.* ☎ *207/780-1506.*

★ Gritty McDuff's OLD PORT   At the foot of Exchange Street, this is practically Portland's living room: good pub food, live music, and a cast of regulars showing up to drink great beers brewed on-site and elsewhere. *396 Fore St.* ☎ *207/772-2739. www.grittys.com.*

★ Three-Dollar Dewey's OLD PORT   One of Portland locals' very favorite Old Port bars is this one, now located at the corner of Commercial and Union streets (downhill a block from Fore St.). Plenty of local beer on tap, plus a super-friendly and peppy vibe. *241 Commercial St.* ☎ *207/772-3310. www.threedollar deweys.com.*

Books
★ Rabelais Books OLD
PORT   Finally, a decent bookstore in the Old Port! It's about time. With a motto of "thought for food," husband and wife Samantha and Don Lindgren run a great little enterprise combining classy, hard-to-find books with deep knowledge of food and wine. Foodie and reader heaven. *86 Middle St.* ☎ *207/774-1044. www.rabelaisbooks.com. AE, DISC, MC, V.*

Yes Books CONGRESS
SQUARE   The legacy of the late Pat Murphy (a talented local poet and full-of-life fellow who passed away in 2009), this bookstore's first editions, philosophy, poetry, history, and prints are wonderfully eccentric. *589 Congress St.* ☎ *207/775-3233. MC, V.*

Edibles
★ Harbor Fish Market OLD
PORT   Another of Portland's waterfront fish markets, it's worth visiting just to see the piles of fish that hardworking guys have pulled out of the bay. You can also buy smoked fish for your bagels and lobsters packed safely for 24 hours worth of traveling. *9 Custom House Wharf.* ☎ *207/775-0251. www.harborfish.com. AE, MC, V.*

LeRoux Kitchen OLD PORT
What's a touristy shopping area without a crack kitchen store? You'll find kitchen gadgets of all sorts, plenty of specialty food products (many of them made in Maine), and a selection of wines at this Old Port shop. *161 Commercial St.* ☎ *207/553-7665. AE, DISC, MC, V.*

Stonewall Kitchen OLD PORT
Stonewall is one of Maine's most popular exports, selling locally made mustards, jams, and gourmet-flavored sauces. You can browse and taste their products here in the Old Port, as

One Longfellow Square showcases folk-oriented music.

well as at the **York headquarters** (p 69). *182 Middle St.* ☎ *207/879-2409. AE, DISC, MC, V.*

Fashion
kids L.L.Bean Outlet Store
DOWNTOWN   Sporting-goods retailer L.L.Bean opened its downtown Portland factory outlet in 1996 (there's another outlet up in Freeport), and Portlanders have been loving it ever since for the discounts. Look for seconds, slightly damaged goods, and outdated fashions, plus a few full-priced items. *542 Congress St.* ☎ *207/772-5100. AE, MC, V.*

Furniture
★★ Green Design Furniture
OLD PORT   This well-thought-out Old Port shop sells lovely wooden furniture that disassembles easily for storage. The "Green" in the name, by the way, doesn't *only* refer to an eco-philosophy (though the wood is carefully chosen): The designer's name is Doug Green. *267 Commercial St.* ☎ *866/756-4730 or 207/775-4234. AE, MC, V.*

Jewelry
★ D. Cole Jewelers OLD PORT
The Coles (a husband-and-wife team) produce lovely handcrafted gold and silver jewelry in their prominently placed Old Port studio/shop. Yet you won't break the bank buying here. Both traditional designs and more adventurous ones are laid out in the cases, utilizing a wide range of precious stones. *10 Exchange St.* ☎ *207/772-5119. AE, MC, V.*

Folia Jewelry OLD PORT Shop owner Edith Armstrong hand-crafts distinctive jewelry and sells it in this tasteful shop in the Old Port, then showcases the work of some of Maine's other top designers, as well. The selection of rings is particularly noteworthy. *50 Exchange St.* ☎ *207/761-4432. AE, MC, V.*

Live Music
★ One Longfellow Square
LONGFELLOW SQUARE Formerly a world-music arts and cultural center, this space has reinvented itself as a rootsier, folksier venue—Ellis Paul, Lucy Kaplansky, Cheryl Wheeler, Chris Smither, Tom Russell, and the like. Directions? "The statue of Longfellow is looking at our front door." *181 State St. (at Congress St.).* ☎ *207/761-1757. www.onelongfellowsquare.com. Tickets $12–$25. AE, MC, V.*

Symphony, Opera & Dance
★★ Portland Symphony Orchestra
DOWNTOWN If you're a classical music buff, don't miss the PSO, a local outfit that knocks your socks off from September through May in a series of pops and classical concerts at the Merrill Auditorium. There are also kids' concerts. *477 Congress St.* ☎ *207/842-0800 or 207/773-612. www.portlandsymphony. com. Tickets $23–$62. AE, MC, V.*

Theater
★ Portland Stage Company
DOWNTOWN Portland theater companies come and go like the wind, but Portland Stage endures. The season runs October through May, with an eclectic schedule of shows such as *Noises Off* and *Much Ado About Nothing*, but also plenty of lesser-known and locally written works. *25A Forest Ave.* ☎ *207/774-0465. www.portlandstage.com. Tickets $26–$36; discounts for seniors & children. AE, MC, V.*

The Portland Stage Company mounts classic plays and lesser-known works by local playwrights.

Portland Dining

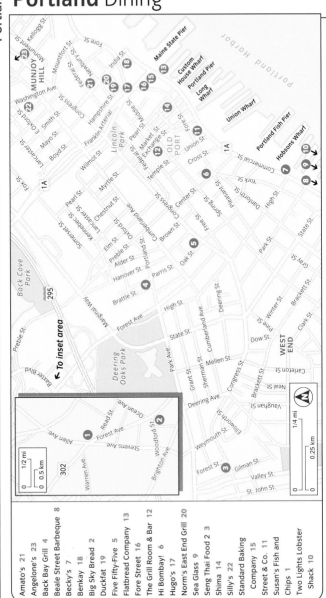

Dining Best Bets

Best **Patio**
Silly's, *40 Washington Ave. (p 115)* *$$.*

Most **Romantic**
★★ Sea Glass, *40 Bowery Beach Rd., Cape Elizabeth (p 114)* $$$$.

Best Place to **Spike Your Cholesterol Count**
★ Duckfat, *43 Middle St. (p 113)* $.

Best **Basic Pizza Pie**
Angelone's, *788 Washington Ave. (p 112)* $$$.

Best **Pizza 2.0**
Flatbread Company, *72 Commercial St. (p 113)* $$$.

Best **Steak**
★★ Grill Room & Bar, *84 Exchange St. (p 113)* $$$$.

Best Place to **Impress a First Date**
★★ Street & Co., *33 Wharf St. (p 115)* $$$$.

Best Place to **Dine in Style**
★★ Back Bay Grill, *65 Portland St. (p 112)* $$$$.

Best Place to **Dine Alfresco**
★ Two Lights Lobster Shack, *225 Two Lights Rd., Cape Elizabeth (p 115)* $$$.

Best **Baked Goods**
★ Standard Baking Company, *75 Commercial St. (p 115)* $.

Brick-walled, romantic Street & Co. has stellar seafood and an outdoor patio.

Most **Authentically Portland**
Becky's, *390 Commercial St. (p 112)* $$.

Most Likely to **Serve Something You've Never Eaten Before**
★★★ Hugo's, *88 Middle St. (p 114)* $$$$$.

Best Use of **Locally Sourced Products**
★★ Fore Street, *288 Fore St. (p 113)* $$$$$.

Portland Dining A to Z

Amato's OLD PORT *DELI* Amato's claims to be the original inventor of the Italian "sub" sandwich, and blue-collar Portlanders still pop in daily for the thick cold-cut sandwiches on simple white bread. This is pretty much all that's left of Portland's once-thriving Italian neighborhood, even if it has zero atmosphere. *71 India St.* ☎ *207/773-1682. Sandwiches $5–$8. MC, V. Breakfast, lunch & dinner daily.*

kids Angelone's BACK COVE *ITALIAN* Way out on Washington Avenue, miles from the sights, Angelone's serves good thin-crust, tomatoey pizzas to an all-locals crowd in an absolutely unpretentious setting. There's a second location in South Portland on Route 77, across the Casco Bay Bridge. *788 Washington Ave.* ☎ *207/775-3114. Pizzas $9–$18. No credit cards. Lunch Mon–Sat, dinner daily.*

★★ Back Bay Grill DOWNTOWN *FUSION* Near the main post office, chef/owner Larry Matthews cooks a New American menu with continental accents and plenty of local ingredients: Maine crab cakes, duck, lamb, grilled filet mignon in wine sauce, and salmon. The fresh homemade pastas are good, too. *65 Portland St.* ☎ *207/772-8833. www.backbaygrill.com. Entrees $17–$33. AE, DC, DISC, MC, V. Dinner Mon–Sat. Closed Sun.*

Beale Street Barbeque SOUTH PORTLAND *AMERICAN* Portland's best 'cue is in this unassuming building across the bridge from the waterfront. Check the board for daily specials and fish entrees. Or get a sample platter of pork, chicken, brisket, cornbread, ribs, beans, and slaw. *725 Broadway.* ☎ *207/767-0130. Entrees $9–$17. MC, V. Lunch & dinner daily.*

Becky's OLD PORT *DINER* This is your basic diner, where fishermen hang out over mugs of coffee before or after a day's (or night's) work—that's why the place opens at 4am. There's nothing fancy here; stay with eggs, pancakes, fried fish, chowder made with just-caught fish, and a bottomless mug of joe. *390 Commercial St.* ☎ *207/773-7070. www.beckysdiner.com. Entrees $2–$8. AE, DISC, MC, V. Breakfast, lunch & dinner daily.*

Benkay OLD PORT *JAPANESE* Affordable and hip sushi joint in a waterfront location. Go for sushi, sashimi, or *maki* rolls, or Japanese bar-food items like tempura (fried

Becky's is a traditional diner frequented by local fishermen.

vegetables), *gyoza* (dumplings), *katsu* (fried chicken or pork cutlets), and *udon* (thick noodles). *2 India St. (at Commercial St.).* ☎ *207/773-5555. www.sushiman.com. Entrees $8–$17. AE, MC, V. Lunch Mon–Fri, dinner daily.*

kids Big Sky Bread WOODFORD'S CORNER *BAKERY* Inside a firehouse, this is a great neighborhood breakfast and lunch spot in Woodford's Corner. Order coffee with a pastry, cookie, or granola, and watch the kids play. There's a branch in downtown in Monument Square. *536 Deering Ave.* ☎ *207/761-5623. www.mainebread.com. Sandwiches $4–$7. AE, MC, V. Breakfast, lunch & dinner daily.*

★ Duckfat OLD PORT *CAFE* Owned by Hugo's (see p 114), this bistro serves Belgian-style fries with curried mayo, truffled ketchup, and other gourmet sauces, plus *poutine* (Canadian-style fries with cheese and gravy), soups, beignets, milkshakes of local ice cream, even a meatloaf-filled panini sandwich. Don't tell your doctor. *43 Middle St.* ☎ *207/774-8080. Entrees $6–$10. AE, MC, V. Lunch & dinner Mon–Sat. Closed Sun.*

★★ Five Fifty-Five DOWNTOWN *CONTEMPORARY AMERICAN* Husband-and-wife Steve and Michelle Corry's restaurant features small plates of soup, salad, cheese, and foie gras—plus a fuller menu of pork chops, veal, lobster mac-and-cheese, hanger steak, hand-rolled pasta, and the like. The wine list is tops. *555 Congress St.* ☎ *207/761-0555. www.fivefifty-five.com. Small plates $6–$15, entrees $31–$35. AE, MC, V. Brunch Sun, dinner daily.*

Flatbread Company OLD PORT *ITALIAN* On a dock overlooking the Casco Bay Lines ferry terminal, Flatbread Company serves delicious pizzas fired in an open wood oven,

Duckfat bistro serves unusual gourmet fare.

adorned with such toppings as nitrate-free pepperoni and organic vegetables. The salads are good, too. *72 Commercial St.* ☎ *207/772-8777. Pizzas $12–$15. AE, MC, V. Lunch Wed–Sun, dinner daily.*

★★ Fore Street OLD PORT *CONTEMPORARY AMERICAN* Chef Sam Hayward uses a wood-fired brick oven and grill in an open kitchen to create memorable, widely acclaimed meals of pork, chicken, steak, and seafood. Desserts might include chocolate soufflé cake, a peanut butter torte, or gelati. *288 Fore St.* ☎ *207/775-2717. www.forestreet.biz. Entrees $13–$29. AE, MC, V. Dinner daily.*

★ The Grill Room & Bar OLD PORT *AMERICAN* Harding Lee Smith works the wood-fired grills in this great Old Port eatery. You can

Meals are cooked on wood-fired grills at Old Port's Grill Room & Bar.

get steak, seared tuna, thin-crust pizza, or grilled fish; the house sauces are a highlight. Go for an outdoor table in good weather, or just hang out at the bar watching baseball. *84 Exchange St.* ☎ *207/774-2333. Entrees $13–$27. AE, DISC, MC, V. Lunch & dinner daily.*

Hi Bombay! OLD PORT *INDIAN* The best Indian food in town, steps from the Old Port: fiery vindaloos, great mango *lassi* shakes, good *shami korma, masala,* and *biryani* dishes—and superb puffed-up *poori* fried breads. Get chutney and yogurt on the side. *1 Pleasant St.* ☎ *207/772-8767. www.hibombay. com. Entrees $9–$14. AE, DISC, MC, V. Lunch & dinner daily.*

★★★ Hugo's OLD PORT *CONTEMPORARY AMERICAN* Chef Rob Evans runs one of Maine's most exciting kitchens, buying local ingredients and crafting unusual meals. The offerings run largely to substantial "small" plates: salads, steak *tartare,* duck, Arctic char, and the like. Dessert could be a goat-cheese cheesecake, a Linzer torte with a green tea froth, or a chocolate parfait. *88 Middle St.* ☎ *207/774-8538. www.hugos.net. Small plates $10–$21. AE, MC, V. Dinner Tues–Sat. Closed Sun & Mon.*

Norm's East End Grill OLD PORT *AMERICAN* This barbecue joint is one of the most convivial eateries in the city. The barbecue is good (as are the biscuits and cornbread), but I also really like the creamy lobster stew. You can order good bar food such as tacos, fishcakes, quesadillas, salads, and fried chicken. *47 Middle St.* ☎ *207/253-1700. www. normseastendgrill.com. Entrees $8–$18. AE, MC, V. Lunch & dinner Mon–Sat.*

★★ Sea Glass CAPE ELIZABETH *SEAFOOD/FUSION* At the house restaurant of the lovely **Inn by the Sea** (p 118), Argentine chef Mitchell Kaldrovich combines European and Latin tastes and influences with fresh Maine fish and lobster. Expect seafood paella, chowder, pork chops, Argentine-style steak frites, and grilled local lobster. *40 Bowery Beach Rd., Cape Elizabeth.* ☎ *800/888-4287 or 207/799-3134. Entrees $19–$31. AE, DISC, MC, V. Lunch & dinner daily.*

Seng Thai Food 2 LOWER CONGRESS ST. *SOUTHEAST ASIAN* For Thai food, this lowbrow corner eatery is the best in town. Most everything costs less than $10, the Thai iced tea is excellent, and the female chefs are unfailingly friendly. The cashew-nut entree with pineapple is a winner, too. Great local experience. *921 Congress St.* ☎ *207/879-2577. Entrees $6–$16. AE, MC, V. Lunch & dinner daily.*

Shima OLD PORT *FRENCH/JAPANESE* Shima opened in 2009, run by a Japanese-Hawaiian chef who trained in France; it successfully fuses sushi with Japanese bar food, Hawaiian pineapples, and those creamy French sauces. It's hip, tasty, and innovative, yet surprisingly affordable. *339 Fore St.* ☎ *207/773-8389. Entrees $8–$20. DISC, MC, V. Lunch & dinner Mon–Sat.*

Hugo's emphasizes local ingredients and "small plates" style dishes.

Silly's food is as creative as its decor.

kids Silly's MUNJOY HILL *INTERNA-TIONAL* Silly's is the funkiest-looking restaurant in Maine—mismatched furniture, an odd fascination with Einstein, and an impromptu back patio. But the food's creative and great for a cheap, calorific bite: roll-up pita sandwiches ("Abdullahs"), fries, burgers, pizzas, and thick milk-shakes. *40 Washington Ave.* ☎ *207/772-0360. www.sillys.com. Entrees $5–$13. MC, V. Lunch & dinner Tues–Sun.*

★ Standard Baking Company OLD PORT *BAKERY* Across from the ferry terminal, this is one of the best little bakeries in New England. Order sticky buns (with or without pecans), focaccia, bread, brioches, or a cookie and a cup of coffee. No tables, but there's a small seating area outside—or take it over to the waterfront. *75 Commercial St.* ☎ *207/773-2112. AE, MC, V. Breakfast and lunch daily.*

★★ Street & Co. OLD PORT *SEA-FOOD* Dana Street's brick-walled bistro, off an alleyway, specializes in seafood, cooked in an open kitchen looking out on a small, divided dining room with a pleasantly rustic decor. Some locals consider it the best seafood house in Maine. There's a small outdoor patio. *33 Wharf St.* ☎ *207/775-0887. Entrees*

$14–$24. AE, MC, V. Dinner Mon–Sat.

kids Susan's Fish and Chips FOREST AVE. *SEAFOOD* Zero pretense, zero frills, zero website—and the best fried fish in town, cooked up in a deliciously sandy, crunchy jacket that's not too heavy. Get fries, and put ketchup or vinegar on them. *1135 Forest Ave.* ☎ *207/878-3240. Entrees $6–$10. AE, V. Lunch & dinner daily.*

★ Two Lights Lobster Shack CAPE ELIZABETH *SEAFOOD* This seasonal takeout shack, festooned in farm implements, cooks up steamed lobster dinners (with cole-slaw and blueberry cake included). Eat in the dining room or out at the picnic tables on the open rocks; try a whoopie pie for dessert. *225 Two Lights Rd., Cape Elizabeth.* ☎ *207/799-1677. Lobsters market-priced. Other entrees $10-$24. MC, V. Late Mar to Oct lunch & dinner daily. Closed Nov to late Mar.*

Standard Baking Company is one of the best bakeries in New England.

Portland Lodging

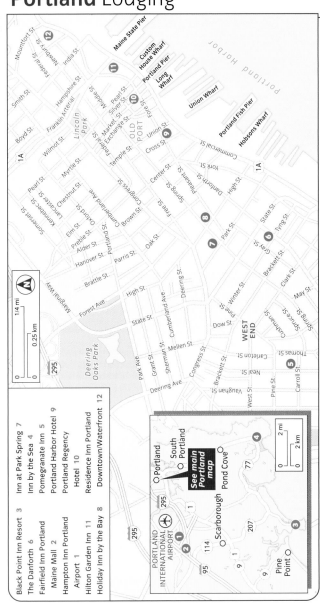

Black Point Inn Resort 3
The Danforth 6
Fairfield Inn Portland
  Maine Mall 2
Hampton Inn Portland
  Airport 1
Hilton Garden Inn 11
Holiday Inn by the Bay 8
Inn at Park Spring 7
Inn by the Sea 4
Pomegranate Inn 5
Portland Harbor Hotel 9
Portland Regency
  Hotel 10
Residence Inn Portland
  Downtown/Waterfront 12

Portland Lodging A to Z

★★★ Black Point Inn Resort

SCARBOROUGH   Just south of Portland, the Black Point is an elegant Maine classic with great coastal views and breezes near Winslow Homer's former studio. Rates are all-inclusive. *510 Black Point Rd. (from U.S. Rte. 1, take Rte. 207 east), Scarborough.* ☎ *207/883-2500. www.blackpointinn.com. 25 units. Doubles $380–$580 w/breakfast, tea & dinner. AE, DC, DISC, MC, V. Closed Nov–Apr.*

★★ The Danforth WEST

END   Once tired, the Danforth is again approaching the status of a grand boutique inn thanks to throw pillows, fireplaces, four-poster beds, televisions, and wingback chairs. The **Victoria Mansion** (p 92) is 2 blocks away, the Old Port a 10-minute stroll. *163 Danforth St.* ☎ *800/ 991-6557 or 207/879-8755. www. danforthmaine.com. 10 units. Doubles $120–$275. MC, V.*

kids Fairfield Inn Portland Maine

Mall MAINE MALL   The Fairfield, on the southern edge of the Maine Mall's sprawl, is a good option for budget-minded families. Rooms all have irons and ironing boards, there's a simple free breakfast in the lobby each morning, and parking's free. *2 Cummings Rd., Scarborough.* ☎ *207/883-0300. www.marriott.com. 118 units. Doubles $69–$250. AE, DISC, MC, V.*

★ kids Hampton Inn Portland

Airport MAINE MALL   Of the hotels clustered around Portland's airport and mall, this is my favorite. There's a pool, a free shuttle van, cookies, Internet, breakfast, good staff, and a quiet-ish location. Downtown is a 10-minute drive away. *171 Philbrook Ave., South Portland.* ☎ *800/426-7866 or 207/773-4400. www.portlandhamptoninn.com. 117 units. Doubles $110–$170 w/breakfast. AE, DISC, MC, V.*

Hilton Garden Inn OLD

PORT   You can't stay closer to the Old Port than at this Hilton, across Commercial Street from the ferry and cruise ship docks and near plenty of restaurants, shopping, bars, and coffeehouses. But it's pricey for a chain hotel. *65 Commercial St.* ☎ *207/780-0780. www. hilton.com. 120 units. Doubles $189–$369. AE, DISC, MC, V.*

Holiday Inn by the Bay WEST

END   Equidistant from the city's three key areas (the Old Port, downtown, and the West End), this hotel is bland but offers good views of the harbor from about half its rooms. *88 Spring St.* ☎ *888/465-4329 or 207/775-2311. www.holidayinn.com. Doubles $115–$210. AE, DISC, MC, V.*

★ Inn at Park Spring WEST

END   This small, friendly B&B in an

The elegant Black Point Inn Resort has great coastal views.

1835 brick home straddles downtown and the West End; the **Portland Museum of Art** (p 85) is close by. All units are corner rooms, most with good light and some with views. *135 Spring St. ☎ 800/437-8511 or 207/774-1059. www.innatparkspring.com. 6 units. Doubles $99–$175 w/breakfast. AE, MC, V. No children under 10.*

★★★ Inn by the Sea CAPE

ELIZABETH This luxury inn gets it all right: seaside location, pool, bar, spa, gourmet food, eco-friendliness, and wonderful rooms and suites with double Jacuzzis. The walkway leads to one of Maine's best beaches. *40 Bowery Beach Rd., Cape Elizabeth. ☎ 800/888-4287 or 207/799-3134. www.innbythesea.com. 57 units. Doubles $189–$369, suites $259-$789. AE, DC, DISC, MC, V.*

★★ Pomegranate Inn WEST

END In a 19th-century Italianate home in the West End, this is the city's top B&B. Eight rooms feature individually distinct design touches, painted floors, faux-marble woodwork, and gas fireplaces. The carriage house room includes a private terrace whose sliding doors open onto a small garden; breakfasts are a highlight. *49 Neal St. ☎ 800/356-0408 or 207/772-1006. www.pomegranateinn.com. 8 units. Doubles $140–$295 w/breakfast. AE, DISC, MC, V. Children 16 & older only.*

Inn by the Sea is next to one of Maine's best beaches.

The stylish Portland Harbor Hotel is close to bars and nightlife.

★★ Portland Harbor Hotel OLD

PORT Adjacent to Portland's bar scene, this townhouse-like hotel is designed to fit with its surroundings. There are good suites with deep tubs, plus a decent gourmet restaurant. *468 Fore St. ☎ 888/798-9090 or 207/775-9090. www.portlandharborhotel.com. 100 units. Doubles $159–$329. AE, DC, DISC, MC, V.*

★★ Portland Regency Hotel

OLD PORT Centrally located in the Old Port, the brick Regency is both historic and thoroughly modern. Corner rooms are best, with city views and Jacuzzis. The health club is among the best in town, and there's an excellent little bar. *20 Milk St. ☎ 800/727-3436 or 207/774-4200. www.theregency.com. 95 units. Doubles $159–$389. AE, DISC, MC, V.*

★ Residence Inn Portland Downtown/Waterfront OLD

PORT Portland's newest hotel is part of a chain, but its location—off the Old Port—and amenities (all units are suites, big and with full kitchens, including dishwashers and stove tops) have already made it a hit. Some units have bay views. There's an indoor pool, Jacuzzi, and health club. *145 Fore St. ☎ 207/761-1660. www.marriott.com. 179 units. Suites $150–$410. AE, DISC, MC, V.* ●

Bath-Brunswick-Wiscasset

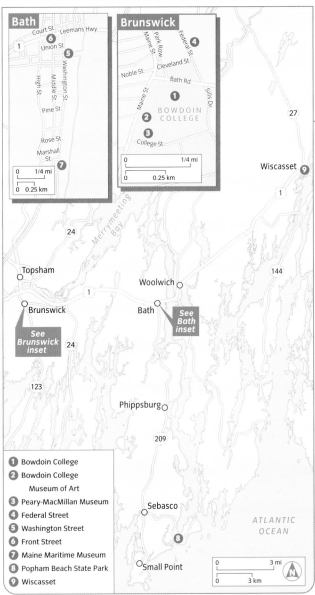

Bath

Court St.
Leemans Hwy.
1
6
Union St.
5
Washington St.
High St.
Middle St.
Pine St.
Rose St.
Marshall St.
7

0   1/4 mi
0   0.25 km

Brunswick

Park Row
Maine St.
Federal St.
4
Cleveland St.
Noble St.
Bath Rd.
Maine St.
1
BOWDOIN COLLEGE
Sills Dr.
2
3
College St.

0   1/4 mi
0   0.25 km

27

Wiscasset **9**

1

Merrymeeting Bay

24

Topsham

Woolwich

144

See Bath inset

1

Brunswick

Bath

See Brunswick inset

24

123

Phippsburg

209

1 Bowdoin College
2 Bowdoin College
       Museum of Art
3 Peary-MacMillan Museum
4 Federal Street
5 Washington Street
6 Front Street
7 Maine Maritime Museum
8 Popham Beach State Park
9 Wiscasset

Sebasco

ATLANTIC OCEAN

8

Small Point

0   3 mi
0   3 km

Previous page: Boats in Camden harbor.

ath-Brunswick is one of the best places to get a compact history lesson in colonial Maine: Both towns prospered in wooden-ship days, and each has taken a different path (education vs. ironworks) to survive in the modern era. I also recommend brief detours to Popham Beach and the village of Wiscasset for fresh air and a third dose of quaintness, respectively. The tour begins at Bowdoin College's central quadrangle, in the coastal town of Brunswick.

START: **Follow U.S. Rte. 1 to downtown Brunswick, which becomes Bath Rd. Turn right on North Campus Dr. and go to the free visitors' parking area.**

❶ Bowdoin College. The campus of Bowdoin College is attractive *and* historic; this "little ivy" was Maine's first educational institution and has one of the lowest admission rates in the U.S. Among the highlights of campus are the squarish, Federal-style **Massachusetts Hall** (when Bowdoin opened, the entire first year's class fit inside the building); a stone chapel; a rambling, Gothic science building; the Pickard Theatre, which comes alive with musical performances during summer; and Coles Tower, a bit of '70s Space Needle architecture that stands aloofly above the lovely old buildings. ⏱ *30 min. Maine St. at U.S. Rte. 1, Brunswick,* ☎ *207/725-3100.*

On the western side of the main quadrangle, look for the domed building with the big steps. This is the

❷ ★★ Bowdoin College Museum of Art. Here's one of the best small museums in New England. The holdings include a number of American artists—some with close ties to Maine, such as the Wyeths and Winslow Homer (1836–1910)—but there's also a significant collection of work from classic European painters and plenty of modern art. The rotunda entrance is grand; the basement was redesigned in 2008 by an Argentine architect to bring in light, color, and style. ⏱ *1 hr.* ☎ *207/725-3275. www.bowdoin.edu/art-museum. Free admission. Tues, Wed, Fri & Sat 10am–5pm, Thurs 10am–8:30pm, Sun 1–5pm.*

The Bowdoin College Museum of Art features both American painters and classic European artists.

Federal Street has many excellent examples of Federal-style architecture.

Walk kitty-corner across the lawn to tall brick Hubbard Hall. Open the huge, heavy doors. On the main floor, you'll find the

❸ ★★ Peary-MacMillan Museum. Just as good as the art museum, in its own way, is Bowdoin's song to the Arctic. Two of history's most famous Arctic explorers, Admiral Robert Peary and Donald MacMillan, graduated from Bowdoin in consecutive years late in the 19th century. When they returned from their polar travels, both men donated items to their alma mater. Among the museum's holdings are the obligatory stuffed polar bears, but also journal pages, native Canadian craftwork, and thousands of photographs of the polar region. ⏱ 45 min. ☎ 207/725-3416. www.bowdoin.edu/arctic-museum. Free admission. Tues–Sat 10am–5pm, Sun 2–5pm.

Backtrack to the parking lot. Cross Bath Rd. (the busy highway just past Massachusetts Hall) at the stop light, then walk along

❹ ★ Federal Street. This straight, mile-long (1.6km) street is home to one of New England's best concentrations of whitewashed, Federal-style architecture. None of the homes here are open to the public, but the sidewalk is public property. The entire street is

attractive and worth a walk (Maine St.'s restaurants are just a block west); if you're pressed for time, the first the ½-mile (.8km) from the college to Center Street is prettiest. ⏱ 15 min.

From the parking lot, turn right on Bath Rd. (U.S. Rte. 1) and drive 8 miles (13km) north. Bear right and exit for downtown Bath, then turn left beneath the underpass onto Middle St. Continue 3 blocks to Oak St. and turn right. In 1 block, you reach

❺ ★ Washington Street. Maple-framed Washington Street was the place the wealthy captains, shipbuilders, and merchants built their ostentatious (for the time) Victorian homes late in the 19th century. Along with Brunswick's Federal Street (see above), it's one of northern New England's best-preserved residential streets. Don't miss the big white Winter Street Church. ⏱ 30 min.

Walk or drive 1 block to

❻ Front Street. Bath's compact downtown, on a small rise overlooking the river, is home to some remarkable brick and stone Victorian commercial architecture. Note especially the blond, stone Richardson-style **Patten Free Library** at 33 Summer Street—its park features a gazebo, fountain, and view of the

Winter Street Church—and the bell tower on the big **City Hall/Davenport Memorial** (its full name) at 55 Front St., built in 1929 with money bequeathed by a local merchant. Its bell, from 1802, was probably cast by Paul Revere (1734–1818). ⏱ *45 min.*

Backtrack to Washington St. and travel about 2 miles (3.2km) south to the

7 kids **Maine Maritime Museum.** This good historical museum, which backs up to the tidal Kennebec River, teaches you and your kids everything about wooden boat building that you ever wanted to know. The site itself is a former shipyard, where more than 40 schooners were built in the late 19th and early 20th centuries. The main building features exhibits of maritime art and artifacts, plus a gift shop. The remainder of the property consists of a fleet of "display" ships and a complete boat-building shop. A kids' play area (with a pirate ship, naturally) offers good diversions for the little ones. ⏱ *1¼ hr. 243 Washington St.* ☎ *207/443-1316. www. bathmaine.com. Admission $10 adults, $9 seniors, $7 kids 6–17. Daily 9:30am–5pm.*

Follow Washington St. south until it ends on High St. (Rte. 209). Continue south on Rte. 209 for 12 miles (19km) until you reach

8 ★ **Popham Beach State Park.** Popham Beach seems like a big, empty beach—and it is—but it's also an important historical and ecological site. This was the location of two of the first colonial attempts at settling Maine. Those efforts failed, but shipping and fishing interests eventually did take hold here. Today, the park is best known for great hard-packed sand and views of Seguin Island and its lighthouse out to sea. Rare birds nest in the sand, so step carefully. ⏱ *1 hr. 10 Perkins Farm Lane, Phippsburg.* ☎ *207/389-1335 or 207/389-9125. Admission summer $4 adults, $1 kids 5–11; fall–spring $1.50 adults, free for kids.*

Retrace your path 15 miles (24km) to U.S. Rte. 1. Turn right and continue north. In about 12 more miles (19km), you come into downtown

9 ★ **Wiscasset.** Wiscasset is a cute riverside town billing itself as "The Prettiest Village in Maine" at the entrance to its compact village center. Dozens of structures here have some form of historic designation. Look for the brick, Georgian **county courthouse** at 32 High Street (from 1824, it's the longest continuously operating courthouse in the U.S.); a gray, granite-slabbed 1811 **jail** at 15 Federal Street, which operated until the 1950s; an old **customs house** at the foot of Water Street; and the 1808 Federal-style **Nickels-Sortwell House** at Main and Federal streets, with its multiple chimneys. ⏱ *1 hr.*

The Maine Maritime Museum has display boats and a children's play area.

Camden to Rockland

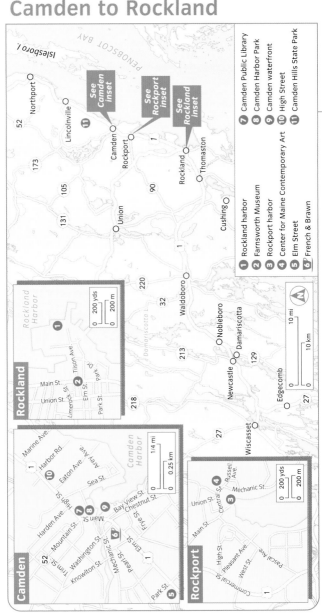

7 Camden Public Library
8 Camden Harbor Park
9 Camden waterfront
10 High Street
11 Camden Hills State Park

1 Rockland harbor
2 Farnsworth Museum
3 Rockport harbor
4 Center for Maine Contemporary Art
5 Elm Street
6 French & Brawn

PENOBSCOT BAY

Islesboro I.

Northport
Lincolnville **11**
52
173
105
131
Union
90
Camden
Rockport
1
Rockland
Thomaston
Cushing
220
32
Waldoboro
213
129
Newcastle
Damariscotta
Nobleboro
Edgecomb
27
Wiscasset
218

See Camden inset
See Rockport inset
See Rockland inset

Rockland

Rockland Harbor
1
Main St.
2 Tilson Ave.
Limerock St.
Union St.
Elm St.
Park St.
Park St.
0 200 yds
0 200 m

Camden

Marine Ave.
Harbor Rd.
1
10
Eaton Ave.
Avey Ave.
Sea St.
High St.
Harden Ave.
7 8 9
Bay View St.
Chestnut St.
Frye St.
6
Mountain St.
Main St.
Elm St.
52
Trim St.
Washington St.
Mechanic St.
Pearl St.
Knowlton St.
1
Park St.
5
Camden Harbor
0 1/4 mi
0 0.25 km

Rockport

Union St.
Central St.
4 Russell Ave.
Mechanic St.
3
Main St.
High St.
Commercial St.
Pleasant Ave.
West St.
Pascal Ave.
1
0 200 yds
0 200 m

0 10 mi
0 10 km

Camden and Rockland are polar opposites, on the face of it. Rockland is a blue-collar town, founded on fishing and fish-processing; Camden was where sea captains built mansions with their booty. Yet Rockland is catching up—it has become a place to dine well, stay overnight, and visit art galleries, and it's home to one of Maine's best museums. Rockport, a tiny fishing village nearby, is a cute detour. START: **Take U.S. Rte. 1 to downtown Rockland. Park on Main St. and walk 1 block east to the waterfront.**

❶ Rockland harbor. Rockland's main square and long Main Street have plenty of brick buildings of architectural interest, but the waterfront and its small park are where you *really* feel the town's character. Watch real windjammers and schooners come, go, or just bob in the harbor; some of the ships and shipbuilders here have acquired national historic designation. ⏱ *15 min. Just east of Main St., from Tilson Ave. to Ocean St.*

From the waterfront, walk back to the main square. Between the two one-way sections of U.S. Rte. 1, flanked by Museum and Elm sts., is the

❷ ★★ Farnsworth Museum. Philanthropist Lucy Farnsworth bequeathed the funds that established the Farnsworth Museum in the 1930s; it has since become one of the most important collections of art in northern New England. The museum holds a superb collection of paintings and sculptures by renowned American artists with

connections to Maine—three generations of Wyeths, Rockwell Kent (1882–1971), and the like. The spaces here are big, well-lit, and stylish; the quality of the exhibits is tops. ⏱ *1½ hr. 356 Main St., Rockland. ☎ 207/596-6457. www.farnsworthmuseum.org. Admission $10 adults, $8 seniors & students 18 & older; free for children 17 & under. Late May to early Oct daily 10am–5pm; early Oct to late May closed Mon.*

From Rockland, drive north 6 miles (9.7km) on U.S. Rte. 1 to Pascal Ave. and bear right. In a half-mile (.8km) the road arrives in

❸ ★ Rockport harbor. Rockport is not just another of Maine's cute little fishing-harbor towns, though it is cute. This is also one of the hidden centers of Maine art, with a thriving photography school and a museum along with that scenic harbor view, a boat landing, a small park, and a cafe. This is a great place to rest after a bike ride or take a short stroll in the sea air with your

The Farnsworth Museum has one of the most important art collections in northern New England.

camera. Park in the small parking lot above the boat landing at Central and Main streets, instead of down on the harbor, which is a place of commerce. ⏱ *45 min. Foot of Main St., off Central St. Free parking on Main, Pascal & Central sts.*

From Main St., walk uphill along Central St. 1 block and bear right onto Russell Ave. Continue ½ block to the

④ ★ **Center for Maine Contemporary Art.** Also known as CMCA, this is still another quality museum in the Midcoast. The gallery showcases the work of local painters, sculptors, mixed-media artists, and the like. There's also a healthy program of artist talks and poetry readings. ⏱ *45 min. 162 Russell Ave.* ☎ *207/236-2875. www. artsmaine.org. Free admission (donations accepted). Tues–Sat 10am–5pm, Sun 1–5pm.*

From Rockport, drive north 2 miles (3.2km) on Russell Ave., which becomes Chestnut St. and brings you into Camden. The street comes to a T-junction with

⑤ **Elm Street.** U.S. Route 1 (Elm Street) suddenly becomes graceful as it approaches the center of downtown Camden; Elm is lined with Federal-style buildings, many converted into bed-and-breakfasts such as the **Blue Harbor House** (p 133) and the **Hartstone Inn** (p 134). Note also the Camden Opera House, on the left at 29 Elm St. As you progress into the very center of town, parking becomes tight, and the buildings become commercial blocks. But seafood restaurants and souvenir shops become ubiquitous. ⏱ *15 min.*

I can't count the number of times I have grabbed a deli sandwich, a piece of fruit, and a drink at the ⑥ **French & Brawn** grocer, then walked across the street to the shady park in front of the St. Thomas Episcopal Church. The grocer features a great selection of local and international wines and beers, plus a small deli area, gourmet Maine snacks and chocolates, and fresh produce. Enjoy the benches and a perfect view of the main street and opera house. *1 Elm St., Camden.* ☎ *207/236-3361. $.*

Park downtown and walk north along Main St. past all the shops to the

French & Brawn is the perfect place to shop for a picnic.

⑦ Camden Public Library. I can't think of a public library with a better ocean view on the East Coast than this one. Camden's library stands high on the town hill, with a little gazebo, benches, and gardens in summer. The library itself dates from 1928 (a high-tech wing was added in 1996). ⏱ *15 min. 55 Main St. (at High St.)* ☎ *207/236-3440. www.librarycamden.org. Mon, Wed, Fri & Sat 9:30am–5pm, Tues & Thurs 9:30am–8pm, Sun 1–5pm.*

Walk a few steps downhill to the

⑧ ★ kids Camden Harbor Park. A natural amphitheater, this public park is attached to Camden's library—the same ocean-view plot of land (which would be invaluable today) was donated by the same generous local woman, Mary Louise Curtis Bok Zimbalist (1876–1970), in the 1920s. Today, it's on the National Register of Historic Places. My favorite time to come is during the annual windjammer festival over Labor Day weekend, when music and big ships fill the view. Bring a picnic. ⏱ *30 min. Between Atlantic Ave. & Main St.*

Walk downhill and cross Atlantic Avenue to find the boats tied up along the

⑨ ★ Camden waterfront. In summer, it's a virtual carnival here, as vendors hawk hot dogs and ice cream, whale-watch tours depart, and shutterbugs click cameras at the yachts and wooden ships (sometimes) tied up on the docks. This is the best spot to sample Camden if you're pressed for time. Also be sure to explore the various unnamed alleys leading down to the waterfront, where there are several good restaurants, a bakery, and curio shops. ⏱ *45 min.*

Leaving town, drive north on U.S. Rte. 1. You'll first pass along

Camden Harbor Park is a great place to relax and enjoy the views.

⑩ High Street. Once again, Camden's character is gracefully revealed, but this time it's as you exit the village center. Some of the very finest private homes and inns in Camden march along High Street on the northern edge of town, including the **Norumbega** (p 134), the **Maine Stay** (p 73), and the **Camden Windward House** (p 133). Foliage and mansards also abound here. ⏱ *15 min.*

From Camden, drive 1½ miles (2.4km) north along U.S. Rte. 1 until you come to the gatehouse on the left at Mount Battie Rd., one of two entrances to

⑪ ★ Camden Hills State Park. This 6,500-acre (2,630-hectare) park may not be as big as the White or Green mountains, but it's got the ocean views those mountains don't. There's a free ocean-side picnic area, more than 100 campsites, and a small toll road to the summit of the "mountain" with awesome Penobscot Bay views. You can take any number of hikes, too (see p 20). ⏱ *1¼ hr. U.S. Rte. 1 (at Mount Battie Rd.).* ☎ *207/236-3109. Admission $3 adults, $1 children 5–11. Mid-May to mid-Oct sunrise–sunset.*

Midcoast Maine Dining

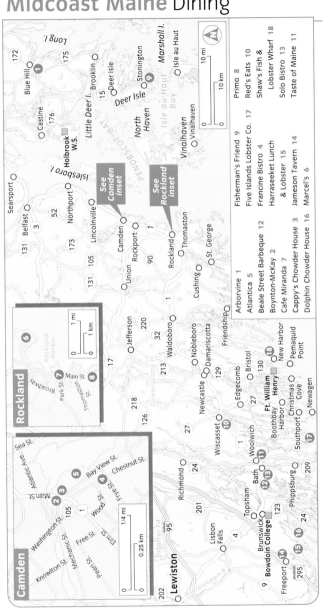

Arborvine 1
Atlantica 5
Beale Street Barbeque 12
Boynton-McKay 2
Cafe Miranda 7
Cappy's Chowder House 3
Dolphin Chowder House 16

Fisherman's Friend 9
Five Islands Lobster Co. 17
Francine Bistro 4
Harraseeket Lunch
& Lobster 15
Jameson Tavern 14
Marcel's 6

Primo 8
Red's Eats 10
Shaw's Fish &
Lobster Wharf 18
Solo Bistro 13
Taste of Maine 11

Midcoast Maine Dining A to Z

★ **Arborvine** BLUE HILL *SEAFOOD* Local seafood (Bagaduce River oysters on the half-shell, broiled Stonington halibut) predominates in this eatery on Blue Hill's cute main village street. But you can also get beef medallions or rack of lamb. *33 Main St. ☎ 207/374-2119. www. arborvine.com. Entrees $27–$30. MC, V. Summer dinner daily; off-season dinner Fri–Sun.*

★★ **Atlantica** CAMDEN *SEAFOOD* Chef Ken Paquin delivers seafood with flair on the Camden waterfront. Expect thick chowders, poached lobsters, seared scallops, and a fresh fish dish of the day. *1 Bayview Landing. ☎ 888/507-8514 or 207/236-6011. www.atlanticarestaurant.com. Entrees $26–$36. AE, MC, V. Apr–Sept dinner Wed–Mon. Closed Nov–Mar.*

★ **Beale Street Barbeque** BATH *BARBECUE* A fancier version of the barbecue joint in South Portland (see p 112), this place delivers the same great smoky ribs, brisket, and side dishes—just in a fancier room. *215 Water St. ☎ 207/442-9514. mainebbq.com. Entrees $9–$17. MC, V. Lunch & dinner daily.*

kids Boynton-McKay CAMDEN *CAFE* A former pharmacy (with bottles and pill boxes still on the wall), this funky downtown diner serves good sandwiches, coffee, and lunch specials like meatloaf to famished families. *30 Main St. ☎ 207/236-2465. Entrees $8–$14. MC, V. Lunch Tues–Sat, dinner Tues–Sun. Closed Mon.*

★★ **Cafe Miranda** ROCKLAND *INTERNATIONAL* One of the craziest, most inventive menus in America, from owner-chef Kerry Altiero. Expect menu items like Ducks of Spanish Pleasure (a sort of duck curry) and Sunday brunches that go beyond eggs to smoked fish cakes and gourmet hot dogs. It's very reasonably priced, too. *15 Oak St. ☎ 207/594-2034. www.cafemiranda. com. Entrees $9–$22. DISC, MC, V. Brunch Sun, dinner daily.*

kids Cappy's Chowder House CAMDEN *SEAFOOD* The name says it all: clam chowder, seafood chowder, fish chowders. They serve fried fish and lobster, too, plus a wine list. *1 Main St. ☎ 207/236-2254. www. cappyschowder.com. Entrees $8–$20. MC, V. Lunch & dinner daily.*

★ **Dolphin Chowder House** SOUTH HARPSWELL *SEAFOOD* Located next to a working-class Harpswell marina, this is the best chowder in the state of Maine. Table or booth, it doesn't matter: You're facing a full bay view and real fishermen. The

Cappy's Chowder House.

muffins are great, too. *515 Basin Point (via Rte. 123 from Brunswick).* ☎ *207/833-6000. Entrees $4–$17. MC, V. May–Oct breakfast, lunch & dinner daily. Closed Nov–Apr.*

Fisherman's Friend STONING-TON *SEAFOOD* On a dock near the Isle au Haut ferry and attached to a general store, this is family dining: broiled and fried fresh fish, plus lobsters cooked 30 different ways. People come from far and wide for the lobster bisque. There's also a wine list and a choice of pastas. *5 Atlantic Ave. (on the dock).* ☎ *207/367-2442. www.stoningtonharbor.com. Lobsters market-priced, entrees $13–$20. DISC, MC, V. Mid-May to mid-Oct lunch & dinner daily; mid-Oct to mid-May, call for hours.*

★ **Five Islands Lobster Co.** GEORGETOWN *LOBSTER* After a scenic drive down a point, this unprepossessing lobster pound on the wharf is a welcome nosh. Zero atmosphere; excellent lobsters. *1447 Five Islands Rd. (Rte. 127).* ☎ *207/371-2990. Entrees market-priced. MC, V. May–Oct lunch & dinner daily. Closed Nov–Apr.*

★★ **Francine Bistro** CAMDEN *FRENCH* A casually elegant bistro manned by a very talented chef, tucked away in little Camden? You bet. The food leans on local seafood, but French favorites like oven-roasted chicken and duck *a l'Orange* pop up on the menu, too. *55 Chestnut St.* ☎ *207/230-0083. www.francinebistro.com. Entrees $17–$25. MC, V. Dinner Tues–Sat.*

★ **Harraseeket Lunch & Lobster** SOUTH FREEPORT *LOBSTER* Next to a boatyard, this off-the-track lobster pound gets crowded—but it's worth finding. Pick out your lobster, pay, and wait. You can also get fish baskets, chowder, and ice cream. *36 N. Main St. From Freeport, take Bow St. to South St.* ☎ *207/865-4888. Lobsters market-priced. No credit cards. May to mid-Oct lunch & dinner daily. Closed mid-Oct to Apr.*

Jameson Tavern FREEPORT *AMERICAN* In the shadow of L.L.Bean, Jameson Tavern is the birthplace of Maine: In 1820, papers were signed here legally separating Maine from Massachusetts. Meals here are hearty: steak, salmon, and pastas. *115 Main St.* ☎ *207/865-4196. www.jamesontavern.com. Entrees $7–$26. AE, DC, DISC, MC, V. Lunch & dinner daily.*

★★ **Marcel's** ROCKPORT *AMERICAN* A fancy room with a fancy view and great food from CIA-trained

The papers separating Maine from Massachusetts were signed at Jameson Tavern.

Primo is located inside a century-old home in Rockland.

chef Tim Pierce of the Samoset Resort (see p 134). Eat steak Diane, lobster Thermidor, filet mignon, bisque, or dynamite pan-seared scallops in citrus cream. *220 Warrenton St.* ☎ *800/341-1650 or 207/594-2511. www.samoset.com. Entrees $24–$36. AE, DC, V. May–Oct dinner daily.*

★★★ **Primo** ROCKLAND *NEW AMERICAN* Chefs Melissa Kelly and Price Kushner dominate the Midcoast dining scene with this incredible bistro, in a century-old home outside Rockland. Expect lots of French and Italian accents, plus one of my favorite dessert menus in all of New England. *2 S. Main St.* ☎ *207/596-0770. www.primorestaurant. com. Entrees $23–$38. AE, DC, DISC, MC, V. May–Oct dinner daily; call for hours off-season.*

★ **Red's Eats** WISCASSET *LOBSTER* A little red shack at the U.S. Route 1 bridge in Wiscasset is the best place to get a lobster roll for miles and miles. That's why traffic stops here—literally. Big chunks of meat on toasted hot-dog rolls, scoops of ice cream, and picnic tables. *U.S. Rte. 1 (at Water St.).* ☎ *207/882-6128. Entrees $6–$16. No credit cards. May–Sept lunch & dinner daily. Closed Oct–Apr.*

★ **Shaw's Fish & Lobster Wharf** NEW HARBOR *LOBSTER* This is one of the best-situated lobster pounds on the Maine coast, with postcard-perfect views. (Hollywood filmed a bit of *Message in a Bottle,* a Kevin Costner movie, here.) Eat on the open deck upstairs or in the indoor dining room. The lobster rolls are considered among Maine's best. *129 Rte. 32.* ☎ *207/677-2200. Lobsters market-priced, entrees $10–$25. MC, V. Mid-May to mid-Oct lunch & dinner daily. Closed mid-Oct to mid-May.*

★ **Solo Bistro** BATH *BISTRO* This bistro/jazz club serves hearty burgers, stews, seafood, and risotto among the possible offerings. The interior's Euro-cool, too—the owners run a design shop next door. *128 Front St.* ☎ *207/443-3373. www.solobistro.com. Entrees $13–$24. AE, MC, V. Dinner Mon–Sat.*

kids Taste of Maine WOOLWICH *SEAFOOD* This is a place to eat big lobsters and big plates of fish: nothing more, nothing less. The marsh-side location is attractive, though, and the prices are mostly right. Family dining at its most quintessentially Maine. *161 Main St. (U.S. Rte. 1).* ☎ *207/443-4554. www.tasteofmaine. com. Lobsters market-priced, entrees $12–$23. AE, MC, V. Lunch & dinner daily.*

Midcoast Maine Lodging

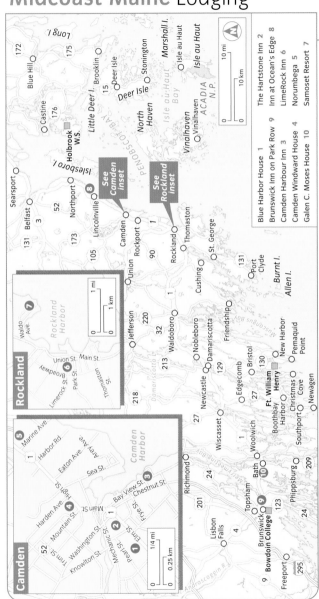

Blue Harbor House 1
Brunswick Inn on Park Row 9
Camden Harbour Inn 3
Camden Windward House 4
Galen C. Moses House 10
The Hartstone Inn 2
Inn at Ocean's Edge 8
LimeRock Inn 6
Norumbega 5
Samoset Resort 7

Midcoast Maine Lodging A to Z

Suites at Camden Harbour Inn are designed with international themes.

★ **Blue Harbor House** CAMDEN
This robin's-egg blue farmhouse
(built in 1810) is dolled up and
dainty, with all the poster beds,
claw-footed tubs, and wicker you'd
expect here. Some rooms have
Jacuzzis; the carriage house is nic-
est. *67 Elm St.* ☎ *800/248-3196 or
207/236-3196. www.blueharbor
house.com. 11 units. Doubles $95–
$155 w/breakfast. AE, DISC, MC, V.
Closed mid-Oct to mid-May.*

★★ **Brunswick Inn on Park
Row** BRUNSWICK Brunswick's
best B&B is also its most central,
located on Park Row a block from
Federal Street. Expect wingback
chairs, homey quilts, and comfortable suites in an historic-looking
building. You can walk to Bowdoin
College in 2 minutes. *165 Park Row.*
☎ *800/299-4914 or 207/729-4914.
www.brunswickbnb.com. 15 units.
Doubles $125–$190 w/breakfast.
MC, V. Closed Jan. No children 5 &
under.*

★★★ **Camden Harbour Inn**
CAMDEN A bit hard to find, this is
one of the Midcoast's coolest over-
nights. Two Dutchman renovated
the 1871 captain's house with king
beds, a spa, a gourmet restaurant,
and wine refrigerators in each room.
Suites are designed with Taiwanese,
Thai, Mauritian, and other themes.
83 Bayview St. ☎ *800/236-4266 or
207/236-4200. www.camdenharbour
inn.com. 22 units. Doubles $175–
$450 w/breakfast. AE, DISC, MC, V.
Closed Dec–Apr. No children 11 &
under.*

★★ **Camden Windward House**
CAMDEN On historic High Street,
the friendly Windward is an 1854
mansion with modern touches in
the guest rooms such as flat-screen
TVs, Jacuzzis, and specially sound-
proofed windows. *6 High St.* ☎ *877/
492-9656 or 207/236-9656. www.
windwardhouse.com. Doubles $110–$280 w/breakfast & afternoon tea. AE, MC, V. No children 11
& under.*

★ **Galen C. Moses House** BATH
This Italianate 19th-century manse
is full of Victorian clocks, antiques,

and original stained glass. Rooms have fun themes: Check out the stripy Safari Room. *1009 Washington St.* ☎ *888/442-8771 or 207/442-8771. www.galenmoses.com. 7 units. Doubles $119–$259 w/breakfast. AE, DISC, MC, V.*

★★ The Hartstone Inn CAMDEN

Great food in a comfortable inn near the water: This is Maine. Rooms are furnished in antiques and lovely interior stylings; suites have Jacuzzis. Do not miss dinner or a cooking class with the owners. *41 Elm St.* ☎ *800/788-4823 or 207/236-4259. www.hartstoneinn.com. 21 units. Doubles $105–$190. MC, V. Closed late Nov to late Apr.*

★★★ Inn at Ocean's Edge LINCOLNVILLE BEACH

On a beautiful piece of water frontage, this inn has become a seriously luxurious place. Spa services, a gourmet restaurant, and a cool vanishing-edge swimming pool are all recent additions. Many rooms have king poster beds, Jacuzzis, and/or balconies. *24 Stonecoast Rd. (U.S. Rte. 1).* ☎ *207/236-0945. www.innatoceansedge.com. 33 units. Doubles $195–$425 w/breakfast. AE, DISC, MC, V.*

★★ LimeRock Inn ROCKLAND

A Queen Anne–style inn a quick walk from the Farnsworth Museum. The owners have revamped with country Victorian furniture and high-thread-count sheets. Rooms include a Provencal-feeling room with private deck and a room in the turret. *96 Limerock St.* ☎ *800/546-3762. www.limerockinn.com. 8 units. Doubles $110–$229 w/breakfast. DISC, MC, V.*

★★★ Norumbega CAMDEN

Nobody could miss this stone castle-like mansion on the northern edge of town. Historic details, like carved wood throughout, abound, and the rooms are immaculate. For a Maine splurge, the two suites are hard to beat for either views or decor. *63 High St.* ☎ *877/363-4646 or 207/236-4646. www.norumbegainn.com. 12 units. Doubles $125–$475 w/breakfast. AE, DISC, MC, V. Children 7 & older welcome.*

★★ Samoset Resort ROCKPORT

This classic Maine resort received several much-needed upgrades recently. A new heated pool and hot tub sport sweeping ocean views and a Tiki bar. Most rooms have balconies or porches, flat-screen TVs, and marble vanities; the golf course and restaurant are among the state's best. *220 Warrenton St.* ☎ *800/341-1650 or 207/594-2511. www.samoset.com. 178 units. Doubles $129–$369, cottages $539–$769. AE, DC, DISC, MC, V.* ●

Samoset Resort has great ocean views from the heated pool.

Bar Harbor

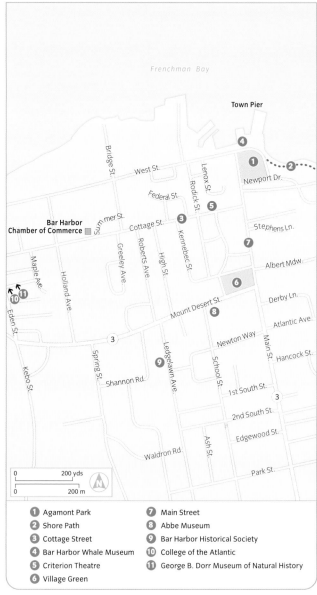

Frenchman Bay

Town Pier

Bridge St.

West St.

Lenox St.

Rodick St.

Newport Dr.

Federal St.

Summer St.

Bar Harbor
Chamber of Commerce

Cottage St.

Stephens Ln.

Greeley Ave.

Roberts Ave.

High St.

Kennebec St.

Albert Mdw.

Maple Ave.

Holland Ave.

Derby Ln.

Atlantic Ave.

Eden St.

Mount Desert St.

Newton Way

Main St.

Hancock St.

3

Spring St.

Kebo St.

Shannon Rd.

Ledgelawn Ave.

School St.

1st South St.

3

2nd South St.

Ash St.

Edgewood St.

Waldron Rd.

Park St.

0	200 yds
0	200 m

1 Agamont Park

2 Shore Path

3 Cottage Street

4 Bar Harbor Whale Museum

5 Criterion Theatre

6 Village Green

7 Main Street

8 Abbe Museum

9 Bar Harbor Historical Society

10 College of the Atlantic

11 George B. Dorr Museum of Natural History

Previous page: A view of Jordan Pond.

ar Harbor is a summer vacation town, pure and simple; it has been that way since the 19th century, when urban tourists began coming to Mount Desert Island. But even so, it's a nice enough place to call a base—there are plenty of good gift shops, inns, ocean views, and lobsters to keep you interested. START: **Agamont Park, at the foot of Main and West sts.**

❶ ★ Agamont Park. The best water views in town are from the foot of Main Street, at grassy Agamont Park. This popular green lawn with a gazebo overlooks not only the town pier, but also the **Bar Harbor Inn** (p 149) and the panorama of Frenchman Bay. Best of all, the park is just steps from dozens of restaurants, bars, and gift shops. ⏱ *45 min. Main St. (at West St. & Newport Dr.).*

Walk through the park to the Bar Harbor Inn. Behind the inn is the

❷ ★ Shore Path. It's only half a mile long (.8km), but Bar Harbor's winding walking trail follows the shoreline along a public right of way and passes in front of elegant summer homes. It's one of the best ways to get a quick insider's peek at the town's period architecture. ⏱ *30 min. Accessed from Bar Harbor Inn (see p 149), Newport Dr.*

Return to Main St. and walk uphill away from the water 1 block. Turn right onto

❸ Cottage Street. Bar Harbor's main commercial drag has a little bit of everything: pizza joints and pubs, T-shirt shops, an Internet cafe with an opera-house theme, a restaurant dedicated to Route 66, an outdoors outfitter, and the town post office. It's not super-scenic, but it *is* a good place to grab a bite or a postcard. ⏱ *30 min.*

Turn right on Rodick St. and walk 1 block north to West St. Turn right to find the

❹ kids Bar Harbor Whale Museum. The huge, soaring skeleton of a humpback whale hanging above the reception desk is a tipoff that you've come to the right place. Inside a shingled, shack-like structure, this attraction is pretty small, yet effective. It's largely geared toward kids. ⏱ *30 min. 52 West St.* ☎ *207/288-0288. www.coa.edu/ barharborwhalemuseum.htm. Free admission (donations requested). June–Oct daily 10am–8pm; Nov–May, call for hours.*

Return to Rodick St., turn left, and walk 1 block back to Cottage

A whale skeleton on display at the Bar Harbor Whale Museum.

The Village Green is a good place to gain insight into local life.

St. Turn left. On the next block, on the left, is

5 Criterion Theatre. When the weather's bad, this theater on Cottage Street becomes one of downtown Bar Harbor's best attractions. Built in the 1930s in classic Art Deco style, this 877-seat house shows mostly first-run movies in summer. The interiors alone are worth the price of a ticket, and while it costs extra, try to sit in the more plush seating upstairs in the balcony. ⏱ *2 hr. for films. 35 Cottage St.* ☎ *207/288-3441. www.criterion theater.com. Tickets $5.50–$10.*

In 1 block, turn left on Rodick St. and walk 2 blocks to the

6 ★ Village Green. Bar Harbor's central green space is a wonderful place to while away an hour or two watching the craziness unfold. You might see anything from war protests to marriage proposals to kids goofing off after school, plus scads of summer tourists. There's sometimes music in the bandstand, and this is also the pickup point for the

Island Explorer buses that crisscross the entire island—for free. Not to be missed. ⏱ *45 min. Mount Desert St. (at Main St.).*

Turn left on Firefly Lane and walk 1 block back to

7 ★ Main Street. If Cottage Street is the commercial hub of this town, Main Street is its tourist hub. You can't throw a stone without hitting at least five restaurants, ice cream shops, groceries, and/or souvenir shops. It's great fun and the one essential street to see when in town. ⏱ *30 min.*

From the Village Green side of Main St., turn right onto Mount Desert St.

8 ★ kids Abbe Museum. Since 2001, this has been the downtown headquarters of the museum originally built at Sieur de Monts spring in Acadia National Park (p 140). It's bigger and better than that museum, showcasing a world-class collection of Native American crafts (check out the baskets) and artifacts. Highlights

The Abbe Museum has an excellent collection of Native American crafts and artifacts.

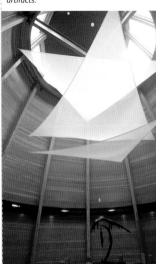

The campus of the College of the Atlantic boasts a beautiful stretch of coastline.

include a glass-walled section where visitors can watch archaeologists labeling and preserving recently recovered items. The changing exhibits and videos mostly focus on the history and culture of the tribes that once lived throughout Maine and New England. ⏱ *45 min. 26 Mount Desert St.* ☎ *207/288-3519. www. abbemuseum.org. Admission $6 adults, $2 children 6–15. Late May to Oct daily 10am–6pm, Nov to late Apr Thurs–Sat 10am–6pm, May Sat & Sun 10am–6pm.*

From Mount Desert St., turn down Ledgelawn Ave. to find the

⑨ Bar Harbor Historical Society. The local historical society is housed in this former convent (dating from 1918), and it holds a decent collection of artifacts from the days when tourism was *really* rip-roaring here: dishes from and photos of those grand old hotels, and exhibits on noted landscape architects and painters. Scrapbooks here also document the 1947 fire that devastated much of the island. ⏱ *30 min. 33 Ledgelawn Ave.* ☎ *207/288-0000 or 207/288-3807. Free admission. June–Oct Mon–Sat 1–4pm; Nov–May, open by appointment.*

Return to Mt. Desert St. Turn left and go ⅓ mile (.5km) to Rte. 3

(Eden St.). Turn right and continue 1½ miles (2.4km) to the

⑩ ★ College of the Atlantic. This school, appropriately, was founded in 1969 to teach environmental education to college kids—it's the only place, to my knowledge, that offers a degree in "human ecology." As a bonus, the campus sits on an attractive stretch of coastline looking out onto the bay and islands, one of which can be walked to at low tide (but ask about the tidal charts first). Spend a half-hour walking this stretch of coast, or at least sitting on benches looking at it. ⏱ *30 min. 105 Eden St. (Rte. 3).* ☎ *207/288-5015. www.coa.edu.*

On the campus of the college is the

⑪ kids George B. Dorr Museum of Natural History. Housed inside the original headquarters of the Acadia National Park, COA's science and nature museum features exhibits on local ecology, geology, small mammals, puffins, and the like. It's not too sophisticated, but good for kids—and in summer the staff leads walks and scavenger hunts. ⏱ *15 min. 105 Eden St. (Rte. 3).* ☎ *207/288-5395. www.coamuseum.org. Free admission (donations requested). Mid-June to late Nov Tues–Sat 10am–5pm; Dec to mid-June, by appointment.*

Acadia National Park

1 Acadia Park Headquarters
2 Eagle Lake
3 Abbe Museum
4 Sand Beach
5 Thunder Hole
6 Otter Cliffs
7 Seal Harbor
8 Jordan Pond
9 The Bubbles
10 Cadillac Mountain

Acadia, put simply, is one of the nation's most scenic (and oldest) national parks. Established as the first national park east of the Mississippi River, it owes some of its grandeur to the largesse of wealthy summer residents who donated much of the land. A drive through the park is a *must* on any trip to Maine. You must buy a park pass ($5 per person, $20 per car) to enter May through October. START: **From Bar Harbor, follow Mt. Desert St. (which becomes Rte. 233 at Eden St.) west 3½ miles (5.6km) to the national park headquarters.**

Travel Tip

There are also several excellent mountain hikes within the boundaries of the park. For information about them, see chapter 9, "The Great Outdoors."

1 ★ Acadia Park Headquarters. Of the island's three visitor information centers, this one is the quietest and biggest. Set in a wooded, quiet clearing on one of the main roads linking up the various towns of the island, this year-round center is full of information and helpful rangers. *15 min. Eagle Lake Rd. (Rte. 233), Bar Harbor.* ☎ *207/288-3338. www.nps. gov/acad. Daily 8am–4:30pm.*

Behind the park offices is a hiking trail circling

2 ★ Eagle Lake. From the back of the park's headquarters, you can hike 6 miles (9.7km) around Eagle Lake—a huge freshwater lake (the island's biggest) that's home to birds, fish, canoeists, and anglers. Landlocked salmon, brook trout, and lake trout can be fished with a license. Or just grab your bike and pedal the loop, which isn't too difficult. Foliage here can be spectacular. *30 min. Behind park headquarters (off Eagle Lake Rd.), Rte. 233. Admission free. Open year-round.*

Follow Rte. 233 for 2 miles (3.2km) east. After the underpass, turn left to merge onto Park Loop Rd. At the stop sign, turn left onto Jordan Pond Rd. After half a mile (.8km), turn left again onto Park Loop Rd.; after 1½ miles

Eagle Lake is the largest lake on the island.

(2.4km), you dip into a wooden valley and come to the right-turn for the

3 Abbe Museum. This is the original Abbe Museum, before the directors decided to open a much bigger, better version in downtown Bar Harbor (p 138). But since you're here, it's worth a quick look if you don't mind paying the small entry fee. The building—behind the nature center and up the hill—features a small but select collection of Native American artifacts. A ticket here gets you a $3 discount at the downtown museum. ⏱ *15 min. Park Loop Rd., Otter Creek.* ☎ *207/288-3519. www. abbemuseum.org. Admission $3 adults, $1 children 6–15. Late May to early Oct daily 9am–4pm. Closed mid-Oct to late May.*

Return to the loop road and continue south about 4 miles (6.4km; pay a $5 per person entry fee at the gate from May through October) to the parking lot for

4 ★ Sand Beach. This small crescent beach is the only sand beach of substance on the island, and it's very attractive, set between two rocky points. Views are stupendous, and there are clean bathrooms and changing facilities, plus a footpath to Thunder Hole (see below); no wonder the strand and parking lot get so packed on sunny summer weekends. However, the water can get frigid, even in summer—don't plan on swimming or wading for long unless you've got the constitution of a polar bear. ⏱ *1 hr. Park Loop Rd., Bar Harbor.*

Continue south by car or on foot along the loop road 1 mile (1.6km) around the point to

5 ★ Thunder Hole. This shallow, ocean-side cavern draws hordes in summer. The pounding waves press into the cave, then shoot up in

Sand Beach has spectacular views and a footpath to Thunder Hole.

impressive geysers—if the ocean and tidal conditions are right. A walking trail on the road allows you to leave your car parked at the beach lot. If the ocean is quiet, skip this stop or just take photos of the open ocean, instead. When the seas are rough, though, this is a must-see; rangers say the best viewing time is about 3 hours before high tide (get a tide chart in town or at park headquarters). Take care on the cliff-side walking trails. ⏱ *30 min. Park Loop Rd., Bar Harbor.*

Continue along the loop road. In about 1½ miles (2.4km), the trees suddenly disappear atop

6 ★★ Otter Cliffs. This set of 100-foot-high (30m) cliffs is capped with stands of spruce. You won't really see the cliffs from the top, but that's okay—you can see for miles and miles from here. Look for spouting whales in summer or rafts of eider ducks floating just offshore in fall. A footpath traces the edge of the crags, but you want to be careful here, especially in windy or wet weather. ⏱ *15 min. Park Loop Rd., Otter Cove.*

Continue around the point on the loop road for 4 miles (6.4km) until the road joins Rte. 3. Turn left and continue 2 miles (3.2km) west to

7 ★ kids **Seal Harbor.** The stony beach and grassy lawn at Seal Harbor are superlative places for a picnic or a walk on the beach. The sea views, public bathrooms, and adjacent grocery store make it all the more so. The beach here is too chilly for swimming, but it's good for beachcombing (or launching a kayak from, if you're experienced at that). As a bonus, you'll sometimes see famous faces in and around the village. *45 min. Rte. 3 (at Stanley Rd.).*

From the beach, turn right on Stanley Rd. and drive 2 miles (3.2km) north on Park Loop Rd. (also called Jordan Pond Rd.) to the parking lots for

8 **Jordan Pond.** A small but lovely oval of water among forested hills, Jordan Pond is often photographed and easily hiked. A 3-mile (4.8km) loop follows the woods along the pond's shoreline, and a network of carriage roads converges at the pond. The view of the Bubbles (see below) is superb. Best of all is the dining: After your hike or mountain-bike ride, don't miss an al fresco meal at the **Jordan Pond House restaurant** (p 148). It's right at the parking lot, no further caloric expenditure required. *45 min. Park Loop Rd. Free parking in lot.*

Exit the lots and turn left. Continue 1½ miles (2.4km) north on the Park Loop Rd. (Jordan Pond Rd.) to the parking lot for

9 ★ **The Bubbles.** These twin, rounded peaks stand at the head of Jordan Pond. Park in the lot just north of the Jordan Pond House; the trail is clearly marked. As you climb (about a 20-minute hike), the forested sides give way to exposed ledges and then a completely clear summit with a picture-perfect view of not only the pond itself, but also the coastline beyond. It's not a very taxing walk, except in a

few steep spots, and well worth the effort. If you're hungry afterward, backtrack to the **Jordan Pond House** (p 148). *1 hr. Park Loop Rd. Free parking in lot.*

Continue 2½ miles (4km) north on the Park Loop Rd. (Jordan Pond Rd.) to the turnoff for Cadillac Mountain. Turn right on Mountain Rd. and climb 3½ miles (5.6km) to the top of

10 ★★★ **Cadillac Mountain.** I've saved Acadia's best and tallest peak for last on this tour. Hordes converge on the mountain at sunrise, not because this 1,528-foot (466m) mountain is the highest peak on the Atlantic coast between Canada and Brazil, but because it's the first place on U.S. soil touched by the sun's rays at daybreak. So the lot at the summit gets filled with chatty tourists. Views are spectacular in all directions, but I'd come in late afternoon or sunset instead to enjoy them—far fewer crowds then. *1 hr. (longer for hikes). Cadillac Summit Rd. (off Park Loop Rd.).*

Cadillac Mountain is the highest peak on the Atlantic coast between Canada and Brazil.

Villages of Mount Desert Island

1. Thuya Garden
2. Asticou Terraces and Azalea Garden
3. Northeast Harbor
4. Somesville
5. Southwest Harbor

Bar I.
Bar Harbor
MOUNT DESERT ISLAND
198
233
Park Headquarters
Eagle L.
Somesville
Champlain Mtn.
Sargent Mtn.
Cadillac Mtn.
The Bubbles
Jordan Pd.
Sand Beach
198
Echo L.
102
Long Pd.
Acadia Mtn.
Thunder Hole
102
3
Otter Cliff
Seal Cove Pd.
ACADIA NATIONAL PARK
Northeast Harbor
Park Loop Rd.
Southwest Harbor
Bear I.
Greening I.
Sutton I.
ATLANTIC OCEAN
Islesford Historical Museum
Little Cranberry I.
Blue Hill Bay
102A
Great Cranberry I.
Baker I.
Bernard
Bass Harbor
0   2 mi
0   2 km
Bass Harbor Head Lighthouse

Mount Desert Island is more than just Bar Harbor, more than Acadia National Park, even. There are plenty of quaint fishing villages, resorts, wooded points of land, cultivated gardens, natural wonders, and small attractions scattered *outside* the park's boundaries, and these make for very pleasant day-tripping. This tour touches on a few highlights. START: **Take Rte. 3 (also known as Peabody Dr.) west from Seal Harbour about 2 miles (3.2km) to Thuya Dr.**

1 ★ Thuya Garden. This garden, part of famous former resident Joseph Curtis's property, was created in 1956 by noted landscape architect Charles K. Savage. It attracts flower enthusiasts admiring the mix of annuals and perennials, students of landscape architecture, and local folks looking for a quiet place to rest. The lawns lead to a pavilion and reflecting pool; the gates were hand-carved of cedar.

⏱ 30 min. Thuya Rd. (off Rte. 3), Northeast Harbor. ☎ 207/276-3727. www.gardenpreserve.org. Free admission (donations requested). Late June to Sept daily 7am–7pm. Limited free parking in lot.

A few hundred feet farther along Rte. 3, on the left side of the road, is the parking area for

2 ★★ Asticou Terraces and Azalea Garden. One of the best

Southwest Harbor is a fishing town that has become renowned for its cuisine.

places for enjoying views of the harbor is from these quiet terraces. Park on the left, cross the road (away from the water), then hike the magnificent gravel path uphill. There's a third garden another few hundred feet down the road (turn right onto Rte. 198 and park): The Asticou Azalea Garden—run by the same organization—is a groomed, Japanese-style wonder of water and plant life. ⏱ *45 min. Peabody Rd. (Rte. 3), Northeast Harbor. www.gardenpreserve.org.* ☎ *207/276-3727. Free admission (donations requested). May–Oct daily dawn–dusk. Closed Nov–Apr. Limited free parking in lot.*

Turn left on Rte. 198 and drive south 1 mile (1.6km) into the town of

❸ ★★ Northeast Harbor. On the tip of the eastern lobe of Mount Desert Island is this staid, prosperous little village. It consists of elegant cottages plus one short main street and a marina. There's a bakery, an excellent small-town grocer, art and craft galleries, the great **Redbird Provisions restaurant** (p 148), a tourist information kiosk—even a laundromat for fishermen on shore leave. This is small-town coastal Maine at its best. ⏱ *1 hr.*

Backtrack to Rte. 198 and turn north, continuing 6 miles (9.7km)

to Rte. 102; turn left. In ½ mile (.8km), you arrive in the town of

❹ Somesville. Believed to be the oldest colonial settlement on the entire island, Somesville is genteel, lovely, and tiny. Founded in 1761, it's as seasonal as a town can be. There's a bookstore, a town hall, a church, a dock with water views, a small repertory theater, and beautiful summer mansions. Yet the town's probably *most* famous for the whitewashed, curving Somesville Bridge, visible from the main road. ⏱ *15 min.*

Continue south 6 miles (9.7km) on Rte. 102 to

❺ ★ Southwest Harbor. Almost directly across the sound from Northeast Harbor, Southwest is a fishing town that went upscale, then became a culinary Mecca. There are more good inns and restaurants here than anywhere else on the island except Bar Harbor—remarkable, given the size of the town. Fishermen and boat builders still live here, too, giving the place an authentic feel. Among the good places to stay or eat here are the **Lindenwood Inn** (p 150), **Kingsleigh** (p 150), the **Inn at Southwest** (p 150), **Beal's** (p 147), and **Fiddlers' Green** (p 147). There's also a bakery, grocer, Internet cafe, ferry dock, and small pocket waterfront park. ⏱ *1½ hr.*

Mt. Desert Is. Dining & Lodging

DINING

Beal's Lobster Pound 6
The Burning Tree 7
Fiddlers' Green 1
Galyn's 11
Havana 20
Jordan Pond House 8
Maggie's Restaurant 13
Michelle's Fine Dining 17
Redbird Provisions 9
Thurston's Lobster
    Pound 10

LODGING

Balance Rock Inn 16
The Bar Harbor Inn 12
Bass Cottage Inn 14
Black Friar Inn 15
The Claremont 5
Inn at Southwest 2
Kingsleigh Inn 3
Lindenwood Inn 4
Mira Monte Inn 19
Primrose Inn 18

Mount Desert Island Dining A to Z

★ kids Beal's Lobster Pound
LOBSTER Some say Beal's is the best lobster shack in Maine. It's certainly got the right feel: Creaky picnic tables sit on a plain concrete pier next to a Coast Guard base. Pick out a lobster from the tank. *182 Clark Point Rd., Southwest Harbor. ☎ 207/244-7178 or 207/244-3202. www.bealslobster.com. Lobsters market-priced. AE, DISC, MC, V. Summer breakfast, lunch & dinner daily; Sept to mid-Oct breakfast & lunch daily. Closed mid-Oct to mid-May.*

★★ The Burning Tree *SEAFOOD* On a busy straightaway of Route 3, this place serves some of the best seafood on the island. Some of the produce and herbs come from the restaurant's own gardens. *69 Otter Creek Dr. (Rte. 3), Otter Creek. ☎ 207/288-9331. Entrees $18–$23. DISC, MC, V. June to late Oct dinner Wed–Mon. Closed late Oct to May.*

★★ Fiddlers' Green *NEW AMERICAN* Island-native chef Derek Wilbur's bistro is a big hit, from the cold seafood bar to small plates of Thai-curried shrimp, fried catfish, grilled *merguez,* and baby back ribs. There are always steaks, pasta dishes, and specialty martinis. *411 Main St., Southwest Harbor. ☎ 207/244-9416. www.fiddlersgreenrestaurant.com. Entrees $16–$32. AE, DISC, MC, V. Dinner Tues–Sun. Closed late Oct to late May.*

★★ Galyn's *SEAFOOD* Charming, unassuming Galyn's gets seafood right, from blackened and grilled Cajun shrimp to daily fish specials and seafood stews. Non-seafood is great, too. Finish with real Indian pudding or the cappuccino sundae. A little street-side deck faces Agamont Park and the bay. *17 Main St., Bar Harbor. ☎ 207/288-9706. www.galynsbarharbor.com. Entrees $7–$31. AE, MC, V. Lunch & dinner daily.*

★★ Havana *LATIN* Chef/owner Michael Boland's menu is inspired by Latino fare, with a New American twist: crab cakes, duck empanadas, fig-and-blue-cheese tarts, beef and pork skewers dusted with cinnamon and vanilla. But there are also variations on lobster. Desserts are creamy, sweet, and good. *318 Main St., Bar Harbor. ☎ 207/288-2822.*

Havana mixes lobsters with Latin cuisine.

www.havanamaine.com. Entrees $24–$32. AE, DC, DISC, MC, V. Dinner daily.

★★ Jordan Pond House *AMERI-CAN* This restaurant is at the tip of **Jordan Pond** (p 25), looking north toward **the Bubbles** (p 165). After-noon tea with popovers and jam is a hallowed tradition here, but they also serve meaty dinners of prime rib, lobster, pasta, and stew. *Park Loop Rd. (near Seal Harbor), Acadia National Park.* ☎ *207/276-3316. www.jordanpond.com. Entrees $12–$23. AE, DISC, MC, V. Mid-May to late Oct lunch & dinner daily.*

★★ Maggie's Restaurant *SEA-FOOD* Only locally caught fish is used here, and you can order other creatively prepared seafoods, from lobster to grilled clams to Gulf shrimp with feta and olives. They also do nice steaks and chicken. Desserts are worth leaving room for, especially the gourmet ice cream sundaes. *6 Summer St., Bar Harbor.* ☎ *207/288-9007. www. maggiesbarharbor.com. Entrees $16–$24. MC, V. Dinner Mon–Sat.*

★★ Michelle's Fine Dining *FRENCH/SEAFOOD* Inside the Ivy Manor Inn is this excellent French restaurant with some New England twists: the bouillabaisse for two includes local lobster, mussels,

clams, and scallops. Finish with a cheese plate or a "bag of choco-late": It comes with berries and is served in an edible chocolate bag. An expensive meal, but worth it. *194 Main St., Bar Harbor.* ☎ *888/ 670-1997 or 207/288-2138. www. michellesfinedining.com. Entrees $24–$54. AE, DISC, MC, V. Dinner daily. Closed late Oct to early May.*

★★ Redbird Provisions *CONTI-NENTAL/SEAFOOD* Right on North-east Harbor's main street, this kitchen cooks up local seafood with Asian, French, and Italian accents. Go for trout salad niçoise, organic salmon with white bean ragout and figs, or a strip streak. The small, porch-side outdoor dining space is nice in warmer weather. *11 Sea St., Northeast Harbor.* ☎ *207/276-3006. www.redbirdprovisions.com. Entrees $9–$34. DISC, MC, V. Lunch Tues–Sat, dinner Tues–Sun. Closed late Oct to late May.*

★★ Thurston's Lobster Pound *LOBSTER* Great views of Bass Har-bor plus lobster dinners, complete with corn on the cob? Sign me up. Eat either upstairs or down—both are convivial. *Steamboat Wharf Rd. (on the waterfront), Bernard.* ☎ *207/ 244-7600. Lobsters market-priced; other entrees $7-$20. MC, V. Late May to early Oct lunch & dinner daily.*

Thurston's Lobster Pound has great views and a convivial atmosphere.

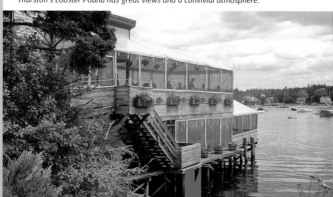

Mount Desert Island Lodging A to Z

★★ **Balance Rock Inn** Down a side alley off Bar Harbor's main drag, the Balance Rock (built in 1903 for a Scottish railroad magnate) achieves a beach-house feel. The swimming pool looks like one from a Tuscan villa; the more expensive rooms feature whirlpools and saunas. *21 Albert Meadow, Bar Harbor.* ☎ *800/753-0494 or 207/288-2610. www.balance rockinn.com. 17 units. Doubles $115–$525 w/breakfast. AE, DISC, MC, V. Closed Nov to early May.*

★★ **The Bar Harbor Inn** Right next to **Agamont Park** (p 137), this inn mixes traditional styling with contemporary touches. Some units have spectacular bay views, and many have private balconies. There's also a newish spa with Vichy showers. *7 Newport Dr., Bar Harbor.* ☎ *800/248-3351 or 207/288-3351. www.barharborinn.com. 153 units. Doubles $79–$379 w/breakfast. AE, DISC, MC, V. Closed Dec to mid-Mar.*

★★ **Bass Cottage Inn** High marks for friendliness, service, luxe rooms, and proximity to the water. Units are decked out in cast-iron beds, woodstoves, silk canopies, love seats, armoires, and the like; some have Jacuzzis and/or views. *14 The Field, Bar Harbor.* ☎ *866/782-9224 or 207/288-1234. www. basscottage.com. 10 units. Doubles $185–$370 w/breakfast. AE, MC, V. 2-night minimum stay on weekends. Closed late Oct to mid-May. No children under 12.*

★ **Black Friar Inn** This yellow-shingled home has quirky interior touches, including replicas of both a London pub with elaborate carved-wood paneling and a doctor's office. *10 Summer St., Bar Harbor.* ☎ *207/288-5091. www.blackfriarinn.com. 6 units. Doubles $120–$175 w/breakfast. MC, V. 2-night minimum stay. Closed Dec–Apr. No children under 12.*

★★ **The Claremont** An old New England sort of summer resort, the Claremont has retained its grace and quality level. Guest rooms are bright and airy, and there are 14 cottages

Many rooms at The Bar Harbor Inn have spectacular bay views.

on the property with fireplaces and kitchenettes. *22 Claremont Rd. (at Clark Point Rd.), Southwest Harbor.* ☎ *800/244-5036. www.theclaremont hotel.com. 44 units. Doubles $152–$308 w/breakfast. MC, V. Closed mid-Oct to late May.*

★ **Inn at Southwest** There's a late-19th-century feel to this mansard-roofed Victorian home, which is spare rather than frilly. All guest rooms are named for Maine lighthouses and outfitted simply—some with touches like sleigh beds and rosewood sofas. *371 Main St., Southwest Harbor.* ☎ *207/244-3835. www.innatsouthwest.com. 7 units. Doubles $105–$185 w/breakfast. DISC, MC, V. Closed Nov to late Apr.*

★★ **Kingsleigh Inn** The Kingsleigh has long been a reliable place to bunk down in Southwest. All rooms are equipped with sound machines, wine glasses, and robes; the penthouse suite brings great sea views and a telescope to see them with. *373 Main St., Southwest Harbor.* ☎ *207/244-5302. www.kingsleighinn. com. 8 units. Doubles $110–$195 w/ breakfast. AE, MC, V. Closed Nov–Mar. Children 13 & older welcome.*

★★ **Lindenwood Inn** This inn features a striking interior decor in a captain's house near the harbor. Most units have balconies and

plenty of windows; some have fireplaces, French doors, and/or private porches or decks. The heated inground pool and Jacuzzi are a bonus. *118 Clark Point Rd., Southwest Harbor.* ☎ *800/307-5335 or 207/244-5335. www.lindenwoodinn. com. 8 units. Doubles $95–$215 w/ breakfast. MC, V.*

★ **Mira Monte Inn** This 1864 home in downtown Bar Harbor has gotten a spruce-up and is now improving. Some rooms have a balcony, fireplace, and/or Jacuzzi, especially those in the adjacent outbuilding. *69 Mount Desert St., Bar Harbor.* ☎ *800/553-5109. www. miramonte.com. 12 units. Doubles $95–$209 w/breakfast. AE, DISC, MC, V. 2-night minimum stay in summer. Closed late Oct to mid-May.*

★★ **Primrose Inn** A Victorian stick-style inn built in 1878, the Primrose is one of the prettiest homes on Bar Harbor's "mansion row" along Mount Desert Street. Recent renovations have brought private bathrooms, balconies, flat-screen TVs, and Wi-Fi access. *73 Mount Desert St., Bar Harbor.* ☎ *877/846-3424 or 207/288-4031. www.primroseinn. com. 13 units. Doubles $99–$229 w/ breakfast. AE, DISC, MC, V. Summer & fall 2-night minimum stay. Closed Nov to late May.* ●

The Lindenwood Inn has a striking interior décor.

The Downeast Coast

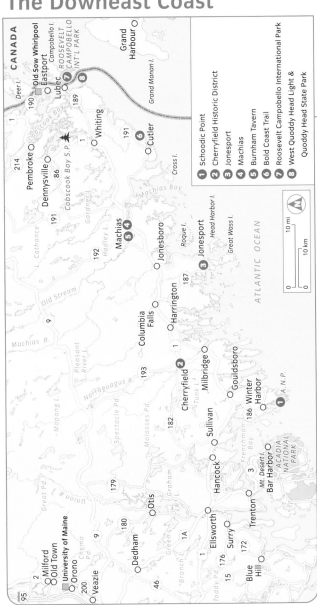

1. Schoodic Point
2. Cherryfield Historic District
3. Jonesport
4. Machias
5. Burnham Tavern
6. Bold Coast Trail
7. Roosevelt Campobello International Park
8. West Quoddy Head Light & Quoddy Head State Park

Previous page: A stretch of rugged shoreline along the Downeast Coast.

Downeast Maine doesn't even get a look from most travelers, and there's a reason why: It takes time to get here, and sites are few and far between once you do. Still, if you enjoy solitude, salty and foggy air, maritime history, or empty roads lined with fir and spruce trees, this is *the* place for you. Bonus: we'll visit Canada. Bring your passport. START: **Begin in Ellsworth and travel north on U.S. Rte. 1 about 18 miles (29km) to Rte. 186; turn right and drive 6 miles (9.7km) to Moore Rd. Turn right again and continue 5 miles (8km) along Schoodic Dr.**

❶ ★ Schoodic Point. This remote, scenic unit of Acadia National Park is just 7 miles (11km) from Mount Desert Island across Frenchman Bay, but it's a 50-mile (80km) drive to get here. It's worth it, though (and free). A pleasing one-way loop road hooks around the point, along the water, and through forests of spruce and fir. Good views of the mountains of Acadia open up across Frenchman Bay. Park near the tip and explore the rocks that plunge into the ocean—but stay a bit back from the edge, as waves can get big after a storm. ⏱ *45 min. Acadia National Park, Winter Harbor.* ☎ *207/288-3338. Free admission.*

Return to Schoodic Dr. and continue around the point. In 5 miles (8km), rejoin Rte. 186 and continue 6 more miles (9.7km) north to U.S.

Rte. 1. Turn right. In about 8 miles (13km), you reach Rte. 193, the turnoff for Cherryfield and the

❷ ★ Cherryfield Historic District. The little town of Cherryfield (population 1,100 on a good day) has few cherries but a surprising number of historic homes packed into its bounds. The historic district takes in 75 acres (30 hectares) on both sides of the river running through town; the striking mansions are in Federal, Second Empire, Italianate, and other styles. The William M. Nash House (built 1840–1888), for instance, is a Second Empire wonder. Get more info at the historic society on River Road. ⏱ *45 min.*

Return to U.S. Rte. 1 and continue 11 miles (18km) north. Turn right onto Rte. 187 and drive about 12

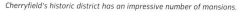

Cherryfield's historic district has an impressive number of mansions.

The fishing village of Jonesport holds lobster boat races each summer.

miles (19km) to the end of the point to reach

❸ ★ Jonesport. This photogenic, lost-in-time fishing village is still mostly the haven of lobstermen, fishermen, and boat builders and fixers. Besides the pretty tableau, salty local color, and dramatic ocean waves, you'll also find some of the biggest puffin colonies in the world here if you decide to catch a local charter boat from the harbor out to Machias Seal Island. The same picturesque harbor is also famed for its wacky summertime lobster boat races. 🕘 *45 min.*

Continue around the point, turning north along Rte. 187 and following it about 11 miles (18km) back to U.S. Rte. 1. Turn right and continue 9 more miles (14km) north to

❹ Machias. The town of Machias (muh-*CHAI*-us) is the biggest town in Washington County, with a university campus, coffee shops, galleries, and other trappings of culture. The river here was the site of the Revolutionary War's very first naval battle in 1775, a story that's told at the **Burnham Tavern** (see below). Historic buildings include the George Foster and Andrew Gilson houses on North Street (both with impressive mansards); a lineup of mansions along Court Street, including

the town offices (in an Italianate former schoolhouse); and the granite Porter Memorial Library, with its ballast from the *Margaretta*. 🕘 *30 min.*

On Main St. (Rte. 192), just after the turnoff from U.S. Rte. 1, is the

❺ Burnham Tavern. This gambrel-roofed tavern (now a museum) was built on a rise overlooking the Machias River in 1770, and it's believed to be the oldest standing building in eastern Maine. In 1775, locals gathered here and hatched a plan: Residents took up sailboats, muskets, swords, axes, pitchforks—anything—and killed the captain of a British ship in the harbor. 🕘 *30 min. Free St. at Main St. (Rte. 192), Machias.* ☎ *207/255-6930. www. burnhamtavern.com. Admission $2 adults, 25¢ children. Mid-June to early Sept Mon–Fri 9am–5pm. Closed early Sept to mid-June.*

Return to U.S. Rte. 1 and continue about 15 miles (24km) north to Rte. 191. Turn right and drive 13 miles (21km) east on Rte. 191 into Cutler. Pass the harbor and continue almost 4 more miles (6.4km) to the turnoff and trail head on the right for the

❻ ★★ Bold Coast Trail. Marked by a sign in a small parking lot, this dramatic trail loops through bogs, barrens, jumbled fields of stone, and forest. But the highlight is a mile-long (1.6km) section along 150-foot (46m) cliffs rising high above the Atlantic—don't go if you fear heights, and step carefully, as there are no railings or fences. You can even see the Bay of Fundy in Canada from these cliff tops. It takes 4 to 5 hours to walk the whole 10-mile (16km) loop, but you can turn around anytime, of course—even after 20 minutes—for a briefer look at the views. ⏲ *1–5 hr. for hikes. Rte. 191, Cutler.* ☎ *207/827-1818. Free admission.*

Continue 10 miles (16km) northeast on Rte. 191 to the junction with Rte. 189.

Decision Time

To continue to Eastport (covered in its own tour on p 156), turn left and continue north on U.S. Route 1 for 16 miles (26km), then turn onto Route 190. If you'll skip Eastport, however, turn right here and follow Route 189 for 6 miles (10km) to the bridge leading to Canada and the next stop on this tour.

❼ ★★ Roosevelt Campobello International Park. President Franklin Delano Roosevelt (1882–1945) made an annual summer trek to this island, in Canadian territory just across the little bridge from Lubec, and you should, too. You can learn a lot about Roosevelt at the visitor center of this peaceful park or during a self-guided tour of the mansion. But also be sure to explore the grounds, which hold plenty of scenic coastline walking trails. (Because this *is* Canada, remember to bring a passport.) ⏲ *2 hr. 459 Rte. 774, Welshpool, New Brunswick.* ☎ *506/752-2922. www.fdr.net. Free admission. Daily 10am–6pm; last tour at 5:45pm. Visitor center closed*

mid-Oct to mid-May; grounds open year-round.

Cross the bridge back to the U.S. and Rte. 189. Head south; after 1 mile (1.6km), turn left on South Lubec Rd. and drive 3 miles (4.8km) south to the access road for

❽ ★★ West Quoddy Head Light & Quoddy Head State Park. The candy cane–colored Quoddy Light marks the easternmost point of United States land. Visitors can photograph it from the park and learn more in the visitor center inside the lightkeeper's house. The park's grounds include the entire headland: 500 acres (202 hectares) of dramatic coast, with trails to the tops of the cliffs. Some of the best views are an easy stroll from the parking lot. ⏲ *1½ hr. West Quoddy Head Rd., Lubec.* ☎ *207/733-0911 (park) or 207/733-2180 (lighthouse). www.westquoddy.com. Lighthouse free admission; state park $3 non-resident adults, $1 seniors & children 5–11. Late May to mid-Oct lighthouse daily 10am–4pm, grounds daily 9am–sunset. Closed mid-Oct to mid-May.*

West Quoddy Head Light is surrounded by 500 acres of parkland.

Eastport

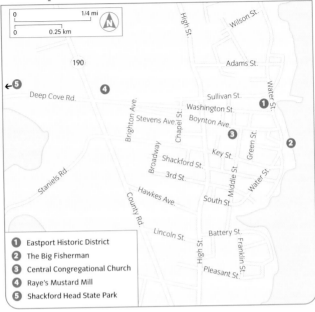

1. Eastport Historic District
2. The Big Fisherman
3. Central Congregational Church
4. Raye's Mustard Mill
5. Shackford Head State Park

ate in the 19th century, Eastport was a boomtown of 5,000 residents and 18 sardine plants. The plants are all gone now, but fishermen remain—as does the handsome architecture, a postcard from those prosperous days. Most of the buildings between the town post office and library are on the National Register of Historic Places. START: **Downtown Eastport on Water St.**

1 ★ Eastport Historic District. Eastport's compact historic district, centered on Water Street, is wonderful. The Boston architect Henry Black designed two-thirds of these Italianate buildings in a hurry, within one year of a devastating 1886 fire that wiped out the downtown. His works include the Eastport Savings Bank at 43 Water St., the Shead Building at 58 Water St., the M. Bradish Bakery at 68 Water St., the Masonic Block at 36 Water St., the Charles & M. A. Jackson Block at 74 Water St., and (probably) the

Hayscale Block at 49 Water St. The street also has views of Campobello Island and Passamaquoddy Bay as a bonus. Boynton Street is similarly lovely. ⏱ *1 hr. Water St. (from Adams St. to Sullivan St. & west to High St.).*

At a gap in the buildings, on the harbor side between Boynton St. and Furniture Ave., is

2 The Big Fisherman. I don't know what else to call it. Eastport's squat, Paul Bunyan-esque statue standing guard over the docks was erected by Hollywood in 2001 for a short-lived reality/murder mystery show filmed in town. Corny or a fitting tribute to fishermen? You decide. ⏱ *15 min. Water St. (near Furniture Ave.).*

Continue south along Water St. to Key St. Turn right and walk 2 blocks to Middle St. and turn right. Halfway down the block is

③ Central Congregational Church.
Eastport's biggest, most impressive church towers over Middle Street, as it has done since 1829, when it was built after a design by Daniel Low, a member of the congregation. Its massive clock faces and triple-arched doorways are Federal Meetinghouse style at its finest. The steeple is sharply pitched and elegant. ⏱ *15 min. 26 Middle St.*

Continue to Boynton St. and turn left. Go 5 blocks to Brighton Ave., turn right, and then turn left onto Washington St. In half a block, on the right, you'll come to

④ ★ Raye's Mustard Mill.
This artisanal mustard factory (painted a dull yellow, of course), just a few blocks from Eastport's historic district, is powered by one of the last stone mills in America. Free tours are given weekdays, and they sometimes show off new flavor variations being rolled out. There's also a gift shop on site. ⏱ *45 min. 83 Washington St.* ☎ *800/853-1903 or 207/853-4451. www.rayes mustard.com. Tours Mon–Fri 10am–3pm, Sat by appointment.*

Continue along Washington St. (it becomes Deep

A colorful array of flavors can be found at Raye's Mustard Mill.

Cove Rd.) ¾ mile (1.2km) to the access road, on the left, into

⑤ ★★ Shackford Head State Park.
This 90-acre (36-hectare) peninsula is quietly spectacular. Among the several miles of easy hiking trails are two (Schooner and Overlook) leading to hundred-foot-high (30m) overlooks with spectacular cliff-top views. You can *also* see the remains of Civil War–era ships at low tide. There's a pebbly beach and public bathrooms—and it's free. ⏱ *1½ hr. Deep Cove Rd.* ☎ *207/941-4014. Free admission. Daily sunrise–sunset.*

"The Big Fisherman" at Eastport's docks.

Downeast Lodging & Dining

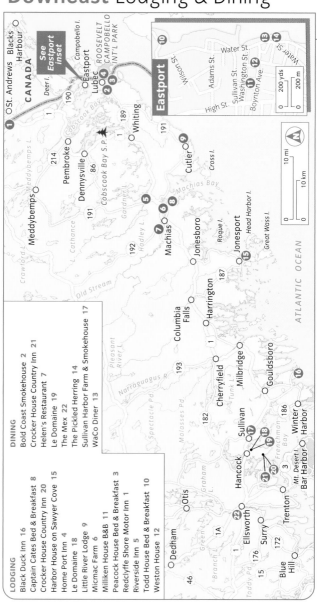

LODGING

Black Duck Inn 16
Captain Cates Bed & Breakfast 8
Crocker House Country Inn 20
Harbor House on Sawyer Cove 15
Home Port Inn 4
Le Domaine 18
Little River Lodge 9
Micmac Farm 6
Milliken House B&B 11
Peacock House Bed & Breakfast 3
Redclyffe Shore Motor Inn 1
Riverside Inn 5
Todd House Bed & Breakfast 10
Weston House 12

DINING

Bold Coast Smokehouse 2
Crocker House Country Inn 21
Helen's Restaurant 7
Le Domaine 19
The Mex 22
The Pickled Herring 14
Sullivan Harbor Farm & Smokehouse 17
WaCo Diner 13

Downeast Maine Lodging A to Z

Black Duck Inn One of the few businesses in Corea, a tiny fishing village far off the beaten track, the Black Duck offers simple rooms (two share a bathroom), a suite, and a waterfront cottage. Furnishings are simple, but water views are excellent. *36 Crowley Island Rd., Corea.* ☎ *207/963-2689. www.blackduck. com. 7 units. Doubles $140–$165 w/ breakfast. DISC, MC, V. Closed Dec to mid-May. No children under 9.*

Captain Cates Bed & Breakfast This trim home in Machiasport was built by a sailor in the 1850s. Most units have ocean views, though all six share three bathrooms. The J. W. Room has a fun mahogany bed and matching commode and dresser. *Rte. 92 (at Phinney Lane), Machiasport.* ☎ *207/ 255-8812. www.captaincates.com. 6 units. Doubles $75–$95. AE, V.*

Crocker House Country Inn Across Frenchman Bay from Mount Desert Island, the Crocker House is tastefully decorated in country decor and solid furniture; nothing fancy, but rooms do have phones.

The dining room (p 161) is the highlight. *967 Point Rd., Hancock Point.* ☎ *877/715-6017 or 207/422-6806. www.crockerhouse.com. 11 units. Doubles $85–$170 w/breakfast. AE, DISC, MC, V. Closed Jan & Feb.*

★ **Harbor House on Sawyer Cove** Once the Jonesport telegraph office, this inn has just two suites, set above an antiques shop. Both feature truly impressive coastal scenery from their third-floor windows and private entrances. Breakfast is served on a great porch. *27 Sawyer Sq., Jonesport.* ☎ *207/497-5417. www.harborhs.com. 2 units. Doubles $100–$125 w/breakfast. DISC, MC, V.*

★ **Home Port Inn** Most of this Lubec inn's rooms possess lovely views of Cobscook Bay and the Bay of Fundy. The living room and fireplace are the focal points; guest rooms vary in size, one occupying a former library and another a former dining room. The house restaurant is good. *45 Main St., Lubec.* ☎ *800/ 457-2077 or 207/733-2077. www. homeportinn.com. 7 units. Doubles*

The Crocker House Inn offers a slice of quaint country living.

$90–$105 w/breakfast. AE, DISC, MC, V. Closed mid-Oct to mid-May.

★ **Le Domaine** About 10 minutes east of Ellsworth, this inn has continental flair. Five rooms are comfortable and tastefully appointed without being pretentious; there are air-conditioning and phones in all units. The dining room (p 162) is excellent. *1513 U.S. Rte. 1, Hancock.* ☎ *800/554-8498 or 207/422-3395. www.ledomaine. com. 5 units. Doubles $200–$370 w/ breakfast & dinner. AE, MC, V. Closed Nov to mid-June.*

Little River Lodge Overlooking Cutler's tiny harbor, this Victorian inn was built to lodge steamship passengers bound from Boston to Canada. Rooms are decorated in nautical themes, but only one has a queen-sized bed. Cash only. *Rte. 191, Cutler.* ☎ *207/259-4437. www. cutlerlodge.com. 5 units (3 w/shared bathroom). Doubles $80–$120 w/ breakfast. No credit cards.*

★ **Micmac Farm** A 1763 farmhouse by a river, plus two woody-rustic cabins in the woods. The single room in the main house is far more luxurious with its king bed, television, and Jacuzzi. *47 Micmac Lane (Rte. 92), Machiasport.* ☎ *207/ 255-3008. www.micmacfarm.com.*

3 units. Doubles & cottages $80– $125. MC, V. Children welcome in cottages.

★ **Milliken House B&B** A friendly B&B steps from Eastport's historic district. All five rooms have marble-top furnishings and nice touches like chocolates, sherry, and flowers. Breakfasts are very good. *29 Washington St., Eastport.* ☎ *888/ 507-9370 or 207/853-2955. www. eastport-inn.com. 6 units. Doubles $75–$85 w/breakfast. MC, V.*

★ **Peacock House Bed & Breakfast** Great name. Peacock House was built by an English sea captain in 1860. The suites are best, including one with an extra daybed and one with a fireplace, four-poster bed, and wet bar. *27 Summer St., Lubec.* ☎ *888/305-0036 or 207/733-2403. www.peacockhouse.com. 7 units. Doubles $90–$112 w/breakfast., suite $105-$135. MC, V.*

★ **Redclyffe Shore Motor Inn** Motels in these parts are hit-or-miss, but this one is unusual: a Gothic Revival manse, plus a cluster of cliff-top motel units with bay vistas. Balcony rooms have the best views, as does the glassed-in dining room. *U.S. Rte. 1, Robbinston.* ☎ *207/454-3270. www.redclyffeshoremotorinn.com.*

Le Domaine has a subtle decor and air-conditioned rooms.

16 units. Doubles $78. MC, V. Closed Nov to mid-May.

★ Riverside Inn More comfy than you'd expect of a motel in these parts: One second-floor unit has a claw-foot tub and skylight, another a wraparound deck, still another a private balcony and small kitchen. *U.S. Rte. 1, East Machias.* ☎ *207/255-4134. www.riversideinn-maine.com. 4 units. Doubles $94–$129 w/breakfast. MC, V.*

Todd House Bed & Breakfast A bright yellow historic house overlooking two bays, this 1775 center cape features classic New England architectural touches like a fireplace with a bake oven. You can walk to downtown. *1 Capen Ave., Eastport.* ☎ *207/853-2328. 6 units (2 w/ shared bathroom). Doubles $50–$90 w/breakfast. MC, V.*

★ Weston House An 1810 Federal home looking out onto the water, this simple Eastport inn features rooms with antiques and

Inside the elegant Todd House B&B.

Asian furnishings; classical music plays in the background. Breakfasts and brunches are elaborate. *26 Boynton St., Eastport.* ☎ *207/853-2907. www.westonhouse-maine.com. 3 units (all w/shared bathroom). Doubles $80–$90 w/breakfast. No credit cards.*

Downeast Maine Dining A to Z

★ Bold Coast Smokehouse *SEAFOOD* Undoubtedly the nation's easternmost smokehouse, this Lubec smokery is perfect when you need provisions for a picnic at Quoddy Head or Shackford Head. Choose from among hot salmon, gravlax, kabobs, and trout pâté. *224 County Rd., Lubec.* ☎ *888/733-0807 or 207/733-8912. www.boldcoast smokehouse.com. Smoked seafood $10–$30 per lb. MC, V. Spring–fall Mon–Fri 9am–4:30pm, Sat 9am–1pm; winter, call ahead.*

★★ Crocker House Country Inn *CONTINENTAL* This inn dining room serves good resort fare:

oysters Rockefeller, scallops, fish, pasta, steak *au poivre,* filet mignon, roast duckling, rack of lamb, and the like. *967 Point Rd., Hancock Point.* ☎ *877/715-6017 or 207/422–6806. Entrees $20–$31. AE, DISC, MC, V. May–Oct dinner daily; Apr, Nov & Dec dinner Sat–Sun. Closed Jan–Mar.*

★ Helen's Restaurant *DINER* This is the original Helen's, a cut-above-the-rest diner and one of the best places in Maine to eat pie. Specials run to pork chops, fried fish, burgers, and meatloaf—but save room for the strawberry rhubarb, blueberry, and cream pies. *28 E.*

Main St., Machias. ☎ 207/255-8423. Entrees $3–$16. DISC, MC, V. Breakfast, lunch & dinner daily.

★★ **Le Domaine** *FRENCH* Not far east of Ellsworth, this country inn serves some of the best French cooking on the coast. The original owner emigrated from Provence to the U.S. during World War II; now, a young Maine chef has revitalized it. *1513 U.S. Rte. 1, Hancock. ☎ 800/554-8498 or 207/422-3395. Prix fixe dinner $35. MC, V. June–Oct lunch Sun, dinner daily. Closed Nov–May.*

The Mex *MEXICAN* This is Ellsworth's go-to spot for Mexican fare, serving all the usual dishes (taco salads, fajitas, and burritos), but also some surprising seafood entrees such as crab enchiladas, ceviche, and haddock Veracruz as a tip of the hat to its Maine home. *191 Main St., Ellsworth. ☎ 207/667-4494. www.themexrestaurant.com. Entrees $12–$17. AE, MC, V. Lunch & dinner daily.*

★★ **The Pickled Herring** *NEW AMERICAN* Out of nowhere, the Herring has become the finest-dining experience in Eastport, and for miles beyond. Eat fire-grilled gourmet pizzas, salmon with dill butter, strip steak, prime rib, and the like. *32 Water St., Eastport. ☎ 207/853-2323. www.thepickledherring.com. Entrees $15–$29. AE, MC, V. May–Oct dinner Thurs–Sun. Closed Nov–Apr.*

★ **Sullivan Harbor Farm & Smokehouse** *SEAFOOD* One of the last independently owned smokehouses around, this operation runs from a farmhouse on U.S. Route 1 near Mount Desert Island. They specialize in locally caught salmon, rubbed with salt and brown sugar, and also do scallops and pâté. *1545 U.S. Rte. 1, Hancock. ☎ 800/422-4014 or 207/422-2209. www.sullivanharborfarm.com. Items priced per pound. MC, V. Mid-Oct to mid-May breakfast & lunch Mon–Fri; mid-May to mid-Oct breakfast & lunch Mon–Sat.*

WaCo Diner *DINER* A touchstone in Eastport for more than 80 years, this diner has evolved from the lunch wagon it began as—but it stills serves big breakfasts of eggs and coffee, plus sandwiches at lunch and dinners of beef and fried fish. Plus cocktails. *47 Water St., Eastport. ☎ 207/853-4046. Entrees $3–$17. MC, V. Breakfast, lunch & dinner daily.* ●

Sullivan Harbor Smokehouse specializes in locally caught salmon.

The Great Outdoors

Acadia's Best **Hiking, Biking & Camping**

Acadia Mountain 6
Blackwoods Campground 5
The Bubbles 1
Cadillac Mountain 2
Day Mountain 4
Flying Mountain 8
Mountain biking the carriage roads 3
St. Sauveur Mountain 7
Seawall Campground 9

Previous page: Kayaking is very popular in Acadia National Park.

M ount Desert Island is chock-full of great opportunities to commune with nature: hikes up ocean-side cliffs; easy, meandering strolls; wide mountain-biking paths. At night? You could sleep in an inn or B&B, but you might also want to sample one of the national park's simple campgrounds. What you give up in luxuries you'll more than gain back through the simple joys of bird song, salt air, fresh grass, campfire smoke, and morning dew on your tent.

Hiking

Acadia Mountain On the western lobe of Mount Desert Island, this mountain takes 1½ to 2 hours to scale and descend; it's not a long hike, but it gets strenuous in spots, especially the final section leading to the summit. With time for lingering and enjoying the views of Somes Sound and the offshore islands with a sandwich and drink, this 2½-mile (4km) loop hike could be a half-day outing. From the trail head, you walk east through mixed forests, then begin an ascent over ledges. The eastern peak has better views; look for pocket clearings at the summit that open up unexpected vistas. Descend via the fire road. *Trail head is about 3 miles (4.8km) south of Somesville on Rte. 102.*

★★ The Bubbles At the northern end of Jordan Pond—accessible via a different parking area at their base—are the twin, oddly symmetrical mounds known as the Bubbles. A trail heads up through mixed woods, then snakes gracefully along open ledges and blueberry bushes until you're presented with a choice: north bubble or south. The southern bubble has a better view. (Also don't miss Bubble Rock, a so-called "glacial erratic" that looks tipsy but can't be tipped.) It's surprising how quickly you get to the top: in 30 minutes, though huffing and puffing is required on some steep sections for kids and the out-of-shape. Up top, you get absolutely stunning views, not only of the pond, but of the

open ocean beyond. *Trail head just south of Jordan Pond.*

★★★ Cadillac Mountain It's only 1,500 feet (457m) high or so, but Cadillac feels grand because its views seem to stretch forever—relatively speaking. This is the best place on the island to get an overview of things: the fractured geology of mountains and islands, the almost Arctic-like vegetation, the subtle color changes of fall, the sea fogs (and cruise ships and ferries) rolling in like clockwork in summer. You can drive to the summit (see p 143) and walk a half-mile (.8km) to the top, but many hikers enjoy the two trails snaking up its flanks. The 4½-mile (7.2km) North Ridge trail is shorter, easier (but not easy), more open, and more ocean-scenic; it departs from a parking lot on Park Loop Road. The 7-mile (11km) South

Day Mountain's winding hiking trail.

Wide and well-maintained, Acadia's carriage roads are ideal for cycling.

Ridge Trail is best left to expert hikers due to its length, verticality, and tricky technical sections—dangerous for beginners. *South Ridge trail head is on Rte. 3, 300 feet (91m) south of Blackwoods Campground. North Ridge trail head is halfway up Cadillac Summit Rd.*

★ **Day Mountain** This easy 2½-mile (4km) hike begins in a nondescript parking lot just west of Otter Creek, and the first stretches are fairly plain. But the trail soon does a dance with one or two of the island's famous carriage roads, where you'll see cyclists and even the occasional horse-drawn carriage or wedding party. The final stretch takes you to an open, safe summit with excellent views stretching south over the Cranberry Islands (p 37). *Trail head is on north side of Rte. 3, about 1 mile (1.6km) east of Seal Harbor.*

★ **Flying Mountain** This isn't a very well-known hike, and it's not demanding at all; thus, excellent for non-hardcore hikers and avid birders. A moderate half-hour walk, through dense fir trees and over boulders and twisted roots, brings you up to a skinny ridge top with views along Somes Sound to Northeast and Southwest harbors and out

to the Cranberry Islands. Birds use the fjord as a flyway, and peregrine falcons are sometimes seen (which can cause the trail to be closed); bring binoculars. *Trail head is on Rte. 102 south; just before Southwest Harbor, turn left on Fernald Point Rd. Go 1 mile (1.6km) to parking area & trail head on left.*

St. Sauveur Mountain This hike doesn't have the greatest views in the park; most of the walk is deep within woods, and even the summit is wooded. But it's a good place to feel the thick evergreen forests of the island around you; in a mist, it becomes a bit magical (though also a bit slippery). The trail head sneaks up on you on a straightaway of Route 102, about halfway between Somesville and Southwest Harbor—it's roughly across from the Echo Lake Beach access road. *Trail head on east side of Rte. 102, about 3 miles (4.8km) north of Southwest Harbor.*

Biking
★★ **Mountain biking the carriage roads** The 57 miles (92km) of carriage roads built by John D. Rockefeller, Jr., (1874–1960) are among Acadia's most extraordinary treasures. Originally built for

horse-drawn carriages, they're also ideal for cruising on a mountain bike—yes, it's allowed and encouraged (except in a few spots where the roads cross private land). Park near Jordan Pond, then plumb the tree-shrouded lanes that lace the area, taking time to admire the stonework on the many bridges you pass over or under. The roads are superbly restored and maintained, with wide hard-packed surfaces, gentle grades, and plenty of good signs. You can find a map online at www.nps.gov/acad/planyourvisit/maps.htm. *Access points include Rte. 3 (east of Seal Harbor), Jordan Pond, Bubble Pond & Eagle Lake.*

Camping
Blackwoods Campground On the island's eastern side, this is the more popular of the national park's two campgrounds, with about 300 sites. The campground has no public showers and no electrical hookups, but an enterprising business just outside the campground entrance provides clean showers for a small fee. The island's free shuttle stops here, as well. *Entrance on Rte. 3, about 5 miles (8km) south of Bar Harbor.* ☎ *877/444-6777*

(reservations) or ☎ *207/288-3274 (campground). www.recreation.gov. May–Oct sites $20 per night, Apr & Nov sites $10 per night; $5 park entry pass also required.*

★ **Seawall Campground** The national park's other campground is on the quieter western half of the island, near the tiny fishing village of Bass Harbor (the island shuttle stops here). Seawall has about 215 sites, and it's a good base for cyclists (this side of the island is nearly traffic-free) or those wishing to take short coastal hikes nearby. But it's a long drive from Bar Harbor's ice cream parlors, souvenir shops, museums, and pizza joints; so, for families traveling with restless kids, it's probably not the best choice. The campground is open mid-May through September, but they do not take reservations. It's first-come, first-served, and lines form early. Note that to reach some sites, you'll need to pack in your tent for a distance of up to 450 feet (137m). There are no electrical or water hookups. *Entrance on Rte. 102A, about 4 miles (6.4km) south of Southwest Harbor.* ☎ *207/244-3600. Sites $14–$20 per night, plus $5 park entry pass.*

A campsite at Acadia National Park's popular Blackwoods Campground.

Best **Ocean Adventures**

Building a boat at The Wooden Boat School 4
Deep-sea fishing in Casco Bay 1
Kayaking Acadia 6
Kayaking the Maine coast 2
Seal and puffin watching Downeast 7
Whale-watching in Acadia 5
Windjamming 3

Since Maine is flanked by a huge ocean split up by numberless bays and inlets, it's not surprising that many of the best adventures here are directly connected to the sea. You can rent a personal watercraft, explore the fishing industry, and even sail off into the glorious sunset on a wooden boat. Here are seven of my favorite ocean adventures.

★ **Building and sailing your own wooden boat.** How cool is this? In Brooklin (on the lovely Blue Hill peninsula), an entire school has been dedicated for more than 30 years to the still-thriving Maine art of building wooden boats. Even the inexperienced can take 1- or 2-week classes in the fundamentals of boat-building and/or seamanship, and return home with sea legs, VHF radio chops, and a knowledge of "lofting" boat plans into finished pieces of wood. Too nervous for all that? There's a duck-decoy carving

class, too. *41 Wooden Boat Lane, Brooklin.* ☎ *207/359-4651. www. thewoodenboatschool.com. Course costs vary; mostly $700–$900.*

Deep-sea fishing in Casco Bay. Maine's fishing grounds are some of the most fertile in the world. Want a piece of that? Pick an outfit with a track record, sturdy boat, and crew of guys tough enough to handle the perfect storm. Portland's **Atlantic Adventures** offers 2-hour, half-day, and full-day tours taking in fish, lobsters, and lighthouses. How tough are these

The Wooden Boat School offers boat-building and seamanship classes.

guys? They've tussled with (and caught) 400-pound (181kg) sharks—multiple times. *Trips depart from 231 Front St., South Portland. ☎ 207/838-9902. www.atlantic adventures.biz. Charters $400–$1,000 plus crew gratuity.*

Kayaking Acadia. Mount Desert Island is more than just hiking and biking. Plenty of summer travelers strap kayaks to their cars and explore inland or coastal waters, though you need some experience before hitting these waves and tides. Tours are run out of Bar Harbor by several outfitters, including Coastal Kayaking, National Park Sea Kayak Tours, and Aquaterra, while crafts can be rented at the town pier. Pack your own lunch. *Coastal Kayaking, 48 Cottage St.; ☎ 800/526-8615 or 207/288-9605; www. acadiafun.com; half-day $48 per person, full-day $72 per person. National Park Sea Kayak Tours, 39 Cottage St.; ☎ 800/347-0940; www. acadiakayak.com; half-day $44–$48 per person, full day $72–$75 per person. Aquaterra Adventures, 1 West St.; ☎ 877/386-4124 or 207/288-0007; www.aquaterra-adventures. com; half-day $45-$55 per person (no full day tours).*

★ **Kayaking the rest of the Maine coast.** The nation's first long-distance ocean trail, the Maine Island Trail, was created in 1987; it's a 375-mile (604km) waterway

Nearly all of the Maine coast can be explored by kayak.

Maine Sea-Life Primer

You might spot some of the following creatures during your travels along the Maine coast:

- **Lobsters:** Sometimes show on the beach or in rocky tide pools. They scour shallow dark waters for food, using a keen sense of smell rather than their eyes. A lobster's hard shell, which it sheds many times in its life, is greenish-black: It turns red only after cooking.
- **Finback whales:** Visit the coast twice a year, migrating between polar and equatorial waters. This is one of the biggest whales in Maine, and one of the most social: It travels in groups (most whales are solitary). As it doesn't like to swim close to shore, you'll need to be on a whale-watching boat to spot it. Look for a triangular head and a fin that sweeps back (like a dolphin's).
- **Humpback whales:** Huge, dark black, and blow lots of water when they surface. They can do incredible acrobatics in the water, and the males sing haunting songs. This whale's population is drastically reduced, though; if you see one in Maine, it's your lucky day.
- **Minke whales:** The smallest, most people-friendly whales in Maine, usually moving in groups of two or three just offshore. It has a habit of approaching boats and ships, making this the whale you're most likely to see. The whale is dark gray. Its black flippers each have bright white bands.
- **Harbor seals:** Related to sea lions. You see them basking in the sun or on the rocks of offshore islands, especially Downeast. These furry, whiskered seals have five claws on each flipper; their necks are thick and strong.
- **Bald eagles:** Live on the coast year-round and even breed in Acadia, though they're shy and difficult to spot. They were nearly wiped out in the 1970s by environmental poisons; now, the birds have begun to recover. Its black body, white head, and yellow bill are unmistakable—no other bird looks like it.

winding from Portland to Machias, incorporating more than 150 islands en route. Members of the **Maine Island Trail Association** can visit and camp on any of these islands for free (though some are closed during seabird nesting seasons). Some of the best stretches include sections in the Stonington/Deer Isle region (lots of islands in a scenic area) and the Muscongus Bay (Bristol-Friendship-Cushing) region in the Mid-coast, which is well sheltered from the ocean sea and possesses some of the prettiest islands on the Trail. Both are ideal places for short, multi-day kayaking trips. Need gear? **Maine Island Kayak** and **Maine Sport Out-fitters** have it. *Maine Island Trail Association,* ☎ *207/761-8225;*

www.mita.org; annual membership $45 adults, $65 families. Maine Island Kayak, Peaks Island; 70 Luther St., Peaks Island; ☎ 207/766-2373; www.maineislandkayak.com. Maine Sport Outfitters, Rockport; 115 Commercial St. (U.S. Rte. 1), Rockport. ☎ 800/722-0826 or 207/236-8797; www.mainesport.com.

★★ **Seal and puffin watching.** If it's seals, seabirds, and puffins you seek, head for the coast of Downeast Maine. Boats here set out for rocky nubs like Machias Seal Island, which boasts no people but thousands of puffins, razorbills, and seals. **Bold Coast Charter** operates cruises out of Cutler's harbor May through August to Machias Seal and Cross Island (another bird-and-wildlife refuge). Bold Coast, Cutler. ☎ 207/259-4484. www.boldcoast.com. Cruises $80 adults, $45 children. Closed Sept–Apr.

★★ **Whale-watching in Acadia.** Bar Harbor is a great place to catch a whale-watching boat. You can see breaching humpbacks, finbacks, little minkes, even (infrequently) the endangered right whale. **Bar Harbor Whale Watching** offers a money-back guarantee that you'll see whales on the 2- to 3-hour tours, which run from late May through late October. 1 West St., Bar Harbor. ☎ 888/942-5374 or 207/288-2386. www.barharbor whales.com. Cruises $27–$56 adults, $16–$28 kids 6–14. Closed late Oct to late May.

★★ **Windjamming.** They don't call it "sailing" up here when you're on a schooner or tall ship: They call it "windjamming," and it brings a full slate of festivals and races during summer. Many windjammers will let you take a day sail or even rent out a boat for an overnight on the water, too. For more info about boats and captains, contact the well-coordinated **Maine Windjammer Association.** 251 Jefferson St., Waldoboro. ☎ 800/807-9463. www. sailmainecoast.com.

Several different species of whales can be seen on boat tours in Acadia National Park.

Maine Coast's Best **Golfing**

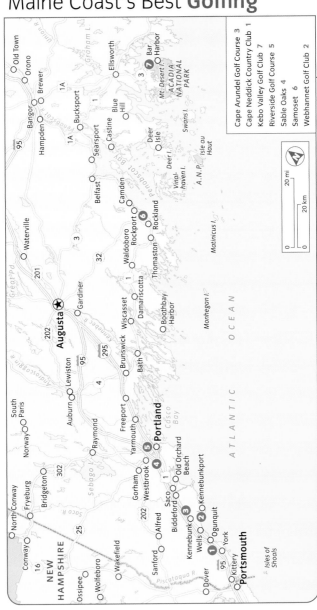

Cape Arundel Golf Course 3
Cape Neddick Country Club 1
Kebo Valley Golf Club 7
Riverside Golf Course 5
Sable Oaks 4
Samoset 6
Webhannet Golf Club 2

Maine's tourism office has come up with a "Maine Golf Trail," but many of this coast's most beautiful courses (in places like Rockport, Falmouth, and Cape Elizabeth) are completely closed to non-members. Fortunately, you can still play a very scenic round of golf—and test your skills—at these seven public and semi-private courses.

The Kebo Valley Golf Club is one of the oldest courses in the United States.

★ Cape Arundel Golf Course
Founded in 1896, this Kennebunkport course is so short that it barely qualifies as a "real" golf course. Yet it's mildly scenic, and the ex-presidents Bush (and their famous friends) like to tee it up here from time to time—George, Sr., is still a member, and his father once held the course record. Also fun: Babe Ruth once played the course. *1447 Old River Rd., Kennebunkport.* ☎ *207/967-3494. www.capearundelgolfclub.com. 18 holes $45–$65. No jeans.*

★★ Cape Neddick Country Club
This Donald Ross–designed (1872–1948) course doesn't show up on the radar, but it's convenient to several resorts and beaches (as well as Ogunquit), occupies a lovely piece of coastal forest land, and often gets misty-valleyed early in the morning or late in the day. Originally designed as an 18-hole track, the course cut back to 9 for the longest time. But in 1997, the full layout was restored. *650 Shore Rd., Ogunquit.* ☎ *207/361-2011. www.capeneddickgolf.com. 18 holes $50–$65; cart optional. No jeans.*

★★★ Kebo Valley Golf Club
The Kebo Valley course, just outside Bar Harbor, can legitimately claim to be one of the oldest golf courses in North America: Some form of it has been operating here since 1888, and it's a beauty. (*Golf Digest* awarded it four stars.) There was once both a casino and a horse-racing track near the 4th hole, but those are long gone—the view of the hills of Acadia is the star. *136 Eagle Lake Rd., Bar Harbor.* ☎ *207/288-3000. www.kebovalleyclub.com. 18 holes $49–$99.*

★★ Riverside Golf Course
As city public courses go, Portland's is not half-bad; in fact, it's pretty good if you can handle the occasional rough patches in the drapery. There are actually two courses—the longer North Course, where hard-core golfers tee it up, and a more casual South Course (with 9 holes), where duffers hack away. I actually think the

The Great Outdoors

Teeing off at Riverside Golf Course.

South layout is more attractive. The driving range across the road is quiet and handy, too. *1158 Riverside St., Portland.* ☎ *207/797-3524. www. ci.portland.me.us/riverside/riverside. asp. 18 holes North Course $22–$36, South Course $22–$30.*

★★ **Sable Oaks** The location, near several malls, hotels, an inter-state highway, and an airport, doesn't seem at all promising at first glance. Yet the architects—it was co-designed by famed course architect Geoffrey Cornish—have done wonders to reclaim this high patch of greenery from the urban sprawl. Today, it's a pleasing 18 that rambles past stone walls and around little bodies of water. Birds often pass through, too. *505 Country Club Dr., South Portland.*

☎ *207/775-6257. www.sableoaks. com. 18 holes $35–$45.*

★★★ **Samoset** With six holes lit-erally bordering the lapping edge of Penobscot Bay (don't shank one here), the golf course at the Samoset Resort (p 134) is unquestionably the state's most scenic and best. It's got history (it dates from back in 1902) and difficulty—things become quite challenging once you combine the deceptive up-and-downs with the shifting sea breezes. There's a golf school here, as well. This is a champi-onship-caliber course, and it gets busy in peak season; serious golfers will want to play it at least once, so reserve ahead. *220 Warrenton St., Rockport.* ☎ *207/594-1431. www. samoset.com. 18 holes $70–$130 (cart required & included).*

★ **Webhannet Golf Club** This Kennebunk Beach course is rather flat and a tad uninspiring, but it's longer than many resort courses in Maine and just a few short blocks from the sea. When it was founded very early in the 20th century, mem-bers hit through a cow pasture and pinch-shaped tees from the clay-like soil, then gathered in a dining room for steaks and drinks afterward. *26 Golf Club Dr., Kennebunk.* ☎ *207/ 967-2061. www.webhannetgolfclub. com. 18 holes $58–$65.* ●

The challenging and picturesque Samoset caters to serious golfers.

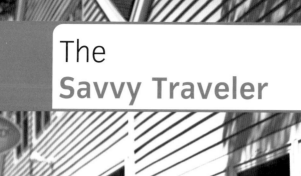

The
Savvy Traveler

Before You Go

Government Tourist Offices

The Maine Office of Tourism (59 State House Station, Augusta, ME 04333; ☎ 888/624-6345 or 207/287-5711; www.visitmaine.com) should be your first call. Nearly all the towns and cities described in this book—except tiny Downeast villages, which maintain a regional office, instead—also operate local tourism offices, often through the local chamber of commerce.

The Best Time to Go

Maine has four distinct seasons. The peak summer season is best for travelers, of course, thanks to the long hours of daylight and mild temperatures. Maine's summer runs from late June through about Labor Day, and crowds surge up the Maine coast during this time. Expect premium prices at hotels throughout the short summer season, since innkeepers need to make the bulk of their annual income during what amounts to a 3-month window.

The off-seasons can be even more wonderful here, especially early autumn. The combination of thinner crowds, colorful foliage, and gorgeous fall weather makes this a perfect time to come—and prices are generally a good deal lower than they are in summer.

Fall foliage season is a wonderful annual spectacle, as the rolling hills of Acadia go ablaze with orange and the cranberry bogs of Downeast Maine turn bright scarlet. It's not to be missed. (Lodging rates kick briefly back up, however.) Thanks to Maine's low elevation and the moderating influences of the ocean, foliage tends to last longer along the coast than it does inland. Sometimes the colors even linger into

early November. Maine maintains a recorded foliage hot line (☎ 888/624-6345; www.mainefoliage.com) to let you know where and when the leaves are brightest.

Winter and spring are not as ideal for visiting the Maine coast. Beach towns and many inns and attractions shut down almost entirely. There are some winter sports options—tobogganing, downhill and cross-country skiing, ice skating on a pond—but the weather is unreliable and sometimes downright ornery. If you're still coming, Portland is a better bet: Its cultural attractions run year-round.

Spring brings deep discounts to lodging, but the weather can be cold and muddy, or warm and wonderful; it's a gamble.

Festivals & Special Events

SPRING Spring is a pretty slow time in Maine, as locals and tourists alike slowly decompress from winter; many inns, restaurants, and attractions don't even open until late May. Still, there are a few distractions, even during this slowest of tourist seasons. Two of the best are the **Boothbay Harbor Fisherman's Festival** (☎ 207/633-2353) in late April, with shucking and cutting demonstrations and plenty of seafood, and Portland's long-running **Old Port Festival** (☎ 207/772-6828) in early June: a sort of outdoor neighborhood block party that serves as the unofficial kickoff to summer for Portlanders.

SUMMER The **Fourth of July** (also known in America as Independence Day) is a big deal throughout the coastal region of Maine, but especially so in Portland, where big fireworks are shot off from the Eastern

Previous page: Winding trails and scenic carriage roads make bikes a great option for getting around.

Promenade. Get to the park very early if you want a good seat—or even a seat at all. Then, way Downeast, Eastport does Portland one better: It takes a full *four* days to celebrate the nation's birth, including fireworks, road and sailboat races, Coast Guard cutters, hypnotists, watermelon- and blueberry pie–eating contests, bingo, a barbecue, and (of course) a parade. As the holiday approaches, you can view a schedule of the events and live music performances at the website **www.eastport4th.com.** Finally, for a Fourth of July of a whole other kind, head for the Downeast fishing village of Jonesport, where the annual **Moosabec Lobster Boat Races** (☎ 207/598-6681) bring out the competitive beast in local fishermen and their powerful fishing boats.

Other good festivals along the coast during the summer include **York Days** in York (☎ 207/363-1040), in late July; the popular **Maine Lobster Festival** (☎ 800/562-2529; www.mainelobsterfestival.com) in Rockland, in early August (which features more butter and bibs that you've ever seen in your life in one place); and the wonderful **Wild Blueberry Festival** (☎ 207/255-4402 or 207/255-6665; www.machias blueberry.com) in Machias a few weeks later, a 3-day series of pie-baking and -eating contests accompanied by quilting bees, a fish fry, footraces, and light musical comedy.

The summer concludes with one of my favorite events in the whole state, the Labor Day weekend **Blue Hill Fair** (☎ 207/374-3701; www.bluehillfair.com) in Blue Hill. It's a 4-day combination agricultural and livestock fair, farmer's market, and cotton-candy-and-fried-dough fest in big fairgrounds near the eponymous hill. The event always includes live country music from a surprisingly big star.

FALL   Things don't stop in Maine when summer ends, though. If anything, festivals get their second wind as tourists dwindle and locals come back out of the woodwork and let their hair down. Camden's **Windjammer Weekend** (☎ 207/236-4404; www.windjammerweekend.com) is a quiet yet impressive gathering of tall old-time sailing ships, for instance, and there's an extremely scenic **marathon** (☎ 207/276-4226) held on Mount Desert Island. Some coastal towns put on some form of a **foliage festival** (or, at least, a single event) to celebrate the annual coming of the bright leaves in mid- or late October. Finally, just when things are threatening to get downright chilly and depressing, Ogunquit throws the late-October **OgunquitFest** (☎ 207/646-2939) over a 3-day period right before Halloween.

WINTER   The pre-Christmas season brings plenty of festivals to the Maine coast, too. Some of the best include the annual **Festival of Lights** (☎ 207/596-0376) in Rockland and a series of holiday-themed events inside the **Victoria Mansion** (☎ 207/772-6828; www.victoria mansion.org) in Portland. But for sheer Maine-ness, it's hard to beat the fun, old-timey **Christmas Prelude** (☎ 207/967-0857; www.christmasprelude.com) in Kennebunkport (Santa arrives in a lobster boat). Nearby, York Village hosts its own **Festival of Lights** (☎ 207/363-4974) a bit later in December.

After the holidays, look for the **U.S. National Toboggan Championships** (☎ 207/236-3438; www.camdensnowbowl.com) at Camden's Snow Bowl ski hill in February:

a slightly rowdy winter carnival of the best kind. As the snows melt away, the **Maine Boatbuilders' Show** (☎ 207/774-1067; www.portlandcompany.com/boatshow) comes to a Portland exposition space, usually in mid-March, to remind us all that summer *will* actually return soon.

The Weather

Being on the coast means dealing with weather on a regular basis. The Atlantic tends to bring lots of moisture and wind ashore—fast—so things tend to happen (or change) dramatically here: Snow or rain can come ashore suddenly, in sheets and buckets, with horizontal winds. Winter storms sometimes wash waves up over the beach and across access roads or parking lots above, tossing boulders and lobster traps in the process. Hurricanes have been known to graze the Maine coast. (On the other hand, the ocean also serves as a sort of natural air-conditioner during the hottest, most humid dog days of summer: Walk to water's edge, and you'll almost certainly feel cooling breezes wafting off it.)

Spring isn't much to talk about along this coast—it's chilly, late to arrive, and sometimes soggy. But summer here is exquisite: not too hot and not too cold. Summer brings long, long days and a wonderfully misty light suffusing early morning, late afternoon, and early evening with a unique glow that legions of artists have made pilgrimages here to paint. (Some of them never left.) It's often warmest or hottest on this coastline late in the morning, until "sea breezes" kick up daily (usually around lunchtime), pushing seaside temperatures back down for the rest of the day. Sometimes a soupy fog rolls in during the afternoon, too, on very hot or very humid days (this can also happen on a warm winter day). On average, at least 1 day in 3 will bring either a sprinkle or a soaking rain, so summer travelers to the coast are wise to come prepared with board games, shopping plans, and rain gear, just in case.

Autumn is one of the best times to visit the Maine coast. The crowds are gone, but the ocean and beaches are still here. The weather improves considerably at this point—in a typical year, it doesn't rain or fog up much at all once the heat of summer has broken—and the first blushes of fall color are sometimes visible even as early as September. Winter? I'd give it a pass most years. Coastal winters tend to be more slushy, rainy, sleety, and icy than deep-white-powdery.

PORTLAND'S AVERAGE TEMPERATURES

	JAN	FEB	MAR	APR	MAY	JUNE
Avg. High (°F)	31	32	40	50	61	72
(°C)	−1	0	4	10	16	22
Avg. Low (°F)	16	16	27	36	47	54
(°C)	−9	−9	−3	2	8	12

	JULY	AUG	SEPT	OCT	NOV	DEC
Avg. High (°F)	76	74	68	58	45	34
(°C)	24	23	20	14	7	1
Avg. Low (°F)	61	59	52	43	32	22
(°C)	16	15	11	6	0	-6

Useful Websites

- **www.pressherald.com:** *Portland Press Herald*, Maine's largest newspaper
- **www.maine.gov:** Maine state government website
- **www.nps.gov/acad:** Acadia National Park
- **www.visitmaine.com:** Maine Office of Tourism
- **www.campmaine.com:** Maine Campground Owners Association
- **www.downeast.com:** *Down East* magazine

Cell (Mobile) Phones
The U.S. AT&T and Verizon networks covers most (though not all) of coastal Maine, usually without incurring roaming charges. T-Mobile, Sprint, and Nextel are notably weaker in coverage. Foreign cellphones may or may not work here due to the poorly developed GSM network; they will probably work on the southern Maine coast, but probably not on the rest of the coast. Foreign phones may or may not be able to use SMS to send text messages.

Getting **There**

By Plane
Portland International Jetport (airport code: PWM) is Maine's largest airport. The airport is served by airlines including JetBlue (☎ 800/538-2583; www.jetblue.com), Continental (☎ 800/525-0280; www.continental. com), Northwest (☎ 800/225-2525; www.nwa.com), United Express (☎ 800/241-6522; www.ual.com), and US Airways (☎ 800/428-4322; www.usair.com). For general airport information, call ☎ 207/874-8877 or see www.portlandjetport.org.

Some regular travelers to Maine fly into Boston's Logan Airport, then rent a car and drive north. (Boston is about 2 hr. by car from Portland, 5 hr. from Bar Harbor.) Almost every major airline in the U.S. (and many others worldwide) flies into Boston daily, so the fare competition can result in a better ticket price.

Remember that Boston's airport can become congested, especially at check-in and security; delayed flights are common; and traffic can snarl. But the fare savings can be large.

When researching fares, also check flights going into Manchester Airport (airport code: MHT) in New Hampshire, a regional hub for Southwest Airlines (☎ 800/435-9792; www.southwest.com). The airport is less than 2 hours from Portland by car, and you can sometimes find deep discounts on routes from Southwest hub cities such as Chicago, Dallas, Orlando, Los Angeles, Houston, and Baltimore-Washington.

Finally, if you need a quick connection directly to Midcoast Maine, check with Cape Air (☎ 800/352-0714 or 866/227-3247; www.cape air.com). This big regional airline operates two to seven daily flights from Boston to the Knox County Regional Airport (airport code: RKD) in the lovely Camden-Rockland region, using small nine-seat twin-engine business jets. If you book well ahead and choose off-peak dates and hours, a round-trip fare from Boston can cost as little as $120 per person. There's even a Budget (☎ 888/594-0822 or 207/594-0822; www.budget.com) auto rental kiosk at the little airport, open daily 8:30am until 5pm (except Sundays, when it opens at 11am).

By Car
From Boston, New York, and points farther beyond, Interstate 95 (I-95) is by far the quickest way to get to the coast of Maine. Note that I-95 is a toll road for stretches through New Hampshire, New Jersey, Delaware, and Maryland—you'll need to pay cash at the tollgate, or go through an "E-ZPass" lane with an electric transponder subscribed to the network. The Maine Turnpike is also a toll road for long stretches, and it also accepts the E-ZPass. To reach Portland, exit the Turnpike at Exit 44 and follow I-295 (a free highway) into the city, then exit for the waterfront (Exit 4) and follow Commercial Street to reach the Old Port and waterfront. To get to Midcoast or Downeast Maine, follow the directions to Portland above, but continue north about half an hour past Portland, then exit onto U.S. Route 1 North.

Road maps can sometimes be deceptive, so keep in mind that Maine is much bigger than it looks on a one-page road map. Budget time for driving accordingly. I have noted driving distances or driving times in this book wherever possible, but a good rule of thumb to follow is that 50 miles (80km) of rural driving takes about 1 hour if there's little traffic. (In summer, passing through a string of busy towns, it might take up to twice that long.) Gasoline in the U.S. is sold in gallons: One gallon is equal to 3.8 liters or 0.85 imperial gallons. Gas in Maine is a bit more expensive than it is in some other parts of the U.S., but still much cheaper than it is in Canada, Europe, Asia, and Australia.

By Train
Amtrak's Downeaster service (☎ 800/872-7245; www.amtrak.com) runs five trains daily between Boston's North Station and Portland. (If you're connecting by train, you'll need to change stations in Boston from South to North—at least a 20-minute taxi or subway ride.) The train stops in Wells (7 miles/11km from Ogunquit), Saco, and Old Orchard Beach before arriving in Portland. Travel time is 2½ hours, and one-way tickets cost $24. Bikes are allowed.

AAA members in the U.S. get a 10% discount on tickets booked at least 3 days in advance (bring your membership card to the station).

Getting **Around**

Mark my words: you'll need a car. Portland's airport (see above) has plenty of rental options. Among the outfits at the terminal are Alamo (☎ 877/222-9075 or 207/775-0855;

www.alamo.com), AVIS (☎ 800/331-1212 or 207/874-7500; www.avis.com), Budget (☎ 800/527-0700 or 207/772-6789; www.budget.com); Enterprise (☎ 800/261-7331 or 207/615-0030; www.enterprise.com), Hertz (☎ 800/654-3131 or 207/774-4544; www.hertz.com), and National (☎ 877/222-9058 or 207/773-0036; www.nationalcar.com).

I've tried to lay out the driving directions to every point mentioned in this book, but there are dozens more peninsulas, points, and villages I couldn't include in these tours due to space limitations. To find some of those, get your hands on a copy of the wonderful Maine Atlas and Gazetteer (☎ 800/642-0970 or 800/561-5105; www.delorme.com), an oversized book of detailed grid maps of the state. With its close-ups of everything from hill contours and historic attractions to hiking trails and even individual boat launches, it's a handy companion. Pick it up at local bookstores, convenience stores, gas stations, or the company headquarters in Yarmouth.

Traffic in Maine is very light compared with that in urban and suburban areas of the East Coast, but the Maine Turnpike and U.S. Route 1 are a couple of notable exceptions during summer weekends. Expect heavy delays at those times and try to travel off-peak if at all possible; mid-week traffic is vastly different from that entering Maine on a Friday evening or departing it on a Sunday night. For what are promised to be live, real-time updates of weather, accidents, and traffic conditions on the state's roads and highways, also check out the website Maine 511 at www.511maine.gov; it's maintained by the Maine Department of Transportation.

Fast **Facts**

ATMS   You will find ATMs (automated teller machines) everywhere in Maine—even on Monhegan Island. Memorize your personal identification number (PIN) and daily withdrawal limit before you get to the machine. Most banks and independent ATMs impose a fee each time you use an ATM to withdraw money, unless it's an ATM with your own bank's name on it; that fee usually starts at $2 (though some banks charge no fee). Ask your bank before traveling. Your bank may also charge a fee (usually about $5) if you are using a bank based outside of the United States.

BANKING HOURS   Bank lobbies on the Maine coast are generally open Monday to Friday, 9am to 3pm; drive-in tellers are usually open 1 to 2 hours later. In places like Portland and York, you can find Saturday banking hours, but it's pretty uncommon in Maine. Sunday, all banks are closed.

BED & BREAKFASTS AND COTTAGE RENTALS   Nearly every town in coastal Maine has at least one simple B&B, though in very rural stretches, this can mean sharing a bathroom and/or sleeping above the owners' own bedroom. For a nicer house or cottage, though, prices are steep: Expect to pay anywhere from $1,500 to $5,000 per week in peak summer season. Local tourist offices can sometimes tell you about local cottage-rental agencies offering discounts and personalized service.

BUSINESS HOURS   Shops in Maine are usually open weekdays from 9am to 6pm, Saturdays from 10am until 5pm to 7pm, and Sundays from noon until 5pm or 6pm. But in bigger cities like Portland, and in shopping-mall and outlet-shop areas, shops stay open as late as 9pm during peak shopping days and/or seasons.

CONSULATES & EMBASSIES All embassies are located in the U.S. capital, Washington, D.C. Most nations have a consulate in New York City, a 90-minute flight or 5-hour drive away, but the United Kingdom and Ireland also have consulates in Boston (a 2-hr. drive from Portland). The **British Consulate** is at 1 Broadway in Cambridge (☎ 617/245-4500) on the campus of MIT. The **Irish Consulate** is on the 5th floor of 535 Boylston St. (☎ 617/267-9330), near Boston's Copley Square. The **Canadian Consulate** (☎ 212/596-1628) is in New York City (at 1251 Avenue of the Americas/6th Ave.), as are the **Australian Consulate** (150 E. 42nd St., 34th floor; ☎ 212/351-6600) and the **New Zealand Consulate** (222 E. 41st St., Suite #2510; ☎ 212/832-4038).

CREDIT CARDS Credit cards are widely accepted in Maine, and you *must* use one to rent a car or hold a hotel room in advance. Most businesses take **Visa** (Barclaycard in Britain) and **MasterCard** (Eurocard in Europe, Access in Britain). Fewer take **American Express,** and fewer still accept **Diners Club** or **Discover.** A handful of establishments here—fast-food eateries, simple B&Bs—do not take *any* credit cards. Foreign travelers to Maine may incur an extra fee on credit card charges made abroad (usually 1% to 3%).

DENTISTS Dentists are readily available in Maine, but often fully booked weeks in advance. In an emergency, they will fit you in if possible, but they may simply not have enough staff. Your best bet for getting seen quickly is in Portland, at one of the city's many dental clinics; or check

the "Yellow Pages" of a local phone book.

DOCTORS All large and small cities in northern New England maintain good hospitals, and some smaller towns have them, too. The quality of service is very good. If health is a serious issue for you, check ahead with your accommodations (or consult the phone book when you arrive) about the nearest emergency-room service or 24-hour clinic.

The largest hospital is **Maine Medical Center** (☎ 207/662-0111; www.mmc.org) at 22 Bramhall St. in Portland. There's also **Mercy Hospital** (☎ 207/879-3000; www.mercyhospital.org), a Catholic-run hospital nearby at 144 State St.; both are excellent. Smaller hospitals are located in York, Biddeford, Brunswick, Damariscotta, Ellsworth, Bar Harbor, and Machias, among other coastal towns. North of Camden, however, they thin out dramatically—you may need to visit a clinic, instead.

ELECTRICITY All plugs in Maine use 110 to 120 volts AC (60 cycles), the same as in Canada but different from the 220 to 240 volts AC (50 cycles) used in most of Europe, Australia, and New Zealand. Converters are almost impossible to find in Maine, so bring one if you will need one.

EMBASSIES See "Consulates & Embassies," above.

EMERGENCIES For fire, police, and ambulance, find any phone and dial ☎ 911. If this fails, dial ☎ 0 (zero) and report an emergency.

EVENT LISTINGS The *Portland Press Herald* is Portland's daily newspaper, with decent listings; the free *Portland Phoenix* is also very handy for listings of concerts, shows at local clubs, and art shows.

GAY & LESBIAN TRAVELERS In general, coastal Maine is welcoming to gay and lesbian travelers. Ogunquit, on the southern coast, is a hugely popular destination for gay travelers and features a lively beach and bar scene in summer. See the website **www.gayogunquit.com**, which has good information on gay-owned inns, restaurants, and shops in town. Portland, as the state's largest city, is also a hub for gay and lesbian culture, with several clubs and bars geared toward that clientele.

INSURANCE **Medical Insurance:** Although it's not required of travelers, health insurance is always a good idea. Many health insurance policies cover you if you get sick away from home—but check your coverage before you travel to be sure.

International visitors to the U.S. should note that the United States does *not* offer free or low-cost medical care to either citizens or visitors. Doctors and hospitals are relatively expensive and sometimes require advance payment or proof of coverage before they even treat you.

Canadians should check with their provincial health plan offices or contact **Health Canada** (www.hc-sc.gc.ca) to learn about their coverage and what documentation and receipts they will need to get in case they are treated in Maine.

British travelers should carry their European Health Insurance Cards (www.ehic.org.uk). Note, however, that an EHIC covers "necessary medical treatment" only, not return flights, lost wages, baggage, or trip-cancellation costs. If purchasing medical or travel insurance, check out **The Association of British Insurers** (☎ 020/7600-3333; www.abi.org.uk); they give advice by phone and publish *Holiday Insurance,* a free guide to policy provisions and prices.

Travel Insurance: If you don't have health insurance, it's smart to buy a temporary travel insurance policy for the length of your trip. It isn't usually expensive; the premium is determined by the length of your trip, where you're going, and how much you think you'll spend on the trip. There are any number of providers, of which I can recommend **Travel Guard** (☎ 800/826-4919; www.travelguard.com) because I have used it more than once, and customer service was exemplary.

Trip-Cancellation Insurance: Trip-cancellation insurance is a way to get a refund when you must cancel a trip or cut it short, or your travel supplier goes bankrupt and cancels it for you. Of course, it's a gamble; chances are, you'll never use it. This insurance usually covers such events as sudden illness and natural disasters. You won't get back *all* of a prepaid trip's cost, of course—but you might recover a substantial portion. Again, there are many providers; recommended insurers include **Access America** (☎ 866/807-3982; www.accessamerica.com), **Travel Guard International** (☎ 800/826-4919; www.travelguard.com), **Travel Insured International** (☎ 800/243-3174; www.travelinsured.com), and **Travelex Insurance Services** (☎ 888/457-4602; www.travelex-insurance.com).

INTERNET ACCESS Many of Maine's public libraries maintain computer terminals with free public Internet access, enabling travelers to check e-mail on the fly. An increasing number of Maine inns and hotels offer free Wi-Fi with your stay; ask when booking or checking in. Internet cafes come and go, but any reasonably hip coffee shop on the coast is also likely to have free Wi-Fi.

LOST PROPERTY Most bus and train stations, stores, and hotels keep lost items. Ask for "lost and found." If your credit card disappears or is stolen, contact your credit card companies immediately. (If theft was involved, also call police and get a printed police report.) Visa's emergency number is ☎ 800/847-2911, MasterCard's is ☎ 800/307-7309, and American Express is at ☎ 800/221-7282. If your baggage is lost on your flight, immediately file a lost-luggage claim at the airport, detailing the luggage contents. For most airlines, you must report delayed, damaged, or lost baggage within 4 hours of arrival. The airlines are required to deliver luggage, once found, directly to your house or destination free of charge.

MAIL & POSTAGE Every town and city in Maine has a post office—in the smallest towns, it may double as a grocer or other business. At press time, domestic letters cost 44¢ (up to 1 oz./28g) and postcards cost 28¢. International rates are always higher. For more information on rates, visit **www.usps.com**.

MONEY Always carry some cash in medium and small bills for small items, tips, and establishments that don't accept any credit cards. Be prepared for a bit of sticker shock during summer: Even motels might charge $100 a night or more for a simple room during high summer season. But other daily expenses, including dining, are quite reasonable—in fact, you can dine extremely well on a budget here.

PASSPORTS If you're a foreign traveler, *always* make a backup copy of your passport's first page and keep it somewhere safe; if you lose your passport, this will be invaluable. Keep your passport numbers and your embassy and consulate phone numbers, too.

For Residents of Australia: You can pick up an application from your local post office or any branch of Passports Australia, but you must schedule an interview at the passport office to present your application materials. Call the **Australian**

Passport Information Service at ☎ 131-232 or visit the government website at www.passports.gov.au.

For Residents of Canada: Passport applications are available at travel agencies throughout Canada or from the central **Passport Office,** Department of Foreign Affairs and International Trade, Gatineau, QCK1A 0G3 (☎ 800/567-6868; www.ppt.gc.ca). Canadian children who travel must have their own passports.

For Residents of Ireland: You can apply for a 10-year passport at the **Passport Office,** Setanta Centre, Molesworth Street, Dublin 2 (☎ 01/671-1633; www.foreign affairs.gov.ie). Those under age 18 and over age 65 must apply for a 3-year passport. You can also apply at 1A South Mall, Cork (☎ 021/494-4700) or at most main post offices.

For Residents of New Zealand: You can pick up a passport application at any New Zealand Passports Office or download it from their website. Contact the **Passports Office** at ☎ 0800/225-050 (in New Zealand) or 04/474-8100, or log on to www.dia.govt.nz.

For Residents of the United Kingdom: To pick up an application for a standard 10-year passport (5-yr. passport for children under age 16), visit your nearest passport office, major post office, or travel agency, or contact the **United Kingdom Passport Service** (☎ 0300/222-0000; www.ips.gov.uk).

PHARMACIES All cities and most towns in coastal Maine have at least one pharmacy; ask your hotel receptionist or check the phone book. Most chain grocery stores in Maine include good in-store pharmacies with late hours. **CVS** (www.cvs.com), **Rite Aid** (www.riteaid.com), and **Walmart** (www.walmart.com) also operate a large number of pharmacies in the state. You won't find any 24-hour pharmacies here.

SAFETY Maine boasts some of the lowest crime rates in the U.S. The odds of anything bad happening are slim. But travelers should still take all the usual precautions against theft, robbery, and assault when on the road: Avoid unnecessary public displays of wealth, and store laptops and valuables securely in hotel safes or safe-deposit boxes if they're available (small inns won't have them).

When traveling at night, gas up and use restrooms in well-lit, busy areas. Don't leave anything in plain view in the seats of your car and lock valuables in the trunk. If you have an electronic security system, use it.

Finally, when traveling on a boat, always wear life vests or other provided safety gear. Also, bring warm, dry clothing in your bag—pants, a sweater—even for a sunny summer cruise; a warm day at sea can turn windy, chilly, or worse fast.

SENIOR TRAVELERS Maine is well suited to older travelers. Senior travelers usually get reduced or free admission to theaters, museums, ski resorts, and other attractions, plus discounted fares on public transit.

The National Park Service's **America the Beautiful Senior Pass** (☎ 888/275-8747; www.nps. gov/fees_passes.htm) gives seniors 62 years or older lifetime entrance to properties administered by the Service—including Acadia National Park, federal historic sites, and wildlife refuges—for a one-time $10 fee. The pass must be acquired in person at an NPS facility. It also grants a 50% discount on some camping, swimming, parking, boat launching, and tour fees. Members of **AARP** (☎ 888/687-2277; www.aarp.org) also get discounts on some hotels, tours, and auto rentals.

SPECTATOR SPORTS Two semi-pro teams play in Portland. The **Portland Sea Dogs** are a Double-A baseball team affiliated with the Boston Red Sox; they play from April through Labor Day at Hadlock Field (217 Park Ave.; ☎ 800/936-3647; www.seadogs.com), a small stadium near downtown that makes for a fine family outing. The **Portland Pirates** (☎ 207/828-4665; www.portlandpirates.com) play AHL hockey at the Cumberland County Civic Center between Spring Street and Free Street from early October until mid-April; they are affiliated with the NHL's Buffalo Sabres.

TAXIS Outside of Portland, you'll be hard-pressed to find a taxi quickly, though small towns sometimes have a local service (check the phone book).

TELEPHONE The area code for Maine is **207**. To make even a local call within Maine, you need to dial this 207 before dialing the 7-digit number. (From within a hotel room, you must also often dial 9 first.) For directory assistance ("information"), dial ☎ **411;** for longer-distance information, dial 1+area code+ 555-1212.

TIPPING If service is good, tip bellhops $1 or more per bag ($2–$3 for a lot of luggage) and maids a few dollars per day (more if you have a large suite). Tip a doorman or concierge if some specific service was performed (calling a cab, booking theater tickets). Tip valet-parking attendants at your hotel $1 to $5 each time you get your car. In restaurants, bars, and nightclubs, tip servers 15% to 20% of the bill (pretax), tip bartenders 10% to 15%, tip coatroom attendants $1 per garment, and tip valet-parking attendants $1 per car. Tip cabbies 15% of your fare, tip skycaps at airports $1 per bag ($2–$3 if you have a lot of bags), and tip hairdressers and barbers 15% to 20%.

TOILETS   In coastal Maine, they're called bathrooms or restrooms. Find them in hotel lobbies, bars, coffee shops, restaurants, fast-food places, museums, department stores, train stations, and some gas stations. (Sometimes, you will need to ask the cashier for a key or make a purchase first.)

TRAVELERS WITH DISABILITIES   The **America the Beautiful Access Pass** (☎ 888/275-8747; www.nps. gov/fees_passes.htm) gives visually impaired and permanently disabled travelers free lifetime entrance to sites administered by the National Park Service and other federal agencies, including Acadia National Park. The pass must be obtained in person at a federal site, and you must show proof of a medically determined disability. All passengers in a pass-holder's vehicle also enter parks free; the pass also gets the holder a 50% discount on some camping, swimming, parking, and tour fees.

Note that many of Maine's coastal towns still use stairs as the primary means of passage, rather than elevators or escalators.

The Maine Coast: A Brief History

16,000 BC A mile-high (1.6km) pile of ice begins receding from the coast, scratching the tops of mountains and depositing boulders and silt.

6500 BC–1000 BC Native American peoples arrive in successive waves and populate sections of the Maine coast; all eventually disappear.

1400 A native population of 20,000 occupies the coast in two bands: the Alonqquin/Armouchiquois (southern Maine) and the Passamaquoddy (Midcoast and Downeast Maine). They sometimes fight each other.

1497 Italian explorer John Cabot, seeking to establish trade for England, sails along the Maine coast.

1604 Explorer Samuel de Champlain sights Mount Desert Island. French colonists settle Downeast on the St. Croix River but soon leave.

1614 Captain John Smith maps the New England coast and calls the area "paradise."

1616–1619 A smallpox epidemic kills as many as 95% of the coast's native population.

1620 The *Mayflower,* carrying 100 colonists, arrives in Massachusetts from England. Colonists begin filtering north into Maine almost immediately.

1624 York Village is settled, the first organized community in the territories that will eventually become Maine.

1775 British ships fire shells on Portland in an attempt to quell revolutionaries. It doesn't work.

1791 Portland Head Light, commissioned by U.S. President George Washington (1732–1799), opens.

1820 Maine, once part of Massachusetts, becomes a state. Statehood papers are signed in Freeport.

1842 A treaty with England finally establishes Maine's contentious northeastern border with Canada.

1844 Artist Thomas Cole (1801–1848) begins painting Mount Desert Island. Summer tourists begin pouring into the region to see the sights he has painted.

1866 A fire sparked by July 4th fireworks levels most of downtown Portland.

1915–1933 Oil magnate John D. Rockefeller, Jr., (1874–1960) finances the construction of 57 miles (92km) of carriage roads on Mount Desert Island.

1919 Acadia National Park (at first called Lafayette National Park) is established. Rockefeller's gift to it totals 11,000 acres (4,452 hectares) of land.

1947 A forest fire burns much of Acadia National Park and Mount Desert Island's trees and buildings.

1972 Maine's Native Americans sue the state, claiming it illegally seized their land in violation of a 1790 treaty. They settle in 1980 for $82 million.

1980s A real-estate bubble hits Portland, creating significant waterfront development. Within a decade, the bubble bursts.

2001 Two terrorists depart Portland International Jetport on a commuter flight to Boston, where they change planes—and change history.

2004 The Boston Red Sox win the World Series, ending 86 years of frustration and triggering wild celebrations from Kittery to Eastport.

2007 Russian President Vladimir Putin (1952–) arrives in Kennebunkport to fish with President George W. Bush (1946–) and ex-President George H.W. Bush (1924–). Anti-war protesters march on the Bush estate.

Eating & Drinking on the Maine Coast

Eating and drinking in Maine is one of the region's signal pleasures.

Lobsters are the star attraction, of course. Live lobsters can be purchased right off the boat at many lobster pounds, or you can buy boiled lobsters with side dishes of corn on the cob or steamed clams. (See my special "Lobsters & Lighthouses" tour on p 40 for some of my favorite lobster shacks.) Wear a bib if you value your clothing.

Lobster rolls are a wonderful permutation of the crustacean:

fresh meat plucked from the shell, mixed with a little mayonnaise, and stuffed inside a hot-dog roll (preferably grilled in butter). Some versions add celery, onions, even gourmet bread; ignore those. You'll find these rolls almost everywhere along the Maine coast. Expect to pay between $9 and $15 per roll (more in lean lobster-harvest years).

Fish is fresh and good everywhere on the Maine coast, as is the chowder: the day's catch of cod or haddock, plus lots of milk, potatoes, and butter. You can also find clam and lobster versions, but I prefer fish chowder. Add plenty of salt and pepper to taste. (If a diner adds thickener, cornstarch, or flour to its chowder, though, walk on by.)

Blueberries are grown and harvested in many coastal towns as you get north of Ellsworth. Look for roadside stands and diners advertising pies made with fresh berries in mid- to late summer. As a bonus, tiny wild blueberries grow along the ground on hills and mountains during summer; even tastier than the commercially grown variety, and they're free.

If it's gourmet dining you want, try Portland (an amazing variety and quality of restaurants) or the Camden-Rockland areas first.

Finally, drink the beer here. The quantity and quality of Maine microbrewed beer is flat-out astonishing. See my "Portland for Beer Lovers" (p 94) for a taste of these riches, though you can also find locally brewed beers in every other corner of the state, too.

Recommended Reading

Fiction
Maine has produced plenty of adult fiction, but little specifically geared toward life on the coast. However, several notable works of children's fiction have been set along this coast: most famously, E.B. White's (1899–1985) classic yarn *Charlotte's Web* (HarperCollins), in which a kindly spider saves a pig from a sorry fate at the Blue Hill Fair. Longtime Deer Isle resident Robert McCloskey also set *Blueberries for Sal* (Viking) and *One Morning in Maine* (Viking), among his other children's books, on this coastline.

Nonfiction
Most of the nonfiction written about coastal Maine has revolved around the drama and grit inherent in its fishing industry. Books like *Lobster Gangs of Maine* (UPNE), by James Acheson, and Linda Greenlaw's *The Lobster Chronicles* (Hyperion) depict this hard life, plus some of the biology and natural history involved.

History
Plenty of robust historical research has been done on the Maine coast, but not a lot has been written for general audiences about its long and fascinating history, which is a shame. (On the other hand, you can find plenty of good nonfiction about Maine's rivers and mountains.) To get the full story of the coast, you need to dig into the archives of the state's museums and libraries, and read historical journals and even the plaques on and inside historic homes. The central office and archives of the Maine Historical Society, located at 489 Congress Street in Portland (☎ 207/774-1822; www.mainehistory.org), is the best place to begin exploring.

Index

See also Accommodations and Restaurant indexes, below.

Photo **Credits**

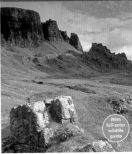